AFTER THEY WERE
PACKERS

THE SUPER BOWL XXXI CHAMPS & OTHER GREEN BAY LEGENDS

JERRY POLING

TRAILS BOOKS
Madison, Wisconsin

Library of Congress Control Number: 2006906031
ISBN 13: 978-1-931599-72-6
ISBN 10: 1-931599-72-6

Editor: Mark Knickelbine
Designer: Colin Harrington
Cover photos courtesy *Eau Claire Leader-Telegram*

Printed in the United States of America by Versa Press.

11 10 09 08 07 06   6 5 4 3 2 1

Trails Books, a division of Big Earth Publishing
923 Williamson Street • Madison, WI 53703
(800) 258-5830 • www.trailsbooks.com

CONTENTS

INTRODUCTION

When I began to work on *After They Were Packers*, I had one overriding goal: I wanted to write about people, not just football players. Professional athletes often seem one-dimensional. We know their jersey numbers, how much they weigh, how many yards they rush for, and so on, but little beyond their football exploits. In other words, we don't really know who they are—what motivates them, their goals, the problems they may have faced in their lives. A player like Reggie White, who publicly expressed his beliefs off the football field, is the exception. A man like Charles Martin, known for one infamous penalty, is closer to the norm.

The format for *After They Were Packers* gave me the chance to look at the lives of Martin and numerous other former Packers beyond football. By talking to them and people who knew them, I hope I have been able to find the person who was at the heart of the football player. Through interviews, I found the late Wayne Simmons—not the linebacker but the young man who wanted to escape poverty. I stood on a Rockford, Illinois, football field with Don Beebe—not the wide receiver but the man who coaches a Christian high school football team for free. I went to a race with Darrell Thompson—not the former running back but the man who has helped troubled youth in Minneapolis straighten out their lives. I talked with Harold "Hal" Van Every—not the Packers' top draft pick in 1940 but the man who survived a year in a German prisoner of war camp. I rode an exercise bike in an empty high school classroom with Steve Okoniewski, who may be remembered as a backup defensive tackle in 1974–75 but should be remembered as a principal who has done admirable things with his talents after football.

The stories in *After They Were Packers* are similar to the ones I wrote in 1996 in *Downfield: Untold Stories of the Green Bay Packers*, although you will find these to be longer and more complete looks at the lives and the careers of these former Packers. Also, one of my goals was to partially focus on the men from the 1996 Packers a decade after they won Super Bowl XXXI. Most of them no longer were playing in 2006, and their memories of having won the game's biggest prize seem to get sweeter with each passing year.

Without the cooperation of the men I profiled, I couldn't have written this book. My sincere thanks go out to them and the other people I interviewed, their coaches, family members, and friends. They gave me hours of their time and their memories. I couldn't have asked for more.

Along the way, I received help from many other people. They include Mark Knickelbine, managing editor of Trails Books, whose critical eye helped shape my stories; Sarah Quick, public relations coordinator for the Green Bay Packers; the *Eau Claire Leader-Telegram*, for use of Packers file photos; Tom Kertscher, reporter for the *Milwaukee Journal Sentinel*; Tom Andrews and Michael Beightol, business associates of Don Majkowski; Tom Pigeon, Packers historian; and last but not least, the love and support of my family, Lynn, Jerad, and Matthew.

— *Jerry Poling*

PART ONE:
THEY WERE CHAMPIONS

FROM THE BOTTOM UP
Wayne Simmons (59)
College: Clemson
Position: Linebacker, 1993–97
Highlight: Started every game at left outside linebacker during the 1996 Super
Bowl season and ranked fifth on the team in tackles.
After football: Owned a restaurant in Kansas City. Died in a one-car auto
accident, August 23, 2002, in Independence, Missouri. He was 32.

On January 6, 1996, the Green Bay Packers were at a crossroads as an up-and-coming football team. In the previous two seasons under Coach Mike Holmgren, the Packers had suffered the identical fate in the playoffs, winning in the first round against Detroit only to lose in the second round to the powerful Dallas Cowboys. Now they were once again in the fateful second-round game, about to face the Super Bowl champion San Francisco 49ers at 3Com Park.

Even though Holmgren and General Manager Ron Wolf had the Packers headed in the right direction—four straight winning seasons and three straight trips to the playoffs—the Packers had something to prove: Could they take the next step as a team? One more win would put them in the National Football Conference championship game. The Packers had gone 11-5—winning six of their last seven games—to win the Central Division title. That success came even after losing Pro Bowl wide receiver Sterling Sharpe, who was forced into retirement after the 1994 season with an injured neck.

Despite the Packers' strong season, overcoming the second-round jinx against the defending Super Bowl champs wasn't going to be easy. The 49ers had Steve Young at quarterback, Jerry Rice at wide receiver, and eight other Pro Bowl players, such as tight end Brent Jones, defensive lineman Dana Stubblefield, and linebacker Ken Norton. That group, led by Coach George Seifert, had beaten San Diego decisively, 49-26, in Super Bowl XXIX.

If the Packers, their coach and their general manager had something to prove, there was no better place than San Francisco to prove it. It was a game Holmgren dearly wanted to win, mostly for his team but for personal reasons, as well. Holmgren grew up in the San Francisco area and had been a star quarterback at

Lincoln High. He began his coaching career as an assistant at a San Francisco high school and went on to become an assistant at San Francisco State in 1981. He was an assistant coach with the 49ers from 1986 to 1991, when they won back-to-back Super Bowls, before leaving to become coach of the Packers in 1992.

With his thick West Coast offense playbook, Holmgren took a cerebral approach to the game, much like his mentor, former 49ers Coach Bill Walsh. On this day, however, Holmgren knew his Packers had all but mastered the Xs and Os. They knew their roles as players, but they needed to take something else with them onto the field. In his pre-game talk, Holmgren told the Packers there was only one way to knock off the Super Bowl champions on their home turf: Kick the crap out of them.

Holmgren's talk hit home with Wayne Simmons. Of all the Packers in the locker room that day, including fierce competitors like Reggie White, LeRoy Butler, and Brett Favre, no one liked the idea of kicking the crap out of the 49ers better than Simmons. At 6-foot-2, 250 pounds, Simmons was far from the biggest player on the team, but he may have been the meanest on the field. He intimidated opponents with his brute strength, inspired teammates with his pointed criticism and comments, and played without fear.

It's no wonder Simmons got along well with defensive coordinator Fritz Shurmur, who once said, "If you don't like to fight, you shouldn't be in this business." Simmons liked to fight. "He brought that toughness and nastiness to the Green Bay Packers," said George Koonce, who started at linebacker next to Simmons in 1996. "Wayne would take a fight in the bar and take it right into the street. He brought that fight to the defense. He was a hell of a player."

Simmons intimidated opponents both physically and mentally. "Wayne was such a great athlete. He could run and jump, but he'd get into your mind. Wayne enjoyed it," recalled Harry Sydney, the Packers' running backs coach from 1995 to 1999.

Buoyed by Holmgren's speech, Simmons made a difference that day in San Francisco. On the 49ers' first offensive play of the game, Steve Young threw a screen pass to fullback Adam Walker, but Simmons saw it coming. He drilled Walker with a vicious hit, jarring the ball loose. Packers rookie Craig Newsome picked up the ball and ran untouched 31 yards to the end zone. It was the first blow in what would become a 27-17 victory, a win that took the Packers to the NFC championship game for the first time since 1967.

Simmons certainly followed Holmgren's admonition to "kick the crap out of them," making 16 tackles (11 solo), including the forced fumble and a sack of Young. He also shut down 49ers star tight end Brent Jones. It was one of the best games of his career. "We knew we had to lay the wood on 'em and hit 'em hard," Simmons told reporters after the game.

The next week, the Packers' Super Bowl hopes once again were ended by the

Cowboys in Dallas, but this time it was different: It was for the NFC championship, and they had a shot at winning. They led, 27-24, going into the fourth quarter before Troy Aikman, Emmitt Smith, and Michael Irvin proved to be too much. The Packers lost, 38-27, but they were one step closer to the Super Bowl, which they finally would reach and win the next season.

For Wayne Simmons, it was a great time to be young, rich, and a Green Bay Packer. Simmons had been the Packers' first-round draft choice in 1993, but he didn't get a chance to fully prove himself until 1995. He started eight games in 1993 and was on the NFL all-rookie team, but he suffered a sprained knee early the following season and started only one game when he couldn't dislodge his replacement, Bryce Paup, from the lineup. When Paup left the Packers early in 1995 for a big free-agent contract with the Buffalo Bills, a linebacker job belonged to Simmons.

Linebacker Wayne Simmons (59) is surrounded by teammates as he helps make a tackle in 1993. The other Packers are George Koonce, foreground, Johnny Holland (50) and Reggie White (92).

PHOTO COURTESY EAU CLAIRE LEADER-TELEGRAM.

Simmons' play, at least initially, didn't disappoint Holmgren and Wolf, who pegged him as one of the key pieces to a Super Bowl puzzle the Packers hadn't put together since 1968. Possessed of a highly prized combination of speed, size, and strength, Simmons was big enough to jam tight ends at the line of scrimmage but quick enough to pick up receivers in zone pass defenses. He also was vocal and not afraid to take charge on the field. When the Packers were in their dime defense, Simmons was the lone linebacker and called the defensive plays.

His career took off in the mid-1990s. In 1995, Simmons was second on the team in tackles (103), led them in tackles during the playoffs, and had four sacks. In 1996, he started every game at left outside linebacker for the second straight year.

That season, he made an eye-opening play against the Chicago Bears. Chicago quarterback Dave Krieg passed in the corner of the end zone to tight end Ryan Wetnight. Simmons, with his powerful arms, ripped the ball from Wetnight's grasp for an interception. The play killed a Bears' first-quarter drive, and the inspired Packers went on to a 37-6 victory.

Simmons finished the season fifth on the team in tackles (76) and helped the Packers achieve the number-one defense in the NFL. As a starter in the Super Bowl win over New England, Simmons had four tackles. Holmgren later characterized Simmons' season as "terrific."

Heading into the 1997 season, with Packers fans anticipating a long-awaited return to the Super Bowl, Simmons couldn't have been a happier man. He was a blossoming NFL star and had a Super Bowl ring on his hand. Plus, he was a free agent. Surely, he was going to get a huge contract, if not from the Packers—his first choice—then from some other team.

Wayne General Simmons—his friends called him "Big Money"—had come a long way up from Low Bottom in South Carolina. Thanks to a big, strong body and unusual determination, he escaped a troubled place and difficult way of life for an idyllic place: Green Bay, Wisconsin. He had come from the bottom and made it to the top.

Tom Gardo sensed something special about Wayne Simmons as a person when he met him in 1985 at Hilton Head High School in Hilton Head, South Carolina. Simmons was a promising freshman on the football team. Hilton Head coaches saw that he was struggling with his grades and could use someone to act as a mentor and guardian. Gardo, a businessman whose daughters were going to the school, had volunteered to help struggling athletes. When the coaches asked Gardo to help Simmons, he agreed.

The first thing Gardo did was give Simmons a ride. He had been hitchhiking 25 miles to school from his home in Low Bottom, a marshy low country near the Atlantic Ocean. Gardo, who owned a conversion van, began taking Simmons home after football practice. At the end of each trip, Gardo began to read books to Simmons as they sat in the van outside his home. Gardo liked to read and thought it would be a way to break the ice, expand Simmons' small world, and get him interested in learning. Simmons could read, but he liked the fatherly attention. No one likely ever had read to him before. Simmons grew up without a father, and his mother, trying to support three children by working three jobs, was seldom at home.

"We just hit it off," Gardo said. "I would take him home from practice three or four times a week, and we really got to know each other. He needed some help in school, guidance in how to study, but he was pretty bright. He never had any direction to study. He literally lived in a shack," Gardo said.

Simmons' mother, Dorothy, tried as best she could to make ends meet in her household, which included her mother, Mamie. She never married Wayne's father. The house, one main room with bedrooms added on, was heated with a wood stove. For firewood, Wayne would take an ax into the nearby woods, chop down a tree, drag it home, and then chop and splinter the wood, according to Bob Arundell, Simmons' assistant football and basketball coach in high school and later his attorney. Arundell, much like Gardo during football season, gave Simmons rides home during basketball season and eventually became a mentor.

One day, when Wayne was 12, he came into the house and found his mother crying. He asked her what was wrong. She explained that she simply couldn't make ends meet financially. She worked five days a week from 6 A.M. to 3 P.M. cleaning bedrooms at the posh Sea Pines Resort on Hilton Head Island, then from 3 P.M. to 11 P.M. at the Speedway gas station. On her two days off from Sea Pines, she worked at Market Express convenience store. Despite her hard work, there seemed to be no way out of crushing poverty. "We had some rough times, and we didn't have anything," she recalls. "I didn't have money to live from day to day."

After explaining to Wayne how poor they were, Dorothy reached a point of despair. In their shack of a home in a poor region of coastal South Carolina, she realized that she never would be able to give her son the material things she thought he deserved. She believed he might have a better life with someone else. The thought previously hadn't crossed her mind, but at that moment giving up her son seemed like the only solution to improve his life and, in some ways, hers, by taking away one of her biggest burdens. "I told him I wanted to put him up for adoption," Dorothy said.

Wayne wouldn't hear of it, and he made his mother a promise. "He told me, if you take care of me to get me where I want to go, then I will take care of you someday. He told me, 'Mom, you're doing alright.'" His vow and vote of confidence reassured his mother. "That gave me some strength to go on," Dorothy Simmons said.

By the end of that day, she decided not to put Wayne up for adoption; she realized that she no longer was in her predicament alone. She had a son and a friend. They were in it together.

At 12, Simmons already had set his sights beyond Low Bottom, where mostly everyone lived near or below the poverty level. A lot of people were unemployed and ended up in prison—like Wayne's older brother, Leon—or spent their lives working for the rich and the tourists among the million-dollar homes, manicured golf courses, and shiny cars and yachts of Hilton Head.

At age 15, Simmons realized that he could escape poverty by working hard and saving his money to go to college. His mother had two years of college, and she didn't want to see him end up in her situation. "I wanted for my son something other than I had," Dorothy recalls. "I literally pushed him and instilled things into him. In order to get somewhere in this world, you have to work hard and fight. When opportunity presents itself to you, you take the ball and run with it, go as far as you can go."

Drawing on his mother's work ethic, Wayne took as many odd jobs as he could handle. As he washed cars at Arnold Palmer Ford in Hilton Head, he dreamed that someday he would be successful enough to own a new car. "The only way I could see out was going to college, becoming successful," Simmons told a reporter in 1993. "Me and my mom went to a bank to get a loan one day, and the bank turned her down. I wanted to become a banker so when someone like Dorothy Simmons comes in for a loan, she'll get it."

Around the time Wayne realized he had extraordinary ability as a basketball and football player, he discovered a zest for life beyond athletics. After their trips home, Gardo began to read classic books to Simmons, who gravitated toward stories that involved knights and castles. "He was fascinated with the Crusades and King Arthur. He never had any exposure to any of that," Gardo said. "It was some of the best times we had.

"We had a good, honest relationship. He didn't have any male figures in his life. Once you were close to him, he was yours and you were his," Gardo said. "Within a year, I was a father figure to him."

Although not regarded by his teachers as "college material," Wayne wasn't a slow learner. He just needed someone like Gardo to give him a push. When that happened, Simmons began to do well in school. He flourished in math, reading, and finance courses. He visited the library regularly, said Gardo, who owns a marketing and public relations firm.

Simmons liked football, but he loved basketball. He was an all-state selection in basketball as a power forward and hoped to get a basketball scholarship. Yet, despite a 35-inch vertical leap, his height, 6-foot-2, wasn't enough to attract college basketball coaches. On the football field, however, his size and 4.5-second speed in the 40-yard dash were definite advantages.

A linebacker and split end, Simmons was all-state and runner-up as South Carolina player of the year in football. In one game as a junior, he had 17 tackles. As a receiver, he caught three touchdown passes for 80 yards or more. Gardo, who often took Simmons to summer games and camps, remembers one University of Georgia camp for high school players. Out of close to 400 kids at the camp, Georgia Coach Vince Dooley singled out Simmons and one other player as possible recruits, calling them out of the crowd to speak with them individually.

Around that time, Simmons' sister, Debra, asked him whether he wanted to meet his father, William Brown. Simmons was stunned at the invitation—he had always assumed his father was dead. Dorothy had never told Wayne about his father. Dorothy had met Brown while he was in the Marines in South Carolina. They had a short relationship, and he left her behind to move to his native state of Kentucky when Wayne was about eight months old. He returned to South Carolina about 18 years later, Dorothy said.

Debra and Wayne drove a short distance to see him. Simmons met a powerfully built, somewhat wild-looking man with long hair and thick forearms, like his son's. "He was all man," Dorothy Simmons said of Brown. There was no attempt to reconcile, no apologies, no love. Simmons left with no desire ever to see his father again.

He did, however, see him again several times, although they never developed a father–son relationship, Dorothy Simmons said. "Wayne let him know in no uncertain terms that I was his mother and his father," Dorothy said. She isn't aware that Brown ever had a career of any sort, and he died some years later when he was stabbed in a fight.

By the time he was 18, Wayne Simmons no longer needed a father. When recruiting letters from all over the country poured in, Gardo helped him sift through the information and come to a decision. "We made a pact. Everybody had to come through me," Gardo said. From among such suitors as Georgia and Louisiana State, Simmons picked tradition-rich Clemson University in Clemson, South Carolina, in the northwestern corner of the state.

For the Clemson Tigers, Simmons became one of the best pass rushers in school history as a two-year starter, ranking fourth all-time with 19 career sacks. Even as a freshman, he opened some eyes with a 73-yard interception return for a touchdown against Florida State. One of his strengths was bursting into the backfield and throwing ball carriers or quarterbacks for losses. Simmons helped Clemson's defense rank in the top five in the nation three times. He was second-team all-American and first-team all-Atlantic Coast Conference. By the time he was a senior, Simmons had every scout in the NFL stopping by Clemson to watch him play.

But with all of his accomplishments on the football field, his academic achievements were at least as important to him. In May 1992, Simmons graduated with a degree in finance after four years. Earning a diploma meant more to Simmons, his mother, and Gardo than the chance to play in the NFL. Simmons had one year of football eligibility remaining, so he entered graduate school at Clemson prior to being drafted by the Packers in 1993. Together, the two achievements represented everything Simmons hoped for as a young man and as the son of a poor, single mother—victory over the circumstances he was born into and financial security for himself and his family.

Wayne's graduation day was one of the best days of Dorothy Simmons' life. "I can't even describe the feeling. It was the proudest moment of my life. It was phenomenal," she said. Dorothy had kept her promise to work hard and persevere financially and emotionally for her son, and he had kept his, to make something of himself. "Football didn't excite him as much as the idea of going to college. He just wanted to be a success. In high school, he saw how the other half lived, and he wanted some of that," Dorothy Simmons said.

Gardo, who talked weekly and sometimes daily with Simmons throughout college to help keep him on track academically, socially, and financially, felt like his son had just graduated. "It was such a huge thing for him," said Gardo, who still has a picture of him together with Simmons in his cap and gown. Simmons was the first person from his extended family to graduate from college.

When Simmons needed an agent for the NFL draft, Gardo still was there for him. Instead of having agents come to them, Gardo did some research, picked one out, and called him up. Gardo laughs at the memory of the call. The agent didn't seem impressed until Gardo explained that he was helping linebacker Wayne Simmons of the Clemson Tigers. "Oh, my God, he's the best linebacker in the NFL draft!" the agent exclaimed.

Simmons became more than a football player to his Packers teammates. With his outgoing, outspoken personality and propensity for practical jokes, he helped keep the locker room loose and always had plenty of friends on and off the team. "He'd mimic everybody around him. He always had people in stitches," Gardo said.

"If he wasn't a football player, he could have been a comedian," Dorothy Simmons said.

But Simmons was no angel. He liked to drink, drive fast, spend his money, listen to loud music, and date a number of women. He had an explosive temper, and it sometimes got him into trouble. At times he was like a big fish that wanted no part of being reeled in. Sometimes, he would talk freely to the news media. Other times, he might not say a word to reporters for weeks.

"If you didn't know him, you'd think he was crazy," said Derrick Mayes, a wide receiver for the Packers in 1996. "But he was probably one of the most loyal individuals I've ever met."

While they possessed some of the same character traits, like fierce determination and extreme competitiveness, Simmons and Reggie White were at the opposite end of the spectrum with regard to social habits. Although he was about 10 years White's junior, Simmons didn't bow down before the much-admired defensive end.

One often-told story is about how White once told Simmons, then on injured reserve, to turn down his boom box in the locker room because players were trying to prepare mentally for a game. Simmons and White began to argue about the music; as Simmons pushed the issue, the two began to wrestle, tumbling over a training table as other players tried to separate them. The next day, however, all was forgotten as they watched morning TV cartoons together in the locker room before practice. Harry Sydney, the running backs coach, admired how Simmons stood up to White. "Simmons backed down from nobody. They gained mutual respect for each other," Sydney said.

Linebacker Wayne Simmons, left, and defensive end Reggie White talk on the sidelines September 22, 1996, when the Packers played the Minnesota Vikings in Minneapolis. The Packers lost, 30-21. It was one of their three regular-season defeats the season they won the Super Bowl.

Mayes believes that Simmons' street-fighter approach to football inspired White numerous times in the huddle. "If Reggie was the heart of the team, Wayne was the bloodline. You knew when Reggie was mad because he'd tell [trainer] Pepper [Burruss] during the game to cut the tape off his hands, and then he'd go out and tear it up."

It happened in Super Bowl XXXI. "Wayne was cussing Reggie out in the huddle," Mayes said, after White played the first half with no sacks and no tackles. At some point in the second half, Simmons tried to verbally motivate White. Immediately after Simmons' pep talk, White went to Burruss and had the tape cut off, freeing up his hands and arms for an all-out attack on New England quarterback Drew Bledsoe. White had three sacks in the fourth quarter. "Reggie even knew that he fed off Wayne. He responded to Wayne just like everybody else did. Them being so opposite, it worked in Reggie's favor. I believe Wayne rejuvenated Reggie," Mayes said.

Simmons didn't mind confrontation; in fact, he seemed to feed off it. In the 1997 Packers media guide, he is quoted as saying, "When I line up across from you, I will destroy you and I will crush you." Maybe Simmons' mean streak can be traced to his naturally high testosterone level. "He was literally over the top, as high as you could get," Gardo said of tests done on Simmons' level of the male hormone. "They couldn't test him for steroids because he had a naturally high testosterone rate," Mayes said.

Whatever Simmons had, women loved it, Gardo said. "He had multiple girl-friends. It was the way he carried himself, so up. He had that kind of physique. Women would put their telephone number in his pants pocket, and they didn't even know who he was," Gardo said, recalling the nights he would jump into a lim-ousine with Simmons and other beefy Packers and head out to the nightclubs. At 5-foot-7, 170 pounds, Gardo didn't look like he belonged with a bunch of Packers so he told people that the players were his bodyguards.

Gardo remembers one night when Simmons walked into a bar in Arizona. Three women who had been huddled around one man took a look at Simmons and immediately were by his side. "Who is that guy?" the first man asked Gardo. The man left in Simmons' wake was baseball star Barry Bonds.

As handsome, popular, and successful as he was, Simmons wasn't egotistical. "He was obviously a gifted athlete, but he was never full of himself," Gardo said.

Simmons liked playing and living in Green Bay. He didn't mind the cold weather. He bought a small house, not far from where Brett Favre lived, in a housing development a short drive from Lambeau Field. He made friends easily, and he especially seemed to bond with the Packers' defensive coordinator, Fritz Shurmur. "He was Fritz's prize possession, and that's saying a lot when you look at who was on that defense," Mayes said.

Other assistant coaches also liked Simmons. Bob Valesente, linebackers coach from 1992 to 1994 and defensive backs coach from 1995 to 1998, marveled at Simmons' physical abilities, especially his unusual hand strength. "Once he got his hands on a tight end, he could rag-doll him," Valesente said. "He had a quick-twitch about him. He could play in the nickel defense because he had the speed to cover. He had all the tools, and he had great attitude and disposition in the locker room."

There seemed to be only one down side to Simmons' Green Bay experience, but it was one that would prove to be his undoing. "He liked everything about Green Bay except Mike Holmgren. They just didn't hit it off," Gardo said.

Maybe the source of his uneasy relationship with the head coach was the impersonation of the often-stoic Holmgren that Simmons used to do for teammates in the locker room. "He had everybody in stitches," Arundell said. "The only one who didn't like it was Mike. Wayne was light and carefree. Mike was very serious."

Holmgren didn't have much patience for players who fumbled on the field or made mistakes off the field. He didn't like disruptions, and Simmons didn't help his future in that regard.

In early 1997, the Packers made a number of changes in an attempt to shore up weak spots and build an even stronger team. They cut ties with aging defensive end Sean Jones, let disruptive kicker Chris Jacke go, parted ways with attention-getting wide receiver Andre Rison, and didn't re-sign Super Bowl MVP Desmond Howard. They had hoped to re-sign Howard but said they couldn't match the big offers he received from other teams as a free agent. They also said they didn't expect to re-sign Simmons, who was now a free agent.

Simmons' off-season activities did nothing to endear him to Holmgren. On March 1, 1997, he was arrested in Beaufort County, South Carolina, for drunk driving. That May, he was convicted and lost his driver's license for six months. His blood-alcohol level was 0.17, well over the legal limit of 0.10 in South Carolina. That same month, after a ceremony at his old high school to retire his jersey number, Simmons was accused of sexually assaulting an 18-year-old girl at a Savannah, Georgia, night club. The girl had graduated from Hilton Head High School that night. Simmons never was charged in the case, but the negative publicity may have sealed his fate with the Packers.

Nevertheless, in late May of 1997, the Packers re-signed Simmons, but only after he had failed to find a suitable contract elsewhere. Simmons believed he could get $3 million a year somewhere in the NFL, but with his drunk-driving arrest and his reputation for being a divisive player in the locker room, he didn't have any takers at that price. He apparently was offered $2 million a year by the Cincinnati Bengals but settled for $1.3 million to return to the Packers. It was a price they couldn't refuse.

Described by Holmgren as high-strung and headstrong, Simmons wasn't around for long, however. Six games into 1997, he had just 27 tackles and hadn't made any big plays. He had quit talking to the media, was fined for being late to two team meetings, and was facing a $5,000 league fine for punching a Minnesota player during a September game at Lambeau Field.

The Packers wanted to give veteran Pro Bowl player Seth Joyner, 32, a free-agent signee in the off-season, more time at linebacker. They were prepared to waive the 27-year-old Simmons rather than demote him, figuring he wouldn't handle demotion well. However, before the trading deadline they worked out a deal and sent him to the Kansas City Chiefs for a fifth-round draft choice in 1998.

General Manager Ron Wolf was matter-of-fact about the trade. "There's an opportunity for us to have a different style player than Wayne and maybe a player that might be just a little bit better. That's why we made the trade," Wolf said. As it turned out, however, Joyner did not return to the Packers in 1998.

Less than a year after being considered one of the best strong-side linebackers in the NFL and about to enter his athletic prime, Simmons was no longer a Green Bay Packer. While Holmgren may not have been sorry to see him leave, some players and assistant coaches were upset by the loss. Shurmur, who treated Simmons like a son, reportedly cried when he was traded. "He could take the dimmest of days and uplift everybody," linebacker Keith McKenzie told reporters after Simmons left.

Sydney, who left coaching in 1999, said the Packers missed Simmons immediately and in 2005 still hadn't found his equal. "He has not been replaced yet with the Green Bay Packers. He was the true nasty, mean, hard-core physical presence."

Simmons was gone, but he made his mark in Packers history as a first-round draft pick, a starter for two years, a Super Bowl champion, and, by some accounts, the player who set the tone for the Packers' defense.

Simmons' life wasn't the same after his expulsion from Green Bay. "When he got traded, that started his downward slide," Gardo said.

Things began promisingly. In Kansas City, Simmons started the second half of the 1997 season and was a starter again in 1998. Then, in a Monday night game against Denver, Simmons, fellow linebacker Derrick Thomas, and defensive tackle Chester McGlockton combined for five personal fouls on one touchdown drive during the Chiefs' embarrassing 30-7 loss to the Broncos. With two ex-Packers Super Bowl champs on their team, Simpson and Andre Rison, the Chiefs had hoped to be contenders themselves, only to watch their dreams fall apart. The day after the Denver debacle, the Chiefs cut Simmons. Thomas, who had three of the personal fouls, received a one-week suspension.

Although Simmons felt, not without some justification, that he had been made the scapegoat for the Denver incident, a simmering flaw in Simmons' character had been exposed: He sometimes had trouble controlling his anger. "His Achilles' heel was always his temperament. He was always prone to explosions," Gardo said.

After being cut by the Chiefs, Simmons was signed by the Buffalo Bills for the final six games of the 1998 season, but they also released him when the season ended. An injured player who Simmons replaced had healed. The Bills weren't disappointed in Simmons' play, Arundell said, and may have re-signed him.

However, Simmons decided to retire. It didn't surprise Gardo. "He didn't like to talk football outside of football. He never liked football all that much. He loved competition and being able to do something well. He didn't like all of what you have to do to be a good football player. He loved basketball," Gardo said.

In 1999, Simmons returned to Kansas City and decided to open a jazz and R&B nightclub and restaurant. "He wanted that restaurant to go so well," Arundell said. Ultimately, it didn't, according to Gardo, Arundell, and Dorothy Simmons. Gardo and Arundell believed Simmons was being led down the wrong path by his friends and business associates, but Simmons, stubborn to a fault, didn't believe his mentors.

The nightclub, 50/50 on Main, took more than a year to open because of problems with the building. The delay was just the beginning of its problems. Simmons reported crowds lined up around the block to get into 50/50, yet he struggled to make money. One time, he opened the restaurant safe to find thousands of dollars missing. Since only Simmons and a couple of other employees knew the combination to the safe, it was an obvious sign of graft, Arundell said.

Then, in February of 2002, Simmons showed up one day and found all the club's expensive sound equipment gone. Again, only a few of his employees and best friends had keys to the restaurant, but Simmons refused to accept that his friends would take advantage of him, Arundell said. The theft was the final blow. Simmons did not renew the club's liquor license in March of 2002.

Simmons' mother confirmed that he lost a significant sum of money in the nightclub project. "Wayne thought everybody was his friend. They stole my son blind," Dorothy Simmons said.

The theft extended to Simmons' personal property. He once returned from a weekend trip to find everything in his apartment missing. Neighbors saw a Mayflower moving truck pull up and assumed Simmons was moving, Arundell said. Although he can't prove it, Arundell again suspects Simmons' friends of the theft because only a few people knew he would be gone that weekend.

Simmons always had a lot of friends, but they disappeared in the spring of 2002 when his money began to run out, Arundell said. "He never spent a lot of money on himself, but he spent a lot on his friends," Gardo said. Arundell remembers the time Simmons invited him and a bunch of kids from Hilton Head to Green Bay to see him play. Simmons paid for everything.

In the summer of 2002, months after the restaurant closed, Simmons told his mother that he was coming home to South Carolina. He never made it. On August 23, 2002, he was out late and had been drinking, Gardo said. Wearing blue jeans and a tan polo shirt, he attempted to drive home alone to Lee's Summit, Missouri, in his green Mercedes-Benz.

On Interstate 70 in Independence, Missouri, Simmons' journey came to a sudden end. Witnesses said he was speeding, passing cars, and driving recklessly. He lost control and left the highway at about 2:45 A.M. The car flipped several times when it hit the ditch and then caught fire. Simmons was unconscious, and bystanders couldn't pull him from the car because he was belted in. Firefighters eventually arrived, put out the fire, and pulled him from the car.

Simmons, 32, was pronounced dead upon arrival at a hospital, but officials believe the crash and not the fire killed him. The cause of death officially was listed as blunt head and neck injury, according to a Jackson County, Missouri, medical examiner's report. Simmons' blood-alcohol level was 0.19, more than twice the state's legal limit, said Thomas Young, Jackson County medical examiner.

The death left Gardo sad but not shocked. He knew that Simmons lived his life on the edge and didn't worry much about the consequences. "He had started drinking again, but he said, 'G, don't worry about it.' He always called me 'G-Dog.' He didn't have a death wish, but if he told me once he told me several times that he was not going to live long. 'I need to live now,'" Gardo quoted Simmons.

Simmons had experienced a similar brush with death before. Two years earlier, his good friend, linebacker Derrick Thomas, asked him along on a trip, but Simmons backed out. Thomas crashed his car on an icy road, was paralyzed, and died soon thereafter. Now, however, Simmons' luck had run out for good.

Gardo spoke at his funeral, which was attended by a number of his Packers teammates. Reggie White spoke at Simmons' wake. A little more than two years later, in 2004, many of those teammates would be together again for White's funeral.

Another person there was Valesente, Simmons' first linebacker coach with the Packers. "He was such a young man. It was difficult to see such a young life snuffed out," Valesente said. "You get to know them [as players and people] and understand them. You develop some pretty strong feelings for them."

Simmons wasn't known as a Christian, but Gardo believes Simmons died a believer in Jesus Christ. "We prayed together more than a few times. He was not a church person, but we did go to church a few times. I'm sure people would scoff at the idea that he's a Christian, but God accepts all of us," said Gardo, 62.

Simmons never married, but he left behind three children. One of his children, a son, was a senior at his dad's alma mater, Hilton Head High School, in 2005–2006. That son was the result of a relationship Simmons had in high school. Wayne Simmons always supported the boy financially, Gardo said. Gardo was aware of a second child that Simmons had fathered. After his death, Gardo learned that a woman was pregnant with a third child that belonged to Simmons.

Though his life was short, Wayne Simmons lived to make good on the promise he made his mother when he was just 12 years old. When he signed with the Packers for $3.2 million in 1993, he told his mother she no longer had to work three jobs, no longer had to work—period.

With his $2 million signing bonus, he bought his mom a log house on the Savannah River in Hardeeville, South Carolina. He also gave her a monthly allowance. "I got to travel and do just about anything I wanted to do. He didn't have to do that because he didn't owe me anything. He didn't have to pay me back. The only thing I did was what a mother would do for her child," she said.

Dorothy Simmons came to Green Bay to watch her son play, and he made his momma proud. "Just to see my son out there on Lambeau Field and play football, that was an experience . . . that was an experience. I just bawled like a baby," said Dorothy Simmons, who was 57 in 2006.

Life changed for her when Wayne died. She had to give up her log home. Wayne was making payments on it, and when he died his entire estate went to support his three children, she said. Most of all, Dorothy Simmons misses the son who always was the life of the party but who also once spent six weeks alone traveling through Europe and falling in love with history. "In the short time he lived, he did everything he wanted to do. When he died, an 80-year-old man couldn't have done what he did. He lived fast and furious. He wasn't afraid to live life to the fullest," said Dorothy, who married, changed her named to Dorothy Bryant, and remained in Hardeeville. "I miss Wayne. I miss everything about him, his laughter, his face, his hugs."

Tom Gardo will miss Simmons, too, the nights on the town in the limousine, Brett Favre giving Simmons big bear hugs in the bars, the thousands of times Simmons made Gardo laugh, the times Gardo read *The Iliad* and *The Odyssey* to the teenage Simmons sitting in a van on a hot August evening in Low Bottom. Even when Wayne Simmons was a grown man, a college graduate who had left his learning-disabled tag in the dust, he would say to Gardo, just for old time's sake, "G-Dog, read to me."

TRIBUTE TO REGGIE
Reggie White (92)

College: Tennessee
Position: Defensive end, 1993–98
Highlight: Had three sacks in Super Bowl XXXI.
After football: Died December 26, 2004, of respiratory failure. He was 43.

It was a Sunday morning in Green Bay, and hundreds of people were pouring through the doors. They came from all walks of life—young, old, rich, poor, the physically robust, and a few who needed wheelchairs.

They milled about but kept their voices to a respectful tone as they waited for the service to begin. Some of the visitors, who had traveled hundreds of miles, took their seats and stared at the image of a larger-than-life man dressed in white at the front of the hall. The image hung in front of a long, black curtain, which made the cavernous facility feel like a temple. A lectern stood below the image.

Ushers handed out programs, and inside were pictures of the man in white. In every picture, the man was doing something good. He hugged people, and they hugged him back. He was the center of attention. In one picture, he stood at a holy place. In another, he helped someone less fortunate than him. In others, he wore the clothes of a warrior and appeared to be engaged in a great battle.

Given the time of day, about 10 A.M. on this Sunday in September of 2005, and the atmosphere of the room, it would have been easy to imagine that I was at a church service. It was obvious that the man in white was about to be praised both in testimony and song.

But I knew better. All I had to do was look around. The image of the man, like God himself descending from the clouds, was Reggie White. The room was actually Shopko Hall across the street from Lambeau Field. The event, billed as a "Tribute to Reggie White," was on the morning of the day when his number 92 would be retired at halftime of the Packers' game against the Cleveland Browns.

I was taken aback, but only slightly. Would the Rev. Reggie White, whose focus was putting God first in people's lives, have approved of this? An entire Sunday morning devoted to him? My guess is that if Reggie had been alive, he would have approved of the event only if it focused on religion. There were no prayers and only a little proselytizing—if you count the Christian songs toward the end of the Tribute and the references to Reggie's Christian beliefs.

On this Sunday morning, pilgrims even could buy a beer and soft pretzel at the concession stand. The bars open early on Sundays in Green Bay.

I suppose it was important to remember a couple of things. Green Bay clergy have been known to schedule their church services around Packers games if there is a potential conflict. Also, White was one of the most beloved Packers ever. In the more than 80-year history of the team, if one player deserved a posthumous, reverent tribute, it was Reggie, who touched people's lives wherever he went.

That's why people attended the Tribute. It wasn't just to remember White but to somehow stay close to the man who became a moral icon for the NFL, a hero to the armchair masses, before he died of respiratory failure, December 26, 2004, at age 43. He died at his home near Huntersville, North Carolina.

Well, yes, there was a little money to be made at the Tribute, too, an offering of sorts. It cost $20 to sit in the general admission section—equivalent to an end zone seat at Lambeau Field. If you wanted to sit in the Tribute's front pews with former Green Bay Packers stars, get their autograph or break bread with them, it cost up to $250. And there was Packers memorabilia for sale—autographed pictures, balls, books, jerseys, and footballs—with prices topping $1,000. Auction proceeds were going to charity, a group called Lombardi Legends made up of famous 1960s Packers and a few others, like John Madden and Reggie White.

The Tribute to Reggie White may have been a quasi-Sunday morning church service devoted to a human being, but it was a good one. Everyone who left Shopko Hall had to feel a little closer to God when they left because they were a little closer to Reggie, who was a pretty effective spokesman for the Almighty.

PHOTO COURTESY EAU CLAIRE LEADER-TELEGRAM.

Reggie White watches from the sidelines in 1993, his first season with the Packers.

The speakers told me things I already knew about Reggie—essentially that he was one fine human being, a person that I could only hope to become—but in a heartfelt way that I had never heard before and with a conviction that left me wishing I had met him. In nearly two hours of testimony, a parade of people came to the stage, all ebullient in their praise of Reggie but not without a story or two that reminded people he most certainly was human. A crowd of about 2,000 people, many of them wearing number 92 Packers jerseys, barely stirred.

First up was Sean Jones, the other defensive end for the Packers when they won Super Bowl XXXI in 1997: "Reggie was the kind of guy that every player wanted to play with, and every team wanted him to play for them." That being said, Jones told how Reggie was the Packers team leader but had a hard time getting teammates' attention when he wanted to chew them out because he didn't swear. After a while, Reggie realized he needed a designated cusser. Jones was his man. When a teammate needed cussing out, he would send Jones.

Former Packers tight end Keith Jackson, one of the key players White convinced to follow him to Green Bay, couldn't attend the Tribute but sent a video message: "I admired him because he was a man of God. I was one of those guys who he helped get his life in order."

Lanky linebacker Bryce Paup, who was the Packers co-defensive player of the year with Reggie in 1994 before he became a free agent and signed with Buffalo, remembers standing up for Reggie once. When serial killer Jeffrey Dahmer of Milwaukee gave his life to God before dying in prison, Reggie said that Dahmer would go to heaven. Packers players were questioning Reggie about what seemed like a hole in the Gospel, to let a mass murderer into heaven, when Paup responded that God says that no one sin is greater than another. Reggie appreciated the support. "Reggie had a huge impact on the way I treat my family," Paup said. "It was amazing to see the love he had for his family." Paup said that when opponents swore at Reggie, they often lived to regret it. "If you wanted to tick him off, just cuss." One of Paup's favorite images of Reggie is of him "always in a huddle in a corner helping people out. His great heart and his love for people and mentoring people to become the best they could be— that's what I remember the most about him."

John Madden, the television analyst and former Oakland Raiders coach, called Reggie one of the rare people who not only was great on the field but great off the field. "There are not a lot of Reggie Whites. If there was a play to be made on the field, Reggie was going to make it. There was nothing too big for Reggie and Sara (White). The NFL and football will never be the same without Reggie here," Madden said by video.

The next man on stage was Willie Davis, one of the Packers' first great defensive ends. Davis was at Green Bay from 1960 to 1969 and joined the Pro Football

Hall of Fame in 1981. He hobbled to the stage because of a bad knee and recent hip replacement surgery. "There has never been a player in the NFL that left a more indelible impression of how to play this game and how to live your life," he said. "One of the things I'd most like to have done is play with Reggie White. He left an example. How you play the game and how you conduct yourself is extremely important." Davis then told a story about seeing a man wearing a number 92 cap. He struck up a conversation with the man, who obviously was a Reggie White fan. The man then looked at Davis and said, "Didn't you used to be somebody?" Davis replied: "I used to be before Reggie White came along."

The procession of players was interrupted briefly when a family video tribute was played. Sara White put together images of Reggie's life and their life together, including the day they were married in 1985 in Knoxville, Tennessee. The video, set to music, left Sara in tears on the stage.

Appropriately, the next person on stage was Robert Brooks, the star wide receiver from the 1990s Packers. Like Reggie, Brooks gave his life to God and became a minister. He was a different person before he met Reggie. "Reggie meant about everything to me. He was the inspiration that changed my life," Brooks said. When he played for the Packers, he called himself the "chief sinner" on the team. Then Reggie came to the Packers, and he began observing the way he lived his life. "I had never seen a Christian [who lived that way]," he said. "Every time I had a party, there was one guy who was never there. It was Reggie White." Brooks got up enough courage to approach White and talk to him about Christianity. White told Brooks to go home and read the Bible. It was the first step that led Brooks to a new commitment to God in his life and led him to where he was in 2005, the pastor of a church in Phoenix. Reggie wasn't afraid to stand up for his beliefs, even if it meant fighting. "Reggie was a guy who would fight (ex-Packers linebacker) Wayne Simmons, and nobody fought Wayne Simmons," he said. Packers players often played practical jokes on each other, including clandestinely dumping jugs of Gatorade on each other while sitting on the toilet. "Reggie still doesn't know I got him," Brooks said.

Former Packers defensive back Eugene Robinson, who became a radio commentator for Carolina Panthers radio broadcasts, sent a tribute by video: "Reggie always had a cause. I said, 'Reggie, we can't save the entire world.' But you know Reggie. He was going to try."

Santana Dotson, who played on the defensive line with White in Green Bay, lumbered to center stage and said he once tried to be like Reggie. So he did what Reggie did, including following his diet. "I gained 12 pounds. One of his biggest weaknesses was breakfast sausages."

Reggie was a leader, Packers safety LeRoy Butler said, but not when it came to picking up restaurant checks. Reggie once ate $250 worth of steak, not to mention other things on the menu, at a restaurant, but "when the check came, he got up and left." Butler once suggested that Reggie offer food to get teammates to team Bible studies. So one time, Reggie ordered some chicken and told everyone about it. Players were slow to arrive, and when Butler and some teammates finally got there the chicken all had been eaten—by Reggie—with a pile of bones in the corner to prove it. "I got hungry," Reggie said. Then he pointed to the bones and said, "That's the way you guys will look if you don't attend Bible study." Butler said he has four daughters. "Their favorite player, including me, was Reggie."

Big Gilbert Brown, who anchored the defensive line at nose tackle in the 1990s, said he had a soft spot in his heart for Reggie, who was like a father to him. "It's hard for me to hold back the tears right now."

White was admired by his Packers teammates, but athletes from around the country attended his funeral in Charlotte, North Carolina, and praised his name, even though he occasionally said something they didn't agree with. White, for example, was not in favor of gay rights because he adhered to biblical teachings that homosexuality was a sin.

The funeral attendees included Major League baseball star Reggie Jackson, former Harlem Globetrotter Meadowlark Lemon, pro basketball player Andrew Lang, and star or former star players from other NFL teams, including Troy Vincent, Michael Strahan, Kevin Greene, Fuad Reveiz, Doug Williams, Irving Fryar, Art Shell, Merton Hanks, Bruce Smith, Cris Carter, Ronnie Lott, and Randall Cunningham.

The Packers were well represented at White's funeral, as well. More than 20 of his Green Bay teammates attended, along with President Bob Harlan, who chartered a plane and brought 50 employees, including Coach Mike Sherman and retired players like Frank Winters and Mark Chmura.

Nine months later, tears still were being shed. The morning of emotional testimonies in 2005 concluded when Sara White and singer Michael Tait of DC Talk sang together, the poised Sara more than holding her own in what was billed as her singing debut. Judging by the crowd's reaction, it likely wasn't her last public performance. Sara and Reggie's daughter, Jecolia, who was on the dais with her brother, Jeremy, then sang a song she wrote about her dad. The lyrics included: "I want to live like you 'cause you showed me the way; you had a vision no one else could see. You made us proud; You fulfilled your destiny."

Reggie's impact, of course, went beyond the men he played football with and against. The people wearing his jersey at Shopko Hall could attest to that. One of them was middle-aged Frank Granacki of Lockport, Illinois, who said, "I have the deepest respect for Reggie White. I loved the Minister of Defense." Granacki once saw White leaving a Packers practice and asked him to say a prayer for his mother, who had recently died. White stopped and prayed. Later that night, Granacki won

$700 playing bingo. He left $200 at the Packers' offices for the Whites to give to a charity of their choice. "I had hoped he'd be able to live to continue his work," said Granacki. "What he stood for was above and beyond football. I'm very thankful God placed a man like him on this earth even for a short time."

While his former teammates and admirers remembered Reggie as a person, they also never will forget him as a Packer player. From the time he signed a four-year, $17 million contract in 1993 until the day he retired in January of 1999, White completed one of the greatest careers in NFL history.

Born in 1961 in Chattanooga, Tennessee, White, 6-foot-5 and 300 pounds, played college ball at the University of Tennessee. He began his pro career with the Memphis Showboats of the United States Football League in 1984 and 1985, recording 23½ sacks. He signed in September of 1985 with Philadelphia of the NFL. In 13 games with the Eagles that season, he had 13 sacks and was the NFC defensive rookie of the year. He played eight seasons with the Eagles. In that time, he had 124 sacks, including an incredible 21 in just 12 games in the 1987 season, which was shortened by a strike.

As a Packer, White's sack numbers tailed off only slightly, even though he didn't arrive until he was 31. He had 68½ in six seasons, setting a team record. But his sack totals told only part of the story. When White signed with the Packers in 1993, he was the first big-name free agent in years who willingly went to a place that had come to be considered the Siberia of the NFL. Thanks in part to White's example, other lesser known but important free agents, including tight end Keith Jackson and safety Eugene Robinson, eventually followed, so that by 1996, the Packers had filled in most of the gaps needed to field a team capable of winning the Super Bowl. White not only attracted good players, he raised the level of play of his teammates. In 1996, the Green Bay defense was ranked number one in the NFL, and White was a big part of that. When opponents would double-team White, other linemen, linebackers, or blitzing safeties suddenly had more opportunities for sacks. He was also considered a strong defender against the run. "He may have been the best player I've ever seen," Packers quarterback Brett Favre said when White died. "He made the defense what it was during our run … the best in the league. He could turn the course of the game in a single play … and did it many times for us."

White had the knack for the big play. On October 10, 1993, the Packers were 1-3 and clinging to a slim lead over Denver in the fourth quarter. White proceeded to sack Denver quarterback John Elway twice to preserve the victory. The win sparked the Packers, and they went on to make the playoffs. White did virtually the same thing in Super Bowl XXXI, sacking New England quarterback Drew Bledsoe three times in the fourth quarter to help seal Green Bay's win.

Reggie White says a prayer with teammates and opponents after a 1993 Packer game. White was a Packer from 1993 through 1998.

White had universal respect among his NFL peers. He played in a record 13 straight Pro Bowl games and was picked for the NFL's all-decade teams for the 1980s and 1990s. Before he retired, he was named to the NFL's 75th anniversary all-time team. He was NFL defensive player of the year twice. He played 15 years, retiring with 198 sacks, a record that since has been surpassed.

White pondered retirement after the 1997 season, when he struggled with injuries and after the Packers loss to Denver in the Super Bowl. He returned in 1998 after having what he called a revelation from God during off-season back therapy. He had 16 sacks, was league defensive player of the year and went to the Pro Bowl. White then retired officially February 15, 1999, in a letter to the Packers, citing God's plans for him as the only reason he was leaving football. White likely heard reports that the Packers could save $4.4 million in salary cap money if he retired, and they needed it to help sign several key free agents.

White, however, returned to play with Carolina in 2000, signing a five-year contract that July. He said location—he and Sara were building a home near Charlotte, the Panthers' home—was a key reason he decided to play again and because he also thought the team had potential. He was a part-time player that season and recorded just 5$\frac{1}{2}$ sacks. One of the Panthers' games in 1998 was in Green Bay and, when White returned, he talked about how much he missed the city.

He retired for good after the 2000 season and turned to his ministry work. For the first year, he focused on giving speeches and sermons. He also was a partner in a Chevrolet dealership in Mount Holly, North Carolina, and was an investor and board member with a new bank in Charlotte, North Carolina. He started Reggie White Motorsports to help recruit black race car drivers. For three years before his death, he largely focused on studying the Bible and learning Hebrew so that he could better understand its teachings. He still attended several Packers games a year and, at Coach Mike Sherman's request, addressed the team several times.

In addition to setting the NFL record for quarterback sacks and bringing people to faith, White's legacy will include giving people hope. One of the sponsors of the Tribute was the Urban Hope Entrepreneur Center in Green Bay. Urban Hope was one of the off-the-field community projects Sara and Reggie White became involved in when they arrived in Green Bay.

Urban Hope, unlike most of the Packers from the 1997 and 1998 Super Bowl teams, still was going strong in 2006. Since opening in 1997, Urban Hope had helped more than 400 people open businesses. Those businesses have created close to 1,200 jobs in the Green Bay area. Among those ventures, 60 percent were started by women and 34 percent by minorities.

Urban Hope's motto is simple: It doesn't give people a hand-out; it gives people a hand-up. Its goal is helping people take control of their lives by teaching them a skill—how to run a business.

I found the Urban Hope offices, not coincidentally, in an urban setting—in a remodeled old office building on West Walnut Street in downtown Green Bay near the gritty Fox River, which flows into Green Bay, the body of water in Lake Michigan that the city is named after. This wasn't the trendy part of town. It was closer to the blue-collar end. I suspect Reggie appreciated that. He made millions of dollars playing football but never seemed impressed with his wealth. He wasn't very good at keeping track of his money. Sara White was known for using coupons.

I stopped in to talk with Urban Hope Executive Director Mark Burwell, who was one of White's good friends. Burwell said that even after nearly a decade of success stories, many people still have a misconception of the program. "It's not a social program. It's based on entrepreneurial concepts that empower people. It's not football-related. It's not religious," Burwell said.

Urban Hope is a business resource center, but it mainly offers classes and programs for a fee. The classes all have football-related names, such as Kick-Off for people ready to start a business; Huddle, for one-on-one coaching; and Game Plan, for developing a business plan. In 2005, one of the graduation programs included 66 people who were starting a variety of businesses, including a snack shop, a hip-hop clothing store, a tile business, a beauty shop, a restaurant, and a cleaning service. The guest speaker that night was Dave Robinson, former linebacker on the

1960s championship teams. At the second graduation program that year, Sara White was the guest speaker.

Burwell said Reggie and Sara didn't just start Urban Hope; they followed through on their commitment to the program. "I have so many stories about Reggie. He was hands-on. He visited the businesses and talked with the owners. He believed in the businesses," Burwell said.

We hopped in Burwell's car, and he drove me through parts of Green Bay's downtown that once had been dead and were being revived. He pointed out business after business run by Urban Hope graduates. One of the graduates of the program, Jenny Erlandson, started a frame shop, Three Thirty-Five Framing, on North Broadway Street not far from Urban Hope's offices.

We stopped in. Erlandson said Reggie was more than a football player. Reggie, she said, had many close friends in the community who were just working moms and dads. Erlandson, who eventually became part of Urban Hope's board of directors, was one of them.

"The success of Reggie is that he knew how to get things done," she said. "People don't see through the football player. They don't see the businessman. He was an easy man to admire, but that isn't what Urban Hope is all about. He taught people to believe in themselves."

The Tribute to Reggie White on Sunday morning was a chance for people to pay their final respects, a wake of sorts for Packers fans. The retiring of his jersey at halftime of the game that afternoon was the moment Green Bay fans officially put him to rest.

A dark green cloth hung like a funeral shroud below the sky boxes in the north end zone of Lambeau Field until halftime. Then, Sara White, Ron Wolf, and Bob Harlan emerged from the south end zone tunnel, arm in arm with Sara in the middle. They were trailed by the Whites' children, Jecolia and Jeremy, who both wore number 92 jerseys. Jecolia sang the national anthem before the game.

Packers radio announcer and former player Larry McCarren conducted a short ceremony at the 50-yard line. As the halftime ceremony began, fans chanted "Reggie! Reggie!" like they had so many times when he played 95 games for the Packers from 1993 through 1998. McCarren, emphasizing that Reggie helped make the Packers winners again, said that from the time White signed as a free agent with the team until 2005, the Packers had more wins than any other NFL team.

In a short speech, Sara White thanked Green Bay and echoed McCarren's thought. "He gave himself to Green Bay, and Green Bay showed its love to him and our family," she said. "And because of the patience of the Green Bay fans for so many years, Reggie helped bring the Super Bowl title, the character of the Packers, the integrity of the city, back home to Green Bay, and we are just honored."

White's number was the fifth retired by the Packers. The others are Don Hutson, 14; Tony Canadeo, 3; Bart Starr, 15; and Ray Nitschke, 66.

The jersey retirement wasn't White's only honor that weekend. On Saturday night, a street named Reggie White Way was dedicated. White's street joins a growing list of streets near Lambeau Field named after Packers heroes.

When the cloth was lifted at halftime, revealing White's name and number in bright yellow lettering against a green wall, Reggie received what most likely will be his last standing ovation at Lambeau Field.

It wasn't, however, the last time his name was chanted. Late in the second half, as the Packers tried to rally to defeat Cleveland, their defense needed to stop the Browns. A sack by the Packers—Reggie was known for getting many of his when they mattered most—would have helped. So fans began invoking the spirit of White by chanting his name over and over. It didn't work. The Packers couldn't muster a sack when they needed it and lost, 26-24.

Reggie may not be around to help the Packers win football games anymore, but one thing was obvious September 18, 2005, the day when fans and ex-teammates paid tribute to him, the day his jersey was put to rest: The spirit of Reggie White will live on in Green Bay, through the people he touched in the community, through pride in Packers football, and through Urban Hope graduates, for many, many years.

PHOTO COURTESY EAU CLAIRE LEADER-TELEGRAM.

Reggie White signs autographs for young Packers fans in 1993.

RIGHT MAN FOR THE JOB
Edgar Bennett (34)
College: Florida State
Position: Running back, 1992–96
Highlight: Rushed for 1,067 yards in 1995.
After football: Packers running backs coach.

Inside the Don Hutson Center, the Green Bay Packers were playing like they had a regular season game coming up that week, even though it was just an April mini-camp in 2005. A stern-looking Mike Sherman made the rounds from position group to position group, spending a few minutes at each corner of the field, where clusters of players gathered with their coaches like secret military corps on training missions.

Maybe Sherman looked serious so early in the 2005 season because the Packers had suffered a rare home playoff loss a few months earlier to the Minnesota Vikings, a loss that would lead to Sherman being stripped of his general manager duties. Sherman's new boss, Ted Thompson, stood along the practice field sidelines, arms crossed and looking casual in a green sweatshirt and black pants, as he watched the action on two perpendicular practice fields.

On one sideline, the wide receiver group caught a variety of passes to test their skills. Donald Driver casually speared a pass one-handed, stepping past reporters with his ever-present smile. Impressed and close enough to look into his eyes, I took the occasion to say, "Nice catch," as he brushed past. He replied, "Thanks, man."

The first-team Packers lined up for a short scrimmage, wearing helmets and shoulder pads but no other protection because there would be no tackling. First-year defensive coordinator Jim Bates, a highly excitable type, sprinted onto the field to give immediate feedback to his unit after each play. When running back Ahman Green broke through the defense and sprinted down a sideline, Bates was livid as he ran full speed toward the defense. It was an odd sight—a small, middle-aged man with skinny, white legs sprinting past gigantic, well-muscled athletes. "That play has not gotten outside in five frigging years," Bates yelled. Then, when the defensive front was pushed back a few plays later by the offensive line, Bates cut loose again while running onto the field. "We've got to have power up the middle with this defense. We can't have a bunch of soft asses!"

Job security in the NFL, for players and coaches, can disappear with a few bad plays, a few losses, or an injury. So perhaps I shouldn't have been surprised when Sherman did something that seemed extraordinary. When one of the defensive line-men jumped offside, Sherman let him have it. "You jumped three times last year!" Is it possible that Sherman could remember such minutiae about one player? Is three times in a season even all that bad? Yet he made his point—mistakes wouldn't be tolerated.

Despite his passion for the game and attention to detail, Sherman, like his players, found out how fickle life can be in the NFL. After numerous injuries to starting players in 2005 and a 4-12 record, Sherman was fired by Thompson. Sherman had one of the best winning percentages in Packers coaching history with a 57-39 record and the fourth most wins among coaches in team history.

Bates, despite transforming the Packers defense into one of the best in the league in 2005, also was gone after the season. He parted ways with new head coach Mike McCarthy.

Although McCarthy fired most of Sherman's assistant coaches, he kept one of the most popular and hardest-working men: Edgar Bennett. In 2006, Bennett again was coaching running backs for the Packers.

The unexpected intensity of the 2005 minicamp nearly pulled my attention away from the real reason I had come—to see Bennett. Just three months earlier, Bennett had a big month. He was promoted by Sherman from director of player development to running backs coach and was named to the Packers Hall of Fame.

It had been nearly a decade since Bennett and Dorsey Levens provided a potent running attack that helped lead the Packers to a Super Bowl win, and he was back on the field where he belonged as one of the team leaders. He wore green athletic shorts that revealed the still well-defined calves of an NFL running back, but at age 36 his running days were behind him. Instead of being the horse, he now was the horse trainer. As Ahman Green ran sprints, Bennett ran behind him with a long rubber band attached to the ball Green was carrying. It appeared as though Bennett was trying to pull the ball out of Green's hands and thereby help Green with his only obvious weakness—a propensity to fumble.

After the morning practice, when everyone else had left the Hutson Center, Bennett and his group of running backs stayed behind. Bennett fed footballs into a machine that spit them out like fat, brown bullets. Tight spiral passes shot at Green, Vonta Leach, Tony Fisher, and others. They caught balls straight on, to their left, and to their right. The players kept track of who dropped the most: the loser would have to buy dinner for everyone in the group.

Bennett was working his backs overtime, but he was not confrontational like Jim Bates or Mike Sherman. Throughout the minicamp, and as I watched him on the sidelines later that season, you'd never know that Bennett was excited about his new job with the Packers. He stayed calm as he watched his backs work in camp, spoke to them one on one and seldom was animated. He didn't raise his voice. It was classic Bennett—a low-key, soft-spoken man who is more likely to win you over with his big smile and sincerity than with his quiet determination.

But don't underestimate his quiet determination. It was that steely will to succeed that made him a favorite with Green Bay fans and coaches in the 1990s and ultimately earned him a spot in the Packers Hall of Fame. Edgar proved the skeptics wrong and got results for an organization that, in the 1990s, was looking for talented, hard-working men like him in its quest for the Super Bowl.

Running back Edgar Bennett, shown in 1993, was drafted by the Packers in 1992 and rushed for 1,067 yards in 1995. He was the Packers' running backs coach heading into the 2006 season.

PHOTO COURTESY EAU CLAIRE LEADER-TELEGRAM.

Bennett, born February 15, 1969, was a fourth-round draft pick from Florida State in 1992. He was considered the best blocker in the draft that year, a guy who Brett Favre eventually nicknamed the "De-cleater" because of his ability to cut-block opponents and knock them off their feet. That ability typecast him in the draft as a fullback, although at six feet, 225 pounds, he really wasn't big enough to play fullback. He ended up there somewhat by default because he wasn't considered fast enough to play halfback.

Consequently, for Bennett's first two years with the Packers, he played in the shadows of Harry Sydney, Darrell Thompson, Dexter McNabb, Reggie Cobb, and others. He showed flashes of what he could do as a runner. In 1992, filling in for the injured Vince Workman, Bennett rushed 29 times for 107 yards in a 17-3 win over the Chicago Bears—the first Packers rookie since 1979 to top 100 yards.

The next two seasons, he gained just under 1,200 yards total while starting 29 of 32 games. His durability, blocking ability, and sure hands made him one of the most dependable players on offense.

Then the Packers put their faith in him. First, Bennett signed a three-year contract in 1995 believed to be worth about $1.3 million a year. Although he turned down the Packers' first offer and hinted at testing the free-agent market, he eventually said he wanted to stay in Green Bay. Then Coach Mike Holmgren switched him to halfback and said he would be the featured runner. Some people scoffed. Bennett wasn't halfback-fast, and at that point his career rushing average was only 3.4 yards per carry. But the Packers saw a good fit—a hard-nosed runner, a back who seldom fumbled, someone who played through injuries and—maybe just as important—a good receiver. Holmgren's West Coast offense relied on having a back who could catch the ball, and Bennett had caught 78 passes for the Packers in 1994, a team record for a running back. At Florida State, Bennett had finished in the top 10 in school history in receptions, surpassing the numbers put up by Fred Biletnikoff, who was later a star with the Oakland Raiders.

Bennett probably could have been a standout wide receiver. He once caught a pass in a regular season game that turned even teammates' heads. He made an outstretched, diving grab on a sideline throw by Favre when it looked like the ball wasn't catchable. "I didn't think he would lay out and catch it the way he did," Favre said. "That was a big time catch—for anybody." Receiver Robert Brooks called it "one of the greatest catches I've seen in a while."

Beyond all of those qualities, there was another reason why the Packers promoted Bennett in 1995: He ran well in bad weather, which was no small factor in Green Bay. "You've got a lot of Porsches out there that are fine until the weather gets bad, and they're slipping and sliding. You get a 4-by-4 like Edgar, they go in rain, hail, sleet, or snow," fullback Harry Sydney said at the time of Bennett's promotion. Bennett's had demonstrated his all-weather ability on Halloween night in 1994 in

Chicago. With 36-mph winds sweeping a cold, hard rain across Soldier Field, Bennett rushed for 105 yards on 26 carries and scored three touchdowns. The Packers won, 33-6. That year, he also rushed for 108 yards on a muddy field against Atlanta.

Bennett was determined in 1995 to make the most of his chance to prove he was a big-time running back. Before the season, he worked with a personal trainer in Arizona. To improve his speed, he also lost 12 pounds, coming to camp at 214. His time in the 40-yard dash fell from a solid 4.5 seconds to 4.37.

In 1995, Bennett broke loose. He rushed for 1,067 yards, becoming the first Packers running back since Terdell Middleton in 1978 to surpass 1,000. He also caught 61 passes. His streak of carries without a fumble increased to 684. All those good things happened after he suffered a serious ankle sprain during the second preseason game, one that left his ankle badly swollen and sore for months. When he got home at night, he had to hang onto the bannister to climb stairs. But he didn't complain and didn't sit out. He wasn't going to miss his opportunity to be the starter. After that season was over, he had surgery to remove bone chips in the ankle.

Bennett broke the 1,000-yard barrier on December 16, 1995, in New Orleans, but his achievement went almost unnoticed. The Packers' 34-23 win put them at 10-5 and sent them to the playoffs. Bennett rushed for 80 yards in New Orleans, but the stars of the day were Brett Favre and Reggie White. Favre completed 21 of 30 passes for 308 yards and four touchdowns. White made a miraculous recovery from a torn hamstring muscle—he said God healed him—when it looked earlier in the week that he might be lost for the remainder of the season.

After the game, Bennett seemed more impressed with Favre's hot hand than his own accomplishment. "Unbelievable. [Favre] was so sharp. I didn't even want to brush up next to him in the huddle. I might have gotten cut," Bennett said. For his day, Bennett simply said he was glad to get the 1,000-yard monkey off his back and thanked his teammates. It was classic low-key Bennett.

The next week, the Packers won their first NFC Central Division crown since 1972, on Christmas Eve, against Pittsburgh at Lambeau Field, when Steelers receiver Yancy Thigpen dropped a pass in the end zone in the closing minutes.

A decade later, Bennett put the 1,000-yard achievement in perspective. "When you basically continue to go out there week in and week out and lay it on the line and get beat up to do something like that, it was special for me as well as the people that helped me achieve that," he said.

After Bennett's 1,000-yard season in 1995, he shared time at halfback in 1996 with emerging star Dorsey Levens. Bennett wasn't happy about being partially replaced after having a great season on a bad ankle, but he didn't complain publicly. The Packers won the Super Bowl that year because they put team goals before individual goals. Bennett was just one of the players who bought into that philosophy. "That's what it's all about. You want to be known as a winner. The most important thing is, did you win? Were you a champion?" Bennett said outside the Packers locker room in 2005, as players and coaches milled about after practice.

He talked about the family-like atmosphere among the 1996 players, many of whom socialized at each other's homes or went bowling together. Packers safety LeRoy Butler was like immediate family to Bennett: the two had played together in high school and college.

Despite his diminished role in 1996—he had nearly 100 fewer carries than in 1995—Bennett still led the Packers with 899 yards and had the best rushing average of his career, four yards a carry. With another 100 carries, he most likely would have been a 1,000-yard rusher again.

Yet he wasn't complaining. Bennett had been working toward the 1996 championship season his entire life, and he was ready when the opportunity arose. In the divisional playoffs in 1996 against San Francisco, Bennett gained 80 yards and scored two touchdowns in the mud in a 35-14 win. His sure-footed, balanced running style and glue-like hands were a welcome sight to Packers coaches and fans. He rushed for 99 yards and a touchdown in the NFC title game win over Carolina on a frigid day at Lambeau Field. In the Super Bowl, he gained 40 yards and caught a pass in the win over New England.

The Super Bowl, however, turned out to be his last game as a Packer. In the 1997 preseason opener against Miami, he tore his Achilles tendon and went on to miss the entire regular season. After Levens proved to be a capable successor in his absence and with his contract up, Bennett signed in 1998 with Chicago, where he led the Bears with 611 yards. He played one more year with Chicago—a team he tormented during his time as a Packer—before retiring.

Despite playing in just one of the two Super Bowls in the 1990s and having just five seasons with the Packers, Bennett was the first player from that group to be enshrined in the Packers Hall of Fame. He got the news in January of 2005, around the same time he was promoted by Holmgren to running backs coach. "I'm overwhelmed," he told reporters. He was inducted in the Hall in July along with quarterback Don Majkowski.

Although Bennett was on a tight schedule, going from practice to team meeting to film session and was in the midst of a typical 5:30 A.M. to 11:30 P.M. day, he didn't seem in any hurry to leave the hallway outside the locker room. Maybe he enjoyed the mental break and the chance to talk briefly about his career. Or maybe he simply wasn't anxious to watch more film. He watches 25 hours' worth a week and also regularly fills notebooks with his observations of the day. One Packers media coordinator said

Bennett isn't crazy about doing interviews, but it wasn't apparent from his demeanor. Maybe corralling him is the hard part. Defensive linemen and linebackers around the NFL who tried to tackle him know the feeling. Once corralled, however, Bennett was at ease. He leaned up against the cement wall and talked casually like an old friend. It was easy to see why easy-going Edgar is liked and respected in Green Bay.

Edgar Bennett actually is Edgar Bennett III, although he doesn't bother attaching the III. His grandfather was Edgar Bennett and his father was Edgar Bennett Jr. He doesn't have a problem with being named after his father. Edgar Jr. largely is why Edgar III has been so successful. After he broke the 1,000-yard barrier in 1995, Edgar gave his father the game ball. When he played for the Packers, the first call Edgar got after the game always was from his dad back in Jacksonville, Florida, where Edgar grew up. His dad was a talented basketball player and became a high school basketball coach in Jacksonville. He wasn't a football player, but he knew athletics. "As soon as I got in my truck after the game, I'd be talking to him on my cell phone," Edgar recalled. "He'd critique every play."

Edgar knew where the conversation always would end up: Pay attention to detail, his father would remind him. "He stayed on me from day one [as a child] about little things. Fundamentals. He played an extremely important role in my life and what was ahead. Every day, I appreciate that."

Edgar and I were speaking on a Monday after the team dropped to 0-2 in 2005. Edgar believed that the lesson learned from his father would be a factor in helping turn the team around. It all starts with individual effort, he said. "Start with yourself," he said. "What can I do to help this situation?" That comment became Edgar's weekly theme as the Packers struggled to a 4-12 record in 2005 and lost Ahman Green and backup Najeh Davenport to season-ending injuries. The Packers ended up relying on third-string runner Tony Fisher and free agent Samkon Gado, who quickly blossomed under Bennett's guidance.

With the injuries, the 2005 Packers rushed for just 1,352 yards, their least since 1982. However, they were fewer than 100 yards behind the 1995 season rushing total, a testament to Bennett's ability to help new players adjust to the system and motivate them.

Bennett told me how he has been blessed with other mentors as well: Florida State Coach Bobby Bowden; former Packers assistant coaches Gil Haskell, Johnny Roland, and Sylvester Croom; and Sherman. "Sylvester Croom has had a tremendous influence on my life. I've not come in contact with a greater person," Bennett said. In 2005, Croom, at Mississippi State, was one of just two black head coaches at major college football programs and was pushing for other blacks, including Bennett, to get the same opportunity.

I asked him what led him to coaching after his football career ended. While hundreds of NFL ex-players wind up in football in some capacity, many have had enough of the profession and simply want to get away from it. And, unlike some ex-players, Bennett had other options. He was a political science major in college and considered being a financial planner, a stockbroker, or a teacher after retiring.

But Bennett, like his dad and the key people he's met in his career, is a mentor at heart. When the Packers, the organization he loved, called and asked him to be director of player development, the position seemed to be a natural fit. It was a wide-ranging job that essentially helped players adjust to life on and off the field. He helped set up teaching internships for some players and helped others stay on track and get their college degrees. Bennett also assisted the running backs coach and attended all team meetings and practices. He was passing down the things his father and his mentors had passed down to him. He was teaching, after all. Bennett held that position until 2005, when running backs coach Johnny Roland left to take a similar job in New Orleans. Sherman, who had originally bypassed Bennett to give Roland the job, this time asked Bennett to join the Packers coaching staff. It wasn't a hard decision. Bennett is eighth all time in Packers rushing history with 3,353 yards, is dedicated to the team, and, of course, pays attention to detail. Sherman, a former teacher, said he always gave Bennett an "A" on his team assignments. Football was in Bennett's blood. "You have to love it. I really, truly believe this is what I'm sup-posed to be doing with my life," Bennett said with conviction. In the locker room, Fisher, Leach, and William Henderson agreed that Bennett is thorough and has high expectations, especially with regard to proper technique and fundamentals, some-thing that was drilled into him by his father. But they also liked him as a person, say-ing he was enthusiastic, easy to talk with, and respectful. "Everybody can come and talk to him," Leach said. "He's a lot more of a teacher."

Henderson concurred: "He hasn't forgotten what it's like to be a player. He's very passionate about the game, but at the same time he's not going to yell and scream and make a scene. That yelling stuff will turn you off." Henderson, who had discussed postcareer plans with Bennett, said, "He's helped me learn different aspects of the game, in case I decide to go into coaching."

Edgar Bennett was a solid if not spectacular performer for the Packers, a man you could count on. In seven seasons of pro football, he ran for 3,992 yards, 3,353 of them as a Packer. He also caught 284 career passes and scored 31 career touchdowns. In 2005, Bennett ranked ninth all time among Packers runners, right behind Pro Football Hall of Fame inductee and 1960s star Paul Hornung and ahead of late 1960s standout Donnie Anderson. Bennett played five seasons for the Packers, and Hornung played nine. The most telling statistic of Bennett's career is his number of fumbles. Between runs and catches, he carried the football 1,399 times in his career and fum-bled just 10 times. He never fumbled more than twice in a season.

The Super Bowl ring. A 1,000-yard season. The Packers Hall of Fame. A coaching job in the NFL. Bennett always has had his eye on the big prizes in life but remains grounded and humble because of his faith. Even when he suffered the season-ending injury in 1997, he talked of the biggest influence in his life, God. As a Christian, he figured his injury was part of God's plan and there was no reason to get down about it. Married and the father of his son and daughter, he also told me how important it is that he be a good role model to his children. His son is Edgar Bennett IV. Edgar III most likely is teaching Edgar IV that little things—as simple as hanging onto the football—are important in life. Little things have a way of adding up. The big things follow. After we spoke for about 30 minutes, Bennett disappeared into the locker room at Lambeau Field like he had been doing since the early 1990s. He had running backs to coach, players to mentor, hours of film to watch and, in a few days, a football game to win.

From his start in 1992 and continuing in 2006, Edgar Bennett has proved to the Packers that, when given responsibility, he will not drop the ball.

IT'S HOW YOU FINISH

Don Beebe (82)

College: Chadron State
Position: Wide receiver, 1996–97
Highlight: Caught 11 passes for 220 yards during 1996 win over San Francisco.
After football: Speed coach for athletes, high school football coach.

A chilly October wind blew across a blacktop parking lot as a tour bus pulled to a stop. The hydraulic front door folded open, and two dozen football players along with a half-dozen coaches spilled out. Except for a few large bodies, they didn't look anything like Green Bay Packers. Some had acne; most didn't yet have facial hair. A few didn't look big enough to be football players. Yet there was a Packer among them—former wide receiver Don Beebe.

Members of Aurora, Ilinois, Christian High School's football team, including Beebe, the head coach, took a quick look at the nearby football field, surrounded by a chain link fence, where parallel white lines turned the thick grass surface into a neat, rectangular playing grid. Then they headed inside to stay warm and get dressed for the game.

At 1 P.M., Aurora Christian would battle Rockford Christian Life in a conference high school football game. With only one loss in the season and hopeful of a playoff berth, Aurora would need this win before facing two of its toughest opponents in the closing weeks of the regular season.

Beebe didn't want to let this one slip away. Aurora was a .500 team but one that Rockford should defeat, he thought. He knew the opponent well: Just as he had in his playing days with the Buffalo Bills and the Packers in the National Football League, Beebe had spent much of his week looking at game film of Rockford. He thought his team had the better talent.

Inside the school, Rockford cheerleaders in blue and white and Aurora cheerleaders in red and white stretched and chatted in a lobby as players for both teams emerged from their locker rooms one by one wearing their pads, girded for battle.

Beebe stood by the lobby window and looked out at the gray, wind-whipped landscape, a pensive look on his face. Few fans were in the bleachers in Rockford, Illinois, a city of 150,000 in the state's northwest corner. Life as a coach for a Division 1A—the small-school division in Illinois—prep football team wasn't anything like the NFL. If this had been Green Bay an hour before kickoff, thousands of people would have been in the stands and thousands more tailgating outside the stadium. Cars passing Rockford Christian School that day couldn't see the football field tucked behind the school and church, and passed without so much as a look.

Rockford's stands were empty, although a few members of the Rockford Christian Life booster club hauled food and drinks to the concession stand. Smoke rose from the grills and quickly blew away in the wind, like memories of football games long ago.

The last time I remembered hearing about Beebe, it was the story of how he chased down Brett Favre in the Superdome in Louisiana moments after the Packers had won the Super Bowl over New England in 1997. Beebe asked Favre if he could have the final game ball. Favre told Beebe, who had suffered through four Super Bowl losses with Buffalo, that he deserved it.

Less than a decade after he was a significant part of the resurrection of one of pro sports' most storied teams, Beebe still was involved in football and not all that far from Green Bay. Yet the accomplishments on the field today would be made by young men who he was trying to teach, not outrun. Born on December 18, 1964, he was old enough to be their father, although he probably still could outrun most of them.

Someone mentioned to Beebe during the week that the struggling Packers still might be able to use him. Not a chance, he said. Pro football was done and gone in his life. He was on a new mission.

It was a mission that didn't involve money, big contracts, or fan or media attention. In 2004, he approached Aurora Christian officials about coaching the school's football team. Beebe grew up in Sugar Grove, Illinois, not far from Aurora—about an hour's drive west of Chicago—and moved back to the area after his final season in the NFL in 1997 with the Packers.

One of many outspoken Christians on the Packers' Super Bowl teams of 1997 and 1998, Beebe was looking for a chance to not only use his football knowledge but impact lives. Aurora Christian was a short drive from his home; his three daughters and one son either were or would be going to the school. He saw an opportunity.

When he told the Aurora athletic director that he was interested in the job, the man, at first, was excited. A former NFL star coaching a high school that had fewer than 300 total students—it seemed too good to be true. Then the athletic director became realistic. "What will it cost us?" he asked Beebe.

"How about free?" Beebe replied.

It was a done deal, although a few of Beebe's family members asked, "What are you thinking?"

Beebe had other offers, including a six-figure salary to coach football at Aurora College, and opportunities to be an assistant coach in the NFL, but he wasn't biting. He took the Aurora Christian job because he wanted to be around home while his children were growing up, and he wanted to influence other children, as well. However, he didn't rule out coaching at higher levels when his children were grown. "I felt my calling is at the high school and what I'm doing here. I'm not in it for myself. I'm in it for the kids. Money never really was an issue," Beebe said.

In 2004, the Aurora Christian Eagles went 10-2 and made the state playoffs, losing in the quarterfinals. The winning was nice, but it was just part of his reason for coaching Aurora Christian instead of at Lambeau Field or some other major stadium—he was building a program. Aurora had just 20 boys on the team the first year. By the second year, 54 boys tried out. Aurora has no home football field and not much of a practice field, but with growing, enthusiasm, a home field was on the drawing board, complete with artificial turf. Children were Beebe's main reason for being at Aurora. Of course, he enjoys responses like that of lineman Ron Keres upon hearing that a former NFL player would be his coach. "We couldn't believe it," Keres said. But it goes much deeper than that. "He's teaching us to be great Christian men first."

Football is football, complete with bone-jarring hits, but at Aurora Christian it's football with a conscience. Before the game against Rockford, Aurora players knelt in a semicircle around Beebe behind one of the goalposts. Dressed in a red-and-black Aurora jacket and black pants, Beebe read a Christian football creed, as he does regularly. He reminded them why they were playing—to honor God with their effort and their physical sacrifices. Although they had heard it all before, not one player took his eyes off Beebe as he spoke.

When Beebe was finished, the public address announcer, like clockwork, said a pregame prayer for players and fans alike. And he reminded folks that Rockford Christian Life was a no-smoking, no-tobacco campus—indoors and outdoors.

Then Rockford kicked off to Aurora. Matt Russell of Aurora took the kick at about the 15-yard line, followed his blockers up the middle, then cut right and raced into the end zone untouched, to give Aurora an early lead. Russell immediately knelt in prayer, then politely handed the ball to the referee. It wasn't the only time an Aurora player would pray during the game. When a Rockford player was injured and needed medical attention on the field, Aurora players held hands, knelt, and formed a prayer circle.

"Don's focus is not on football but on making guys good Christians, molding them into good husbands, good employees. He wants them to focus on God's will, not their own," said Marshall Johnson, an Aurora assistant coach and teacher at the school.

Beebe had to be pleased to see his players pray on their own—it's part of the discipline he's trying to instill. And pleased to see the burst of speed from Russell, the team's star running back who had 20 touchdowns and more than 1,300 yards rushing going into the Rockford game. After all, speed was Beebe's trademark—it's what got him to the NFL and kept him there.

His work ethic didn't hurt him, either. He got it from his father, a meter reader for a northern Illinois gas company, and his mother, who worked part time while raising five children. He knew that at 5-foot-11 and 170 pounds, his only chance to get to the NFL was to work harder than the competition. In both college football and track, Beebe trained and trained to get faster. "If I didn't have the moral fiber my dad taught me, I'd never make it. I was one in a million to make it—or one in 10 million."

Not recruited by major colleges, although he was all-state in football, basketball, and track at Kaneland High School in northern Illinois, Beebe initially went to Western Illinois University. He then transferred to Aurora College to play basketball. After leaving college to work for two years, he returned to Western Illinois in 1987 and then went to Division II Chadron State in Nebraska in 1988. He earned a degree in management and marketing with a 4.0 grade point average, but the pro scouts were most impressed with his speed. Beebe could fly like a bullet. At Chadron, he set a school record in track and ranked fifth in the nation when he ran the 60-yard dash in 6.14 seconds. "He was fast in high school. He got really fast in college and the pros," said Don's younger brother, David, an assistant coach at Aurora Christian. Although he played college ball at the lowest sanctioned level, Beebe had blazing 4.21 speed in the 40-yard dash, as fast as anyone in the NFL. With that going for him, the Buffalo Bills drafted him in the third round in 1989, although he was a diminutive receiver and had no major college experience. Playing with the star-crossed but talented Bills teams of the early 1990s, Beebe was named Bills rookie of the year in 1989. That season, he returned a kick 88 yards for a touchdown. His first pro catch was a 63-yard touchdown reception from Jim Kelly. When he tucked the ball under his arm, Beebe was hard to catch. He was a backup wide receiver through 1990 before breaking through on September 15, 1991. In that game, he caught 10 passes from Kelly, including four for touchdowns, as the Bills beat Pittsburgh, 53-34, defeating a Steelers defense that had been the best in the NFL the year before.

Life with the Bills was exciting if not ultimately fulfilling. Beebe was part of three Super Bowls with the Bills, missing the first one in 1991 with a broken leg. Unfortunately, the Bills lost them all. Still, he was able to do something most players only dream about. He caught four passes in the 1992 Super Bowl (against Washington), two in 1993 (against Dallas), and six more in 1994 (again, against Dallas), including two touchdown passes.

He also was part of the greatest comeback game in NFL history. In January of 1993, the Bills started the playoffs by beating Houston, 41-38, in a wild-card playoff game after trailing, 35-3. Beebe played a role in the comeback with a 38-yard touchdown catch from Frank Reich.

Playing behind stars Andre Reed and James Lofton, Beebe re-signed with the Bills for $475,000 in 1993. He played again for the Bills in 1994 before signing with Carolina in 1995. He seldom was used by the Panthers, catching only 14 passes for 152 yards and one touchdown. "It was the worst time in my career. I had a hard time with some things that were going on," Beebe said. He didn't want to give details, but he didn't fault Panthers Coach Dom Capers.

He wanted out of Carolina and, with the Packers on the way up, he knew where he wanted to go. "I told my agent to contact the Packers. I wanted to win a Super Bowl," Beebe said. "I wanted to walk up the tunnel a winner. I felt the Packers had a good team on the way up."

In April of 1996, he signed for about $300,000 with the Packers, along with free agent Jeff Query. Both were considered longshots to make the team at receiver; however, Beebe didn't hurt his chances any when he was clocked by the Packers at 4.25 in the 40, still one of the fastest times in the NFL. Beebe, then 31, was a hard-working player with Super Bowl experience. He was just the kind of guy Packers General Manager Ron Wolf wanted around in case of injury to a starter.

In October of 1996, Beebe got his chance. In the seventh game of the season, starter Robert Brooks suffered a season-ending knee injury on the first play of a Monday night game against San Francisco. Beebe proceeded to play like an all-pro instead of a backup. He made two catches on a drive that set up a Chris Jacke field goal, tying the game at 20. He made another key catch in overtime that helped set up Jacke's 53-yard field goal, a kick that gave the Packers a 23-20 victory and vaulted them into first place in the NFC Central Division at 6-1.

PHOTO COURTESY EAU CLAIRE LEADER-TELEGRAM.

Wide receiver Don Beebe is pulled down by two Minnesota Vikings during a punt return September 22, 1996, at the Metrodome in Minneapolis.

The Packers wouldn't have gotten to overtime without another big play by Beebe. About halfway through the third quarter, Brett Favre hit Beebe with a 29-yard pass. He went down to the turf, and it appeared he was touched by 49ers defender Marquez Pope. However, Beebe didn't hear a whistle, got up, and ran untouched another 30 yards for a score.

For the night, Beebe had 11 catches for 220 yards. It was just the ninth time in team history a receiver topped the 200-yard mark in a game and the first time since James Lofton in 1984. Only Billy Howton, with 257 yards in 1956, and the great Don Hutson, with 237 in 1943, had bested the mark. "The little guy can play, can't he?" Holmgren said after the game.

Beebe's value to the team was more than catching and running. Pound for pound, he was one of the toughest players on the field. In November of 1996, against Detroit, Beebe had 106 yards receiving on four catches despite taking two big hits—a helmet in the midsection after a catch and a helmet-to-helmet collision with the Lions' Bennie Blades. "Beebe had the biggest heart on the team," said Derrick Mayes, a rookie receiver that year. "To be as gutsy as he was to go over the middle at that size. . . ."

In addition to his super-sub role at receiver, Beebe performed well as a kickoff returner for the 1996 Packers, averaging 26.9 yards on 15 returns that season. Beebe had a 90-yard kickoff return for a touchdown on October 6 that year against Chicago. As the team's injuries mounted in 1996, including one that temporarily sidelined receiver Antonio Freeman, the Packers picked up Andre Rison. When Freeman returned from injured reserve, he and Rison started in the Super Bowl against the Patriots with Beebe as a backup.

Before the Super Bowl, Holmgren called on Beebe and backup quarterback Jim McMahon, both of whom had Super Bowl experience, to talk to the Packers about the pitfalls of the big week in New Orleans. McMahon, who led the Chicago Bears to the 1986 Super Bowl title, was an extrovert who loved to party. "It was a funny thing," Beebe said of the speeches he and McMahon gave. His role was to tell players how to act during Super Bowl week, while McMahon's job was to tell them how not to act.

Beebe didn't catch any passes in the Packers' 35-21 win over New England, although he did play. Afterward, Beebe took the game ball Favre had given him to his family members and walked off the field with his wife, Diane, holding his son and with a brother at his side. He stayed in uniform and hung onto the Lombardi Trophy in the media interview area long after the game had ended. "It was the greatest moment you can experience, I'll be honest," he said. "So many thoughts go back to players in Buffalo. I wish Jim Kelly, Thurman Thomas, and [owner] Ralph Wilson could have experienced what I experienced. Nobody on that [Packers] football team enjoyed that game more than me. Nobody on that team had experienced a [Super Bowl] loss, and I had experienced it four times."

The Packers re-signed Beebe in March of 1997 for two years. He received a bonus and $325,000 a year. It looked like he had found a home in Green Bay. That September, however, an old nemesis came back to haunt him. He suffered a concussion early in the 1997 season, at least the sixth serious head injury of his career, when Lions defenders Stephen Boyd and Mark Carrier converged on him after he caught a slant pass from Favre. Beebe's head snapped back, and he was knocked out for four minutes. His wife had suggested as early as 1994 that he retire because of his multiple concussions, and she suggested again that he quit after the latest one.

He didn't quit, but he didn't have the kind of season he hoped for, either. In 1997, Beebe played in just 10 games as he struggled with a hamstring injury and saw other players, including Derrick Mayes, move ahead of him in the lineup. He caught two passes for 28 yards and returned six kicks for a 22.3-yard average.

Despite his decreased playing time, he was still caught off guard when he was put on the inactive list for the Super Bowl against Denver. Coach Mike Holmgren told Beebe five days before the game, saying the Packers were activating receiver Ronnie Anderson, a practice squad player, to prevent Anderson from being picked up by another team. Beebe didn't understand Holmgren's unusual move. Anderson never had caught a pass in the NFL, while Beebe had more Super Bowl experience than anyone on the team. He felt slighted. Anderson didn't play in the Super Bowl and never played a game for the Packers.

Beebe's improbable journey had come to an end. He retired with 219 career receptions and an impressive career average of 15.6 yards per catch. The latter figure wasn't as good as Hall of Famer James Lofton's 18.3-yard average but was better than that of former teammate and Bills standout Andre Reed, who had a 13.9-yard average.

Beebe left the game with more than good statistics. An underdog, an overachiever, a man with integrity, he also left with admirers across the country and in his own locker room. "Don helped show me the ropes on the field, but he showed me more as a person and as a man as anything on the field," Mayes said.

Beebe's ability to inspire others with his competitive drive and integrity also were at the heart of his most famous play. His greatest career moment came during Super Bowl XXVII when the Buffalo Bills were losing, 52-17, to Dallas. Lineman Leon Lett of the Cowboys picked up a Bills fumble and was running it back for a seemingly easy touchdown. His score would add another wound to Buffalo's already long and painful day.

However, as Lett approached the goal line, he slowed down and began to celebrate. That was all Beebe needed. He hadn't given up on the play, racing down the field to catch Lett even though the Bills trailed by 35 points and had no chance to win. Lett's touchdown would have been meaningless, but not to Beebe. "My team was getting whupped, and I was very frustrated," he said. Beebe was taught never to give up, always to finish the play. This time was no different. He caught up to Lett and punched the ball out of his hands, preventing the score.

When he reached the sidelines, Beebe received a few pats on the back from downtrodden teammates whose spirits temporarily were lifted by his all-out effort, but Beebe didn't think much about his heroics; that was just the way he always played. Only in the locker room did the impact of the play begin to sink in. Bills owner Ralph Wilson sought out Beebe after the game and said to him, "Son, you showed me a lot today. You showed me what the Buffalo Bills are all about. You should be proud of what you did today."

Beebe never has forgotten those words and still gets goosebumps when he thinks of them. The impact of that play went far beyond personal self-esteem, respect from the team owner, or some kind of redemption from a bad game. Today, if people remember one thing about Don Beebe, they remember that one play, the time he didn't give up when all hope of winning was gone. That play has become an often-cited example of how people should approach their lives.

In the weeks after the game, Beebe received boxes of fan mail from teachers, coaches, and parents. "I thought I was Brett Favre or somebody," Beebe said. Some of the letters had tear stains. One was from a dad who used the Lett moment to talk to his son about determination in life. "This has changed my relationship with my son," the man wrote to Beebe.

The Beebe–Lett play was featured in *Sports Illustrated* magazine. It often is seen at Super Bowl time as one of the great plays in the event's history and often ranks near the top of lists of the best hustle plays of all time. As much positive publicity as the play brought Beebe, it brought equal amounts of negative publicity for Lett. Beebe eventually met Lett, and the two talked about the play. "He really was a nice guy, a quiet person. I told him, 'All you had to do was finish,' and he said, 'I know,'" Beebe recalled.

The Lett play strengthened Beebe's faith in God. "We were just getting killed, 52-17. Out of this comes something so glorious. This is how God works."

When he retired from football and considered his next career, Beebe stuck with what he knew best: physical speed. He started a business called House of Speed in Sugar Grove, Illinois. The goal of his business is simple—to train athletes to run faster. When Beebe isn't coaching Aurora Christian, he and partner Dr. Jeff Schutt work with athletes who would love someday to run a 40-yard dash as fast as Beebe did. House of Speed holds group classes and camps, and offers private lessons to middle school athletes all the way up to professionals. He started with a handful of athletes and now trains hundreds each year. A few of his protégés play for Aurora Christian.

Beebe doesn't spend much time telling his players about life in the NFL. He often has the juniors and seniors over to his house for a barbecue. They get to watch the big-screen TV in his basement, see a replica of his locker, and peruse his memorabilia. But that's about it. He knows many of his players never saw him play.

The one NFL story that Beebe does make a point to tell his Aurora players is the Lett fumble. In that story, he knows there is a lesson that young people can learn—do not give up, finish what you started. "No matter what the scoreboard says, we're going to play hard," Aurora assistant coach Marshall Johnson said.

Beebe isn't a traditional football coach. He doesn't yell much and certainly doesn't curse, but his expectations are high for Aurora players. After they beat Rockford, 42-0, he complimented the players but let them know that the big games—including the playoffs—were coming up, so they needed to be ready for new challenges.

Aurora eventually made the Illinois state playoffs in 2005 but lost in the first round and finished with an 8-3 record. Beebe's record as coach after two years, 18-5, was a marked improvement over Aurora's 23-26 mark in the previous several seasons. With his record of achievement throughout his life, it came as no surprise that he still was a winner, although at Aurora Christian character development and stronger faith were as fundamentally important to Beebe as wins and losses.

During the game in Rockford, Beebe criticized players little, unless someone missed an assignment. As might be expected, he focused intently on every play, pacing the sidelines. After a 20-yard Rockford pass play, Beebe yelled to an Aurora defender, "You gotta' hit him, right? Let's do it right!"

Mostly, Aurora did it right. It mixed long runs with a variety of pass plays, including a couple of touchdown-producing screen plays that Mike Holmgren couldn't have diagrammed better. Beebe's team runs a West Coast-style offense, like Holmgren's Packers did. Aurora has 76 passing plays and the players know them all, Beebe said, with obvious pride at his ability to get the team to play at a high level of competence.

Beebe's younger brother, David, is the defensive coordinator, and their father, Don Sr., 69, is the team's videographer and, according to David, the man to whom the coaches often turn for wisdom about difficult issues. The extended Beebe family, which spends a week together each summer at a northern Minnesota resort, is a tight-knit group.

Young Don takes the coaching job seriously, his brother said, not unlike the way he approached football in college and the pros. Coaching Aurora Christian has helped Don bridge the gap from the NFL to his second career. "He taps into that competitive channel he lost when he left the NFL," said David Beebe, six years younger than Don and one of his biggest fans while growing up.

Don would agree. "It's the first time since I retired that I've had some of the same feelings I had when I went to the Super Bowl," he said. "I still have competitive drive, and I can live it in the athletes I train."

Yet Beebe knows he's working with teenagers and that, on average, only one percent of athletes will be able to do what he did. He's not instilling false hopes in the athletes he trains at Aurora and at House of Speed, he says, just hope that they can be better athletes and better people. He believes young people can benefit from the life lessons that athletics teach them.

Beebe's goal is to give back some of the blessings, football and otherwise, to a segment of society he believes is most at risk—young people. So many of them never get pointed in the right direction, and even the ones who do can use an extra push and another firm hand. When he took the Aurora job, Beebe asked about one player on the team, a 6-foot-2, 260-pound lineman. The player often missed practice and lacked direction. "People said, 'He won't be around,'" Beebe recalled. "I said, 'We'll see.'" By the end of the season, the boy had become one of the team leaders. "The dad told me, 'Coach, I gave you a boy and you gave me a man.' That's what it's all about. I feel every kid on the team has gotten better in life. They got better in football, too, but that's not the most important thing," Beebe said.

"If I can make an athlete better, great. If I can make an athlete a better person, even better. I've gotten more comments from parents on that aspect—that what I instill in a kid lasts a lifetime. That tells me God has me doing what I'm supposed to be doing," Beebe said.

After the game against Rockford, Aurora coaches, players, and the few dozen family members who had made the hour-long trip from Aurora all gathered around Beebe in the end zone. Two Rockford players, he noted, refused to shake hands with Aurora players. "Don't ever act like that," Beebe told his players.

Beebe should know. It's how you finish that makes an impression on people.

KOONCE! KOONCE!
George Koonce (53)
College: East Carolina
Position: Linebacker, 1992–99
Highlight: Led the Packers in tackles in 1996 with 117.
After football: Business owner, graduate student, and assistant to the athletic
director at East Carolina University.

I still can hear the chants. "Koonce! Koonce! Koonce!" And it wasn't even at Lambeau Field.

It was the night before the Packers' third game of the 1996 season. They were 2-0 coming off a Monday night win over Philadelphia in Green Bay, and hopes were high that the team would bring the Lombardi Trophy back to Green Bay.

My son and I had heard where the Packers were staying Saturday night before the September 15 game against San Diego. We also heard that a group of former Packers were gathering at an airport-area hotel. It was alumni weekend, the one game a year when ex-stars are invited back to have dinner with their buddies, play golf for charity, watch the game from the sidelines, and be introduced at halftime.

We had to bluff our way in. The hotel was so jam-packed with people that a security guard was posted near the main driveway. He was turning away everyone unless they had a reason to be there, but I said I had to drop something off and we were past the castle gates.

Inside, we spotted famous ex-Packers in a suite off the main lobby. Jerry Kramer was talking to Max McGee. Paul Hornung walked past. There were others, some I didn't recognize but probably should have. We did have something to drop off—a picture and book to be autographed. Then we left like we said we would, inquiring on the way out whether the current Packers had arrived yet for the night. Someone told us to go behind the hotel, where they likely would be arriving.

When we drove around to the back parking lot, I began to realize how hungry Green Bay fans were for a championship. Hundreds of them lined a roped-off area. Many were in their Packers gear—hats, shirts, green-and-gold beads—and carried cameras and Sharpie pens, hoping to get autographs. And this was only the night before a game.

One by one, the players arrived. From behind dark windows of luxury sedans and large SUVs emerged defensive coordinator Fritz Shurmur, fan favorite Gilbert Brown, Mark Chmura, Frank Winters, Tyrone Williams, Brett Favre, Robert Brooks, and others. They received rousing cheers and catcalls like Oscar nominees walking the red carpet in Hollywood.

And George Koonce. When Koonce stepped from his car, the chant began.

"Koonce! Koonce! Koonce!" Big George smiled broadly, acknowledged the fans with a wave and, unlike some of the other players, walked over and signed autographs for his fired-up fans before disappearing into the hotel.

The next day, the chants were a little louder. Lambeau Field was packed with 60,584 fans yelling the name of the starting linebacker from North Carolina. They yelled "Koonce! Koonce! Koonce!" when he was introduced. They yelled it when he made tackles.

Something about that name was fun to yell.

There was something about George Koonce, too, something Packers fans liked.

Maybe the fans liked Koonce because he was humble. Like many of the blue-collar Wisconsin factory workers and farmers who follow the team, Koonce knew what it was like to worry about his future and not take success for granted.

In the summer of 1991, Koonce was an undrafted free agent trying to work his way onto the Atlanta Falcons' roster. He was cut on the final day of training camp by Coach Jerry Glanville. The Falcons had another young player on the roster that

PHOTO COURTESY EAU CLAIRE LEADER-TELEGRAM.

Linebacker George Koonce (53) listens on the sidelines during the 1996 season. Other players in on the discussion are Wayne Simmons (59), foreground, and nose tackle Gilbert Brown (93).

summer who didn't impress Glanville—rookie quarterback Brett Favre. Glanville traded Favre to a team up north the next year.

Koonce didn't give up on his NFL dream, however. In the spring of 1992, he signed with the Ohio Glory of the World League of American Football—the minor leagues of pro football. He figured it was his last shot at making the NFL. Because the World League played in the spring, NFL scouts often were at the games with the hopes of finding overlooked talent.

One day that spring, Koonce was playing his heart out, even though it was just a preseason scrimmage in San Antonio against the Frankfurt Galaxy from Germany. Koonce had about 14 tackles, a sack, and broke up a few pass plays.

During the game, he noticed a man walk over to one of Ohio's offensive linemen and ask a question. The man was Ted Thompson, assistant director of player personnel for the Packers. Thompson, a former NFL player himself, began asking questions about Koonce, whose play had caught his eye. "Who's that guy?" Thompson asked. "George Koonce," the player responded. "Man, he's a good athlete," Thompson said.

Thompson talked with Koonce after the scrimmage and said the Packers would be watching him during the World League season.

It was all Koonce needed to know. Growing up on the East Coast, he didn't know a whole lot about Green Bay, but he knew the Packers were in the NFL, and that was motivation enough. He led the World League in tackles that season with 91 in just 10 games, despite the Glory's very inglorious record of 1-9.

Koonce signed a free agent contract with the Packers on June 2, 1992. His football season wasn't over, and neither was his career. They were both just beginning. "They said they would guarantee me an opportunity, and they did," Koonce said.

Still, his chances of making the Packers didn't look good. They had a veteran group of linebackers led by Brian Noble, Johnny Holland, Tony Bennett, and Bryce Paup. They also drafted Mark D'Onofrio in the second round.

At only 6-foot-1 and 238 pounds, Koonce wasn't big. He wasn't experienced, either; although he had been a standout linebacker at East Carolina University after two years at a junior college, East Carolina hardly was a collegiate football power. Beyond that, despite a few exceptions like 1960s Packers star Willie Wood, free agents seldom make it big in the NFL, especially since teams began to develop highly sophisticated scouting departments.

Koonce, however, was fast. A player's speed in the 40-yard dash is one of the keys that opens the door to the NFL, and Koonce could run the 40 in 4.6 seconds. The ability to go from standing still to top speed in a flash on the limited space of a football field translates to saving touchdowns and, thus, games.

Above all, Koonce was determined, the one intangible quality absolutely essential to NFL success, and one that hard-working Packers fans recognized and admired.

Koonce remembers arriving in Green Bay and staying first at the Midway Hotel across the street from Lambeau Field and near the old Packers Hall of Fame site. "I knew a little about Green Bay, but we didn't have a pro football team then in North Carolina and I didn't follow pro football too closely growing up. So I walked over to the Hall of Fame. I said, 'Man, this is something.' I spent about two and a half hours there. I read all the bios of the players inducted there. The hair on the back of my neck was standing up. I thought to myself, 'Man, this is the place I want to be.' I fell in love with the whole mystique of Lombardi, Lambeau, the 1960s teams, Starr, Nitschke, Don Hutson. I was in awe of the players who came before me. I had no idea I was going to a franchise like the Green Bay Packers," Koonce recalled.

After his trip to the Packers Hall of Fame, Koonce knew more than ever that he wanted to succeed with the Packers. With a new coach and a team that had plenty of room for improvement, he had some hope that he might be part of Green Bay's rise to success.

He applied himself in training camp, and good things began to happen. An injury to linebacker Johnny Holland in camp helped Koonce get playing time with the first team, and he didn't disappoint. In the team's intrasquad scrimmage on August 2, 1992, he had seven tackles; he went on to lead the team in tackles in the preseason. Defensive coordinator Ray Rhodes and linebackers coach Bob Valesente took notice.

Still, Koonce remembered playing well in Atlanta's training camp and not surviving the team's final cut. He was worried about making the Packers roster. "I didn't know until that morning [of the final cut] that I had made it. From the start of training camp until that day, I had no idea if I was going to make the team," he said.

That year, he began to make a name for himself. He played in every game in 1992 and started in 10, was seventh on the team in tackles, and played well on special teams. He finished strong, making 14 tackles in the final regular season game against Minnesota. He was quite a bargain for $150,000 a year, at a time when the average salary for a starting linebacker in the NFL was $763,000.

One of Koonce's hallmark traits as a Packer was his versatility. He eventually started more than 30 games at each linebacker slot. By early 1993, he had already switched positions four times. Koonce was moved to inside linebacker in September 1993 after Brian Noble was injured, although people questioned whether he was big enough to stop the run. "I could run as well as any linebacker in the NFL. I had the ability to hit and play within the framework of a defense. I did what the defensive coordinator and linebackers coach wanted me to do. I could stop the run or drop back and cover the tight end," he said. "I tried to play to the best of my ability for the Packers family. They're knowledgeable fans. If you're dogging it, they know it."

Even *The Sporting News* took notice. In 1994, columnist Bob Glauber called

Koonce one of the top 10 most underrated players in the NFL. "He is one of the most versatile 'backers you'll ever see. The Packers can plug him in just about anywhere. He is easily the team's best run-stopper," Glauber wrote.

In 1994, Koonce signed a two-year contract for a total of $825,000. He became one of the team's most reliable players in the mid-1990s, when they were among the elite of the NFL. He led the team in tackles in 1994 and 1996. His highlights were many, like an 18-tackle game against Chicago in 1993, 11 tackles in one of his first career play-off games in 1994, and 13 tackles in the 1995 NFC championship game loss to Dallas.

Valesente, linebackers coach from 1992 to 1994 and defensive backs coach from 1995 to 1998, was proud of how Koonce blossomed in 1995 and 1996. Koonce relied on speed, strength, and instinct at first and then put it all together when he learned the Packers system, Valesente said. Koonce also advanced quickly because of the help of teammate and fellow linebacker Johnny Holland, who Valesente said took extra time to work with Koonce.

Koonce also was one of the strongest players on the Packers. He could bench press 315 pounds up to 15 times and was one of the leanest players with just 11 percent body fat. "There aren't three guys in the league that look like that," Ralph Vitolo, Koonce's agent, said at the time. In assessing Koonce's abilities, Packers general manager Ron Wolf once compared Koonce to a garbage collector: No job was too dirty for him, and he cleaned up anything that came his way. For the Packers, he did it all, and cheers began for the ex-free agent from East Carolina.

Seeing a player reach the peak of his ability was the greatest joy Valesente got from coaching, and Koonce was one of his triumphs. "I'd work extra hard with his techniques and run-fills. He became what I think was one of the best run-stoppers in the defense," Valesente said. "He just took off. He was a complete linebacker."

The day after my son and I crashed the homecoming celebration in 1996, Green Bay blew out San Diego, 42-10; the Packers were 3-0 and on their way to bringing a title back to Titletown. The game was a harbinger of things to come that season: The defense was tough, Desmond Howard returned a kick for a touchdown, and Brett Favre threw TDs to Antonio Freeman, Keith Jackson, and William Henderson—whomever was open.

Koonce was on his way to an outstanding season, as well. He would go on to lead the Packers defense in tackles that year with 117, including 76 solo stops, and intercept a career-high three passes. He returned one of them 75 yards for a touchdown against Minnesota.

Unfortunately, the '96 season ended two games too soon for Koonce. In the first round of the playoffs, he suffered a knee injury in the second half of the Packers' 35-14 win over the San Francisco 49ers on January 4 in Green Bay. After missing a tackle on 49ers fullback William Floyd, who cut to the right after a pass reception, Koonce slipped to the turf in muddy conditions. He tried to continue playing before taking himself out of the game. He had surgery five days later to repair a torn anterior cruciate ligament in his right knee and was forced to watch from crutches on the sidelines as the Packers defeated Carolina in the NFC championship game at Lambeau Field. He also had to watch as his teammates won the Super Bowl over New England in New Orleans.

The second half of the 1990s weren't as kind to Koonce. He missed nearly half of the 1997 season and Super Bowl while still rehabilitating his knee. He was also forced to take a 50 percent pay cut while on injured reserve; the Packers needed to save money to meet the NFL salary cap. He lost close to $32,000 a week just a year after his best season.

In addition to recovering from the injury in 1997, he lost his dad to a heart attack and his 32-year-old sister to a drug overdose. Two first cousins also died; one, 18, was shot to death, and another, 13, died when her appendix burst. "I played with a heavy heart," he said, remembering that year when he was just 27 years old.

Koonce returned with a solid season in 1998 and proved that his knee injury was a thing of the past. With his four-year contract of $5.2 million finished, the Packers re-signed Koonce in February of 1999 to a four-year deal worth $11 million. His life was back in order.

But then came a divorce from his first wife, the settlement of which made headlines when it went to the state appeals court, and the Packers' 8-8 season in 1999 under new head coach Ray Rhodes. The plan by Rhodes to use the speed of linebackers Koonce, Bernardo Harris, and Brian Williams was one of a number of things that he tried unsuccessfully in his one year as head coach.

It was Koonce's last season in Green Bay, too. With the Packers trying to find room in the salary cap, his contract looked like a good place to trim, even though Koonce agreed to a pay cut of $600,000. "They said I didn't play up to my contract. I told them I was fine with that. I have no hard feelings toward the Packers," he said.

Koonce left Green Bay the way he had arrived—virtually unnoticed. The Packers cut him loose and he signed with Seattle in June of 2000, while most Packers fans were focused on the sexual assault and child enticement charges against tight end Mark Chmura, who was acquitted in 2001. Teammates, and the few fans who noticed, were sad to see the departure of one of the rags-to-riches heroes of the Super Bowl champions.

At Seattle in 2000, Koonce started for Mike Holmgren again but wasn't the same player he had been in the mid-1990s. He appeared to have lost a step, as armchair critics are wont to say. He retired the next year.

A decade after helping the Packers bring back the Lombardi Trophy, Koonce still was close to his roots, living in Greenville, North Carolina, 40 miles north of his hometown, New Bern. He was working and taking classes at East Carolina University, where he had starred in football years before.

He was more than happy to talk about his days in Green Bay, making it clear that the Packers were one of the best things that had ever happened in his life. Sometimes when he's driving in his truck in North Carolina these days, he'll turn off the radio and think back to his career in Green Bay. And it all comes back to him—the days of watching Brett Favre grow up as a quarterback; seeing Reggie White come to Green Bay and deliver on the field and off; observing as Coach Mike Holmgren, General Manager Ron Wolf, and President Bob Harlan built a championship team and a winning organization.

Koonce also thinks about his good fortune—making it to the NFL and then landing in a place like Green Bay. Koonce has more than good memories of Green Bay. The things he experienced there changed his life well beyond football.

Wide receiver Derrick Mayes, who eventually became one of Koonce's teammates in Seattle, has remained friends with him. "George was never the most talented player on the field, but he was the best, if you know what I mean. He's such a great individual. His intensity and leadership were like none other," Mayes said.

As assistant to the athletic director at ECU, Koonce helps with on-campus recruiting for all sports, is involved in fundraising campaigns, and helps with marketing. "I kind of float all around," he said. It's similar to his role with the Packers.

His business, Koonce Properties—apartments, duplexes, and single-family homes that he rents—has grown to about 140 units, including one 72-unit apartment building that he bought in the 1990s with his Packers salary. Because his mother, Lina, and wife, Tunisia, help him run that, George is able to pursue something else that means a lot to him—more education.

"As an undergraduate, I wasn't focused on academics. I was focused on playing football and hanging out with friends. I was a marginal student. I was lazy and didn't have my priorities straight. It was not an indication of the type of person I was. Although I got the degree, I wanted to go back to school and right some wrongs," he said.

While Koonce was still with the Packers, he finished his bachelor's degree in industrial technology management, with a concentration on construction management. Since leaving the NFL, he has been working on his master's degree in sports management. He plans to pursue a doctorate in education, with the goal of becoming a college athletic director or joining an NFL team as general manager or director of operations. He has a team in mind, he said. "The only place I would even consider is Green Bay because they gave me so much in the eight years I was there," Koonce said.

Koonce wasn't referring to money or fame. Playing for the Packers taught him how to balance his priorities, balance his time, and set his goals high. "I was in Green Bay eight years, and I was in school the whole time. Every hour of the day was accounted for. I wanted that structure. Yes, it was a time to develop into a man, but I also learned how an organization is run, how to treat people, how not to treat people. I learned how to win and how to lose," Koonce said, thankful he was part of an organization that taught him to do things the right way.

Many of the Packers from the 1960s championship teams went on to successful business careers; those Packers gave credit to Coach Vince Lombardi for instilling in them the will to succeed. Similarly, the lessons he learned from Harlan, Wolf, Holmgren, and the Packers' assistant coaches in the mid- and late-1990s are carrying over into Koonce's life. "The feeling the Packers gave me, and a lot of players, got us ready for life," Koonce said.

Koonce never will forget the other reason he is thankful for playing in Green Bay—Packers fans. "The big games with the Packers—they all were great and it was a great experience, but the whole area up there in Wisconsin and the dedication they have to football is something special. If you're a football fan, you have to go to Green Bay. If you want to see fans who are behind you, win, lose, or draw, you have to go to Green Bay," he said.

I asked him about the "Koonce! Koonce! Koonce!" chant and why he thought that Packers fans connected with him.

"I think it's because of the way I came up with the team," he said. "I wasn't a first-round pick. I worked my way onto the team. I didn't have a big signing bonus, a limo, or a press conference when I came to town. We're a blue-collar city and a blue-collar team. If you asked the average Packers fans if they could try out for the team, how would they like to do it, they'd say, just like me. 'Just give me a helmet, just give me a chance.' That's where the chant came from. Packers fans could identify with me."

Koonce had one last aspect of unfinished business with the Packers. In 2006, he planned to sign a one-day contract with the Packers, then officially retire from the NFL. He wanted to retire as a Packer.

The man who will sign him to that one-day contract is Ted Thompson, the Packers' general manager. Thompson is the same man who spotted Koonce 15 years earlier in San Antonio playing his heart out in a World League scrimmage—the day that changed the course of George Koonce's life.

THE RING-BEARER
Mike Prior (39, 45)

College: Illinois State

Position: Safety, 1993–98

Highlight: Special teams captain and intercepted a pass in Super Bowl XXXI.

After football: High school baseball coach and Indianapolis Colts youth football commissioner.

A decade after he first slipped it on his finger at the team's private party in June 1997, the luster hasn't worn off Mike Prior's Super Bowl XXXI champion ring—and he has worn it often.

Prior, however, doesn't spend much time looking at the exterior beauty of the ring, the centerpiece of which is a large "G" formed with dozens of small diamonds. He looks past the gold and jewels to the 12th week of the 1996 season. There he sees the Super Bowl champions' true shining moment.

The Packers were 8-3, and their confidence was slipping. After starting the season 8-1 and living up to the preseason predictions that they were the team to beat in the NFL, they had lost two straight games. In mid-November, they fell 27-20 at Kansas City and 21-6 at Dallas. Suddenly, even confident Packers fans were ready to admit that Dallas was the team to beat and that the Packers, like the three previous seasons, might not be good enough to beat the Cowboys in the playoffs.

The 1996 Packers were at a crossroads. That week, the players rallied around each other during practice. They reminded themselves that they were on a mission—to get to the Super Bowl—and that it was time to get serious. "We said, 'We're not getting any younger here. We've got to run the table to get home-field advantage,'" Prior said in 2006.

It wasn't going to be easy. The Packers' top receivers were out with injuries: Robert Brooks was having knee surgery, Antonio Freeman had a broken arm, and Mark Chmura was recovering from a torn arch. Brooks would not return for the rest of the season. Also, the Packers had to go on the road for the third straight week, at St. Louis. Although the Rams had just a 3-8 record, it would be an indoor game and the Packers hadn't been playing well in domes or on artificial turf. They lost earlier in the season at the Metrodome in Minnesota.

The Packers were worried but focused. "Everybody was on the same mission," Prior said as he recalled that week. "We said, 'What have we got to do to make it to the Super Bowl?'"

That attitude, which prevailed throughout the 1996 season, was a key component in the Packers' success, Prior said. Players not only were unified within their ranks but with the various position coaches, as well. Often, game plans that season were a combination of coaches' strategies and players' suggestions.

At St. Louis, the Packers' week of soul-searching and renewed cohesiveness paid off. Trailing 9-3 at halftime, they held the Rams scoreless in the second half and pulled away to a 24-9 win. When the Green Bay offense was struggling, the league's top-ranked defense played harder. Doug Evans returned an interception 32 yards for a touchdown in the second half, and Brett Favre threw two short scoring passes.

The Packers went on to win their final four games, three of them at home, to finish 13-3 and secure home-field advantage in the playoffs. "The guys rallied. We won the last five games, and it put us in the driver's seat," Prior said. Home playoff victories over San Francisco, 35-14, and Carolina, 30-13, sent the Packers to the Super Bowl.

Prior, the 6-foot, 208-pound reserve safety, was part of the reason for that late-season rally. He had been in the league for more than a decade, as long as Reggie White. They were among the veterans who believed that the 1996 season might be their best shot at winning a Super Bowl ring before retiring. Against the Rams, Prior turned in a strong performance. He led the team with three special teams tackles and recovered a kick that led to a Packers field goal.

It wasn't the Super Bowl, but without that much-needed victory on the road in Week 12 they wouldn't have had home-field advantage and might not have brought the Lombardi Trophy back to Green Bay in 1996.

Prior knew how to keep a dream alive.

A fleet centerfielder and power hitter in high school and college baseball, he was a fourth-round draft pick of the Los Angeles Dodgers in 1985. (He also was drafted by the Baltimore Orioles in 1984 and Houston Astros in 1986.)

He was good at more than baseball, however. He also was a Division I-AA all-American in football at Illinois State. Prior, a native of Chicago Heights, Illinois, wanted to try football first. He was a seventh-round draft pick by Tampa Bay in 1985 and played mostly special teams that year. The Buccaneers cut him in 1986, and he sat out the season.

He didn't give up on football, however. In 1987, he tried to resurrect his career with the Indianapolis Colts and made it to the final cut before they let him go on August 31.

Fortunately for him, NFL players went on strike in 1987 and he returned as a strike replacement player on September 24 of that year. He had another chance and made the most of it. When the strike ended, he was playing so well that he was one of five replacement players the Colts kept on the team. By the end of 1987, Prior was starting and leading the Colts in special teams tackles and interceptions. He was on his way to a long and successful NFL career.

Prior was happy he landed in Green Bay in 1993, although he didn't get the job he expected. He signed with the Packers as a free agent after they lost Pro Bowl safety Chuck Cecil to free agency. As one of the Colts' leading tacklers and twice intercepting six passes in a season, he was disappointed to be named a backup safety in Green Bay. He played behind LeRoy Butler, George Teague, Eugene Robinson, Darren Sharper, and others in the next six seasons. "I was able to adjust to my role. That's part of life in the NFL," Prior said.

A special teams standout and regular on the Packers' passing-down defenses, Prior was a solid performer, playing in every game for the Packers from 1993 to 1998. He often led the team in special teams tackles. He was one of the key performers on their successful kick return and kick coverage teams in 1996.

Going to the playoffs every year and winning the Super Bowl helped make up for the disappointment of not starting with the Packers. "You hope every player in the league at one time has a chance to be part of a Super Bowl. You put in so many hours and put your body through so much. It's a chance to take it all in," Prior said, recalling Super Bowl XXXI festivities in New Orleans, where his family also spent the week.

Prior was Green Bay's special teams captain in Super Bowl XXXI and intercepted a Drew Bledsoe pass in the second quarter. The interception led to a Packers score that put them ahead, 24-14, at halftime. They wound up defeating the Patriots, 35-21. Today, Prior has that interception ball on display in his basement.

After the Super Bowl win, Prior came back strong. In 1997, he had one of his best seasons as a Packer when he intercepted four passes, one behind team leader LeRoy Butler. One of Prior's steals was the 7,000th career pass attempt by Miami quarterback Dan Marino. The pickoff came during a 23-18 win over the Dolphins on September 14, 1997, at Lambeau Field. The Packers were 2-1 and on their way to another Super Bowl appearance.

Despite his strong play, the Packers released him in February of 1998, a month after Super Bowl XXXII. They re-signed him a month later. He played the 1998 season and had one interception, raising his career total to 35, the same as his age.

If all of Prior's interceptions had come in Green Bay, he would have ranked sixth in team history, right behind Darren Sharper (36), Butler (38), and Herb Adderley (39). Bobby Dillon, who played in the 1950s, is the team record-holder with 52, while Willie Wood, from the 1960s, has 48.

After the 1998 season, Prior asked General Manager Ron Wolf whether the Packers planned to bring him back. "He said, 'No, Mike, we'll be moving in a different direction, but thanks for all you did here,'" Prior said, recalling their phone conversation.

Safety Mike Prior (39) grabs some water while cornerback Bucky Brooks (22) encourages defensive end Reggie White during a 1996 regular-season Packer game. Prior had an interception against New England during Super Bowl XXXI.

So Prior and his wife and children, who had been living in Green Bay half the year, returned to live full-time in Indianapolis. With his daughters already in school in Indianapolis and not knowing how long he'd be in Green Bay, Prior and his wife, Diane, kept their home in Indiana when he signed with the Packers. They sent their children to school in Green Bay in the fall and Indiana in the spring. Shuffling his family was difficult, but the excitement of being in Green Bay during winning seasons made it worthwhile. "It was a great period of time for us," Prior said.

After retiring, he began to work with children in the Indianapolis area. He coached baseball and football at local high schools and was the athletic director at a Catholic elementary school for five years. He earned a bachelor's degree in business administration from Illinois State. In 2005, he became youth football commissioner for the Colts and was an analyst on the team's postgame radio show.

He watched the Colts start the 2005 season 13-0 before fading and losing in the playoffs. "It brought back a lot of memories of '96 when we went to the Super Bowl. I look back at what we had to do to get there—it's not as easy as it looks," Prior said.

Some of his memories were revived when, in January of 2006, he traveled with team marketing personnel, the team mascot, and cheerleaders on the Colts Playoff Tour to build interest in the team's drive to the playoffs. The tour covered more than 1,000 miles in four days, stopping in four cities. It drew more than 5,000 fans, including some who hauled out their old Mike Prior Colts cards for autographs.

Prior's new duties with the Colts are varied. He sets up 90-minute Big Blue youth football camps at Indianapolis-area grade schools. At the camps, part of an NFL effort to promote football, children practice such skills as throwing and catching, and get a chance to see the "Colts in Motion" interactive trailer, which includes a replica player's locker and a mini-museum. He also coordinates a Colts program that recognizes a high school coach each week.

Prior helps with the NFL Grassroots program, which gives money to programs in NFL cities through the NFL Youth Football Fund; he helps oversee the Colts Youth Football Fund, which supports local youth football programs; and he helps at the team's women's football clinic. He has become a team ambassador, signing autographs for special events and making appearances with current players.

Among the benefits of working for the Colts is that Prior can enjoy regular work hours and be around to see his daughters finish high school. With an office at the Colts headquarters, he also is in a pro football environment again. He has considered coaching full-time, including in the NFL, but for now he is content to stay near home as much as possible.

Since the day Wolf let him go, Prior has put his permanent second-career plans somewhat on hold until his children are grown. "I'm still trying to adjust to a normal life. I'm still finding out what I'm supposed to do. Maybe it's to be a teacher and help these kids make the right decisions," he said.

A decade after they first made him happy, Mike Prior's Super Bowl rings are making others smile in Indiana. He always lets children at the Big Blue camps get a good look at them. "It's fun to see kids get a charge out of it. Having that little piece of jewelry really goes a long way. They look up to you," Prior said.

When children take a look at Prior's rings, they also get some advice from the owner. "I tell them that it shows you can do anything you want to if you put the time and effort into it."

GETTING A GRIP
Ken Ruettgers (75)

College: Southern California
Position: Tackle, 1985–96
Highlight: Played in 156 games as a Packer, 12th most in team history.
After football: Founded *GamesOver.org*, a career counseling and transition
program for professional athletes.

In November of 1996, Ken Ruettgers was at a personal crossroads. His aching left knee hurt so badly he could barely walk onto the football field. However, the Packers were 9-3 and by all accounts headed for their first Super Bowl in three decades.

Should he retire? Could he give up the very thing he'd been playing for as a Packer for 12 seasons?

He had experienced pain before—cracked ribs, a broken shoulder, a broken back, broken ankles, a broken hand, and multiple knee surgeries, not to mention humid July training camps, insufferable hours in the weight room, and long months of rehabilitation after his surgeries. But not pain like this.

Yet Ruettgers also had suffered another kind of pain: the agony of living through too many losing seasons under Coaches Forrest Gregg and Lindy Infante. Three times he was on teams that had seven-game losing streaks; some of those years were so bad and he had grown so tired of losing in Green Bay that by 1992 he began to believe he'd had enough. He asked to be traded before the season, when the Packers were starting over again with new General Manager Ron Wolf and Coach Mike Holmgren. With his physical problems piling up, Ruettgers didn't know how many years he had left. He wanted to play for a winner, or at least closer to Bakersfield, California, where he grew up, and the University of Southern California, where he starred in college. "I needed a change," Ruettgers said, remembering his first meeting with Wolf early in 1992. "Ron encouraged me to meet with Holmgren and [offensive line coach] Tom Lovat. I said to Wolf, 'Trade me to the Oakland Raiders. You've got connections. I want to go back home to California.' It had been seven lean years. I told Ron I had paid my penance."

Wolf said no. He looked at Ruettgers, a 6-foot-6, 295-pound specimen who was one of the mainstays of the Packers offensive line, and figured the team needed him, even though Ruettgers was on crutches, recovering from a torn hamstring and arthroscopic surgery on a knee. But Infante's last year with the Packers, when the team went 4-12, hadn't been pretty; it also was lineman Tony Mandarich's disappointing last year with the team. "There was a lot of stuff going on. It was just a weird year for the linemen, plus with losing there was a lot of pressure," Ruettgers said.

Then Ruettgers went to minicamp with his new head coach. He liked Holmgren.

Ruettgers felt like he was with a new team. "It was a fresh start in Green Bay," he said. The Packers began to win, and Ruettgers enjoyed some of the best years of his career from 1992 through 1995. He was one of just three players from the Infante era still with the Packers in 1996, and he was the last player remaining from the Gregg era, which had ended in 1987.

The lean Gregg and Infante years were over. Talented players began to arrive. Reggie White, Brett Favre, Santana Dotson, Eugene Robinson, Sean Jones, Edgar Bennett, Keith Jackson. There were playoff games. High expectations. Super Bowl talk.

The Holmgren era was nothing like Ruettgers' first seven years in Green Bay. In 1993, when the Packers surged late in the season to finish 9-7 and make the playoffs for the first time under Holmgren, Ruettgers was a human wall on the line—he didn't allow a sack that year until early November.

Heading into the 1996 season, Ruettgers was excited. "Sheryl, we're going to the Super Bowl this year," Ruettgers told his wife. "We had the key people in the right positions. People kept their egos in check. We had the right coaches, the right attitudes. I thought, 'Man, this is it.'"

But while the Packers seemed to be on the verge of their long-awaited comeback, it wasn't at all clear that Ruettgers would be able to make it there with them. The off-season had brought two surgeries on his degenerative left knee. Despite extensive rehabilitation, the knee wasn't getting better and the pain wasn't going away.

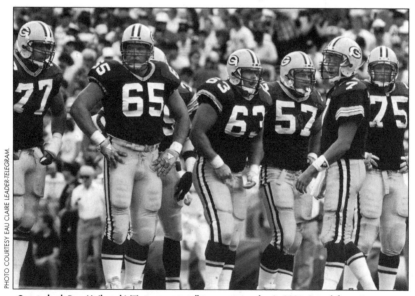

PHOTO COURTESY EAU CLAIRE LEADER-TELEGRAM.

Quarterback Don Majkowski (7) prepares to tell teammates a play in 1991. From left are Tony Mandarich (77), Ron Hallstrom (65), James Campen (63), Rich Moran (57), and Ken Ruettgers (75). Ruettgers retired during the 1996 season, missing by only a couple of months his goal to play in the Super Bowl.

Ruettgers met with Holmgren during training camp and told him he probably wouldn't be able to make it through the 1996 season. Like Wolf back in 1992, Holmgren didn't want to give up on Ruettgers. He told him to hang on, see if the pain got better, and try to play. "He didn't have to twist my arm," Ruettgers said, holding out hope that he might be able to get a Super Bowl ring.

The Packers thought Ruettgers might miraculously recover. He had done it before. In 1995, after the final preseason game, Ruettgers woke up and couldn't move his legs. Only with the help of his wife was he able to make it to a hospital, where doctors found four cracked bones at the base of his back. He was expected to miss three or four regular season games but returned, without pain, in 12 days. Ruettgers, a Christian, said God played a role in healing him so quickly, a scenario that Packers fans would hear again later in the season when Reggie White claimed that God healed his torn hamstring.

But this was 1996 and it was Ruettgers' oft-injured knee, not his back. He was another year older, and his knee had even less cartilage than it did the year before. This time, there would be no miracle.

He didn't play until October 27, as a backup, and then returned to the starting lineup on November 18, 1996, against the defending Super Bowl champion Dallas Cowboys. He played well, but it was a painful experience. Ruettgers had to grit his teeth and play in constant pain. "The more I played, the worse it got. I needed crutches just to walk out on the field and to get off the field. It took every ounce of focus just for me to play," Ruettgers said.

Two days later, he knew that he had no choice. It was his day of reckoning: November 20, 1996. This time, Holmgren didn't try to talk him out of it, although he was somewhat surprised because Ruettgers had played well. But the constant pain in his knee simply was too much to handle. The day that most pro athletes dread arrived for Ruettgers: His athletic career, the work that had defined his life to that point, was finished.

Ruettgers called a news conference at Lambeau Field to announce his retirement at age 34. His wife, Sheryl, was there, along with Holmgren. He made it clear to the media that he didn't want to quit. "I cannot do it anymore. I'm going to miss my teammates and just the whole culture of football," Ruettgers said that day as tears came to his eyes and his words became choked with emotion. "What's making this very difficult is that I still have a great passion and desire to play. I still love the game and everything about it."

Ruettgers proved his love for football during the 12 seasons he wore a Packers uniform. He was one of the best tackles in the NFL for years, even though he never made the Pro Bowl. He probably would have earned individual honors if the

Packers had had better teams in the late 1980s and early 1990s before his injuries began piling up. Still, he played well after Holmgren arrived, usually ranking among the top three on the team in player evaluations after games.

Ruettgers, the top draft pick in 1985, was with the Packers longer than all but five players in team history. It was a career marked by steady improvement and consistent, solid performances, not unlike that of Hall of Fame member Forrest Gregg, Ruettgers' first pro coach.

By his second year, Ruettgers' talent was beginning to show. On December 20, 1986, the Packers closed out their regular season against the New York Giants, losing, 55-24, but in that game Ruettgers neutralized Giants pass rusher Lawrence Taylor, denying Taylor the one sack he needed to set the NFL single-season record. The Giants went on to win the Super Bowl that season.

He continued to turn heads in 1987. He gave up just $3\frac{1}{2}$ sacks in a strike-shortened, 12-game schedule. He was so dominating that Wisconsin media voted him the offensive player of the year, the first time since 1971 an offensive lineman had received such an honor. One of his favorite years was 1989. The surprising 1989 team was 10-6 and tied for first in the NFC Central Division, but missed the playoffs on a tiebreaker. "That team felt like if we could get to the playoffs, we would have a chance to go all the way," Ruettgers said. "We were playing well. That team won against adversity. We all went home saying, 'Man, talk about a missed opportunity.'"

He was glad Wolf and Holmgren convinced him to stay in 1992. Ruettgers enjoyed 1992 much like 1989 because the Packers won when they weren't expected to and had fun. The Packers went 9-7, reversing the 4-12 record from the year before. "That year was the most fun. Holmgren was excited and energetic. Favre was coming in and fun to watch."

Some observers say 1992 also was Ruettgers' best year as a Packer. He picked a good time to play well because his contract was up. In 1993, after he held out for 45 days, missing training camp, he signed a four-year, $8 million deal. With that contract, he became the highest-paid player on offense in the team's 75 years of existence. After he signed, he said, "The business part of this game leaves a bitter taste in your mouth, but the good thing about it is, once you get done, you can put it behind you and get on with what you love to do."

As a lineman, Ruettgers appreciated the West Coast offense used by Holmgren because the quarterback used only a three- to five-step drop before setting and throwing. Under Infante, the quarterback used a five- to seven-step drop, forcing the linemen to hold their blocks longer. Because of that challenge, Ruettgers believes 1989 was his best year as a lineman. Even with the long quarterback drops, Ruettgers gave up just one sack until the final game of the year, when he gave up two.

At left tackle and with a right-handed quarterback, Ruettgers was a key part of a passing offense, protecting the quarterback's blind side from pass rushers. He took pride in shutting down defensive ends. One occasion came early in 1993 when he went against feared Chicago defensive end Richard Dent, a 6-foot-5, 265-pound pass rushing specialist who still was a force at age 31. Ruettgers was notorious for studying opponents; he kept a book on their favorite moves, their history, their personality types. "You know my old moves, but I still can beat you," Dent told Ruettgers early in the game. "You take away my bread, I'll go over to my butter."

Yet the Packers won, 17-3, that day at Lambeau Field, often running the ball away from Dent, who had just one tackle and no sacks against Ruettgers. It was a classic one-on-one battle in the trenches, with Dent complaining that he was being held by Ruettgers and Ruettgers refusing to let Dent get past him. Near the end of the game, Dent took a swipe at Ruettgers out of frustration. That Bears game provided the kind of competition Ruettgers missed when he retired.

During his career, Ruettgers played for the sometimes-controversial Gregg and with one player who often faced criticism, Sterling Sharpe. Ruettgers liked them both.

Gregg was known for criticizing players in front of their teammates, which didn't sit well with many Packers, but Ruettgers never took the criticism personally. "If you understood him, he was an easy guy to play for. He was hard-working, wanted to win, and very encouraging and forgiving," Ruettgers said.

Gregg certainly understood what Ruettgers was going through as a player. Considered one of the greatest offensive tackles of all time, Gregg thought Ruettgers was someone special when he drafted him in 1985. "We have a football player that we have coveted for a long time. We think he is outstanding," Gregg said that day. Ruettgers was assigned number 75, the same number that Gregg had worn.

Sharpe often didn't talk with the media, seldom signed autographs in public, and was roundly criticized when he once held out for a bigger contract on the eve of a regular season. "Sterling probably was one of my favorite guys. I appreciated his willingness to share about racial issues as they related to the South. He was recruited to play quarterback in college [at the University of South Carolina] but was told he was the wrong color," Ruettgers said.

Ruettgers played in 156 games with the Packers. At one point, he started 52 straight before the back injury that kept him out of the 1995 season opener. When he retired, only two linemen had played more than Ruettgers' 12 seasons with the Packers. They were Gregg, with 14 years, and Charles "Buckets" Goldenberg, with 13. Larry McCarren also played 12 years.

Despite the losing seasons, Ruettgers is proud that he played his entire career in Green Bay. Once, after a game, he and his wife went out to a supper club to eat. In most NFL cities, an offensive lineman wouldn't be recognized. But this was Green Bay. Fans stopped to talk and ask about the game. "Here, people not only know who you are, they respect you," he said.

The day he retired, just before Thanksgiving in 1996, Ruettgers had put one big decision behind him but faced an even tougher one: What was he going to do with the rest of his life? He had had a fine NFL career, but that didn't mean a lot when he needed to find a new line of work, one that wouldn't involve physical labor. His well-developed muscles and pass-blocking skills had become all but useless. He had a wife and three children, had written a book, *Home Field Advantage*, about being a good role model and father, had a master's degree in business administration, and did community work. In short, he had his priorities straight and planned for retirement better than any other players he knew. Still, he wasn't prepared.

He quickly realized one thing: "Our capitalistic society doesn't dwell too much on guys that 'used to be.'"

The Packers went on to win the Super Bowl, with Ruettgers watching on the sidelines. He got his Super Bowl ring when they were passed out at the Oneida Country Club team party in Green Bay. But while the organization and fans celebrated and geared up for the next season, Ruettgers went on a personal journey of discovery. He got football out of his system as an assistant coach in the fall of 1997 for West DePere High School near Green Bay. Then he and Sheryl and their children moved to Oregon, where he took a job working with authors at a small book-publishing company.

The first day he drove to work, he realized he no longer was in the company of wealthy athletes. "I looked around and said to myself, 'Where's all the Mercedes, Beamers [BMWs], SUVs? With the Packers, I never saw a car older than three or four years old. Even the rookies had new cars." There were other rude awakenings. For the first time in his life, he had to work in a co-ed environment. He had never worked with women while playing in the NFL. Also, outside of football games, he wasn't used to working weekends in an office. And he was working year-round, the first time in his life he didn't have a seasonal job. "I didn't know what it meant to do a regular job," he said.

He was 36 years old and realized that, in a social sense, he was about 17. Starting when he went to USC, he had lived in a false world. At USC, as a pampered scholarship athlete, his tuition was paid for. He didn't have to wait in line to get classes. Food and housing were provided. In the pros, he made $1 million a year in the early 1990s (that's $19,231 a week or $481 an hour based on a 40-hour work week). Then, his contract doubled in the mid-1990s. There was extra money from shoe contracts, speaking engagements, promotional appearances, and all the adulation he could handle. And his days were structured for him by the team.

"They treat you like a god, and you start thinking you're a god. Sheryl once said to me, 'You think the world revolves around you, don't you?' And I said, 'Yes, it does.' After football, you wonder, 'What happened to my agent? He said I was such a great guy. What happened to all the cousins I never knew existed until they wanted tickets?'" said a bemused Ruettgers.

Despite a sometimes rough transition away from football, Ruettgers was adjusting. He was promoted at the publishing house before he realized something: If he was prepared for retirement from the NFL and was still having a hard time, what was life like for players who weren't prepared? The insight led him into a new line of work: He wanted to help athletes make the transition from the pampered world of professional sports to the real world. In 2000, he started *GamesOver.org*, a Web site and nonprofit counseling service. His motto: Where a new season begins.

In 2005, Ruettgers worked with about 100 active and retired pro athletes and their wives. *GamesOver.org* offers classes and resources to help athletes deal with the vagaries of life beyond the kingdom of the NFL and other pro sports. He is associated with career advisers, marriage and family advisers, and a chaplain. He also made a video, *When the Cheering Stops*, that features 25 former athletes, including former Packers Brian Noble, Don Majkowski, Rich Moran, and John Michels, the player who replaced Ruettgers at left tackle in November of 1996.

People in the working world may have a hard time accepting that the very people who seemingly have it all—pro athletes—need help and more attention. Few people are going to reach out and help them, unless it's one of them. Ruettgers has no problem arguing his point that these people are at risk and need help. He can rattle off vital statistics about the sordid lives of ex-athletes like they were part of some big NFL game he just played:

- Two years after they retire, 87 percent of NFL players are either bankrupt, divorced, or unemployed.
- Half of them have no college degree or job experience.
- 65 percent have permanent injuries.
- More than half feel they've lost their purpose in life, a feeling that often leads to depression.
- The suicide rate for active and retired NFL players is six times the national average.

The reason for all the problems is simple, Ruettgers said: Athletes are dealing with the death of their identity.

Ruettgers tries to help athletes realize they can live productive lives after retiring. Despite their perception that their lives are over, they should actually be able to live more productive lives than the average person at their age because of the resources available to them, including money, time, and name recognition.

The first step, however, often is the hardest. Most men, and certainly ex-athletes who have come to believe they are superhuman, don't like deflating their egos and asking for help. "I get more calls from [athletes'] wives," Ruettgers said. "They say, 'I don't know what to do with him. I'm worried. He's driving me nuts.'"

Early in 2006, his Web site featured an interview with retired Hall of Fame lineman Anthony Munoz; excerpts from a book, *Daddy's Home at Last,* by retired Chicago Bears linebacker Mike Singletary; and an interview with Andrea Novoselsky, the wife of retired Minnesota Vikings tight end Brent Novoselsky.

In a welcome letter on the *GamesOver.org* Web site, Ruettgers tells visitors he's there to help. "It hurts to get kicked out of the NFL Palace and end up on the streets of the unfamiliar.... It's difficult to maintain the illusion that you have it all together after you leave the game. It can cost you time, money, your marriage. You have what it takes to conquer life after the game is over. You are a world-class competitor."

Ruettgers still is bothered by the left knee that forced him to retire. He has no cartilage left in the joint, which is arthritic, hurts 24 hours a day, and swells when he overuses it; a 30-minute walk can mean agony. The rest of his body feels pretty good. "If not for that one spot on my knee the size of a penny, I could have kept playing. In my dream world, I would have played another two or three years," he said. He might even have settled for another two or three months—enough to get him on the field in Super Bowl XXXI. He was there, but watching the game from the sidelines wasn't his idea of fulfilling a dream.

However, he left pro football with the satisfaction of having played well. After 1995, his last full season, *Milwaukee Journal Sentinel* reporter Bob McGinn had this to say about him: "He has been the team's best lineman for most of his 10-year career. A self-made, quality pass protector who practices and plays as hard as anyone on the roster. Doesn't blow anyone up in the running game but usually crafty enough to get by. You can't put a price tag on a left tackle who neutralizes the game's premier rushers and never gets shook."

After football, Ruettgers faced a new challenge. Could he achieve the same level of success in his personal life? By 2006, he had climbed the first hurdle: He was content with his second career and had made strides to become a well-adjusted husband and father. He was ready for the next opponent. Could he help other pro athletes do the same? At *GamesOver.org,* Ruettgers found that the end actually is a beginning.

COACHING BOYS TO MEN
Harry Sydney (42)
College: Kansas
Position: Fullback, 1992
Highlight: Played in all 16 games and caught 49 passes in 1992.
After football: Packer running backs coach 1995 to 1999, founder of My Brother's
Keeper mentoring service in Green Bay.

On game days, the bars near Lambeau Field overflow. Fans listen to live music, dance, drink, and eat before and after the game. Stadium View, The Bar, and Andruzzi's are a few of the hot spots where fans gather, crowding the streets and forcing traffic to slow to a crawl. Brett Favre's Steakhouse, just down the street, always draws a big game-day crowd. Many people gather at fenced-off tour group parties.

At Stadium View prior to a 2005 game, big Gilbert Brown and little Robert Brooks of the 1990s Super Bowl teams were signing memorabilia outdoors, a few feet from a tent where bartenders poured cold ones and fans danced near the street. So many people were crammed on the Stadium View grounds that, believe it or not, it was hard to spot the 345-pound Gilbert. I asked one employee where I could find him; the employee had no idea, although it turned out that Gilbert and Brooks were just 20 feet away in the mass of people. Inside Stadium View, people waited in line to get a free autograph from 1980s running back Gerry Ellis, whose old jersey still fit him just fine.

In the midst of the pounding rock music, dancing, drinking, and smoking, it seemed an odd place to find Harry Sydney. Or maybe it wasn't.

After Sydney coached Packers running backs from 1995 to 1999—and wasn't retained by new coach Mike Sherman in 2000—he started a mentoring service for boys and men in Green Bay. My Brother's Keeper Inc. helps put males on the right track in life. On Holmgren Way, Sydney probably knew that some of the revelers could use a little talking to, but he wasn't there on a recruiting trip.

After home games, Sydney sits on a makeshift stage at The Bar with a radio host and talks football on WDUZ The Fan, a Green Bay radio station. On this day, dozens of people danced to music outside The Bar as the DJ asked, "How many drinkers do we have out there tonight?" Dozens more partied inside The Bar, the floor wet with spilled beer. Many of the inebriated customers were oblivious to the radio show going on a few feet in front of them, although it was being broadcast in the bar as well as over the air.

Sydney hadn't been part of pro football for more than five years, but he hadn't completely gotten it out of his system. He doesn't pass up the chance to talk about the Packers, both on the postgame radio show and on a weekly late-afternoon radio show on the same station. It shouldn't be surprising. He isn't afraid to tell people how to straighten out their lives. He has no problem offering his opinions on the Packers, even on Brett Favre. With the Packers and Favre struggling in 2005, Sydney said the aging Favre finally was paying the price for his unconventional style of throwing off his front foot. Other great quarterbacks, such as Joe Montana and John Elway, played well late in their careers because they were mechanically sound throwers. The Packers weren't playing well, and Sydney dared to say that Favre was part of the problem.

Heresy amid the throngs of the faithful, perhaps, but Sydney was just doing what he does best: Telling people the truth.

Sydney had a hunch when he started My Brother's Keeper that there was a need for a male guidance program in the Green Bay area. Soon after he opened the office on West Mason Street, he realized he was right.

In less than a year, he had helped dozens of boys and men. In two years, he helped more than 250. And his business keeps growing. He helps paroled convicts from the prison in Green Bay, works with juvenile offenders at a prison like facility (Lincoln Hills, in Wausau, Wisconsin), and regularly goes to the juvenile detention center at the Brown County Jail to talk with troubled adolescents. He talks to men off the streets who are down to their last dollar.

With his wife, Madonna, taking care of scheduling and welcoming sometimes-hesitant men and boys into the office, Sydney has opened himself up to the not-so-pretty underside of blue-collar Green Bay, the side he and most of his teammates seldom saw while playing for the Packers. He helps men who are alcoholics, criminals, adulterers, homeless, abusers—anyone who's willing to take a step forward in his life. "I deal with every male issue there is. Insecurity, failure, sexual problems, anger management," Sydney said.

He charges for his 45-minute sessions—if people can pay. If they can't, he takes them into his office anyway. Once he gets them inside, Sydney knows he has a better than 50-50 chance of turning them into new people and putting them back on the streets as productive citizens again.

I didn't go into Sydney's office looking for any advice, just a few stories about his new career and his old one. But it was impossible to leave My Brother's Keeper without thinking more deeply about life and how I could take charge to make it better. Sydney has an upfront, confrontational style of speaking that would make anyone take notice, especially someone who needed just a glimmer of hope.

A muscular, 250-pound former NFL fullback with a shaved head and a booming voice, he leans forward in his chair and looks straight at you. A man whose dad was a Green Beret and who grew up indoctrinated with a military approach to daily living. Just you and him in a small office, surrounded by pictures of his successes—playing for the Super Bowl champion San Francisco 49ers and the Packers. He used to flatten linebackers for a living.

You have problems. He might be your last chance. You are intimidated, which is good in a way, but then you realize this man really has it in his heart to help you. He seems to understand.

He often starts with, "How's life been working for you? Do you like where you're at?"

You tell him you've made mistakes, big mistakes. You're in a pit, and you can't get out.

"It doesn't matter where you've come from. It matters where you're going," he says.

You tell him you're nothing, a failure.

"Why aren't you a man of integrity? You need a foundation built on integrity. If it's not, it's built on quicksand. We have to clean you out," he says.

You think he's being a bit rough. You don't need someone else to come down on you.

"I'm here to tell you the truth," he shoots back.

You tell him you need money and a job.

"I'm not here to pat you on the back."

He sends you home with a plan and a little homework, and wants to see you in another week to see what you've accomplished. You're not sure what just happened, but you have an inkling not only that this guy likes you but that he's onto something—something that hit straight at your soul.

These days, Sydney doesn't knock people over. He lifts them up.

Sydney realized after he got out of coaching that numerous counseling organizations in the Green Bay area were geared toward women, not for men. The need for a men's mentoring program, he believes, is critical because men are at the root of many societal ills and many of the problems women face.

Men, he says, are examples of the duck philosophy. On the surface, they look calm but beneath the fascade "they're paddling their butts off trying to stay afloat," he said. Like the classic male who doesn't want to ask for directions when he's lost, Sydney helps boys and men who need direction in their life but don't seek it until they are about to drive off the map.

"The majority of people, I've at least given them a choice to see a different way. With some of them, all of a sudden you can see a light go on when I'm talking with them," Sydney said as we sat in his office, with the week's saying, courtesy of Franklin Delano Roosevelt, staring us down: "You have nothing to fear but fear itself."

Most of the men and boys he sees have experience at failing but not at succeeding. Sydney's goal is to help them succeed one step at a time, starting with his

IRS code—integrity, respect, and standards. "If you have that, what is there to fear? You then have the ability to make the right choices," Sydney said. "It's straight talk. I shoot straight. They respect the truth."

Sydney speaks from experience. He's been through many of the same things as the men he's guided. He also knows what it's like to pull himself out of a tailspin and succeed beyond even his wildest dreams.

First, the good times. He made a name for himself at Kansas, where he studied criminology and juvenile justice, and was an all-Big Eight running back in 1980. But his first attempts at making the NFL ended when he was the last man cut by both the Seattle Seahawks and then the Cincinnati Bengals in 1981.

He played three years in the United States Football League with the Denver Gold and the Memphis Showboats (where he was Reggie White's teammate), and one year with the Montreal Alouettes of the Canadian Football League. Then the USFL folded and his Canadian team folded. Without a football career, he was back to doing the odd jobs he had held during the off-season—cook, factory worker, soft drink truck driver.

PHOTO COURTESY EAU CLAIRE LEADER-TELEGRAM.

Fullback Harry Sydney looks for running room in 1992, his only season with the Packers. He was running backs coach in 1996, when the Packers went 13-3 and then won the Super Bowl.

"I was at a big crossroads. I went back home to North Carolina. Anytime there's pressure, you have to run home to mom, you know. I was substitute teaching a psychology course and telling kids how to be successful—what a joke. I also was working at a factory as a forklift driver. I remember a man came up to me and said, 'Are you Harry Sydney, the pro football player?' I told him I was. He said, 'No, you're not. You're a forklift driver.' The reality is, I was," Sydney said.

It was the kind of "wake up and take a look at yourself" advice Sydney needed and the kind he would be giving men in Green Bay two decades later.

Hit between the eyes with the reality that his pro football dream was slipping away, Sydney sent a résumé to every NFL team. Only one of them answered—the San Francisco 49ers. It was serendipity. Coach Bill Walsh had remembered Sydney playing well against the 49ers in a preseason game years before when he was in camp with Seattle. Walsh invited him for a tryout.

Sydney's forklift days were in the past. He played fullback for the 49ers for five seasons during their glory years, helping them win the 1989 and 1990 Super Bowls with Joe Montana at quarterback and a host of other talented players like halfback Roger Craig, wide receiver Jerry Rice, and defensive back Ronnie Lott.

Sydney wasn't a starter, but he was special-teams captain during the Super Bowls. After the first win, realizing that he still might be driving a forklift if not for a co-worker who gave him a dose of reality, "I laughed, I cried. I laughed, I cried. I never thought I'd get there," Sydney said.

As a backup at fullback to Tom Rathman, Sydney rushed for just 50 yards in 1988, 56 yards in 1989, and 166 yards in 1990. But he also caught passes, was a special-teams warrior, and did all the little things that kept him on the 49ers roster year after year.

In 1992, he joined Holmgren and helped the former 49ers assistant coach institute Walsh's West Coast offense in Green Bay. Holmgren had thought about picking up Sydney in the Plan B draft that year. Then, on August 31, just before the 1992 season started, he saw that the 49ers had waived Sydney. He grabbed him. "Harry adds a lot to the team at this point because we have [rookies] Dexter McNabb and Edgar [Bennett]. It's nice to have another veteran who they can learn from. He knows the system," Holmgren said at the time.

Then 33 and called "old man" by Holmgren, Sydney knew that his role in Green Bay was to help the Packers start over, show players how to practice the way the champion 49ers practiced, and to teach them how to win. Holmgren cleaned house of numerous Packers veterans that summer; Sydney was the exception.

Besides, Sydney had a secret weapon. He had been a wishbone quarterback for two years at Kansas and still was pretty handy at throwing the halfback or fullback option. In fact, Sydney was tabbed by Holmgren in 1992 as the Packers' emergency quarterback if Favre and Ty Detmer were injured. It was a role Sydney had played in San Francisco for a while, once throwing a touchdown pass to Jerry Rice.

The Packers signed him for $400,000, the biggest salary of Sydney's career. That season also was one of his best. He rushed for 163 yards and caught 49 passes for 384 yards. One pass never got to him, however. When Favre made his Packers debut and threw his first pass, it was intended for Sydney. But it was batted back toward Favre by Cincinnati lineman Ray Seals and caught by Favre for a seven-yard loss.

Sydney was waived in 1993 when the Packers brought in younger and more versatile fullbacks, and he retired. He was a staff assistant in 1994 under Holmgren before landing the running backs coaching job in 1995. It was the same year Edgar Bennett broke through and had the Packers' first 1,000-yard rushing season since 1978. Then came the Packers' Super Bowl win, in which Sydney helped meld the talents of two emerging star runners, Bennett and Dorsey Levens, in the backfield.

Sydney also proved his mettle when he recommended that the Packers draft fullback William Henderson, a powerful lead blocker, in 1995. It turned out to be a great piece of advice. By 2005, Henderson had become a Pro Bowl player and was one of the few Packers from the 1990s Super Bowl teams still on the roster. In March of 2006, under new coach Mike McCarthy, Henderson signed a two-year contract.

Sydney left his mark as much in Green Bay as he had in San Francisco, even though not everything went well for him in Titletown. He suffered through a divorce there before remarrying. "We just grew apart," he said of his first marriage. Part of the reason he didn't pursue other coaching jobs after 1999—he had a chance to coach in Detroit with former Packers assistant Marty Mornhinweg—was that his children were in Green Bay. It was time for him to stay in one place, leave behind the long hours of the NFL (which, Sydney jokes, stands for No Family Life) and be the best father he could be.

Green Bay, he realized, was his kind of town. "It's what the all-American dream is about—safe, respectful, good schools, good sports. I wasn't thinking of setting roots down in Green Bay; it was a pit stop. But I started noticing it's a little bit different community. I used to call this place Mayberry. I loved the way words meant things here. If a guy says something here, you can count on it. Handshakes and words are people's bonds," Sydney said.

The amiable small-town environment of Green Bay is a sharp contrast to the world Sydney lived in as a child. The only place Harry Flanroy Sydney III ever has lived in longer is his hometown in North Carolina, and he doesn't plan to leave anytime soon. He doesn't want to go back to the scene of his childhood, which was nothing short of a nightmare.

Sydney's dad was a tough man with little capacity for compassion. A Green Beret who taught at Fort Bragg, he had been a heavyweight boxing champion in

France while in the military and still was running five miles a day in his 60s. Born on June 26, 1959, Harry grew up with two brothers and two sisters near the base in Fayetteville, North Carolina.

"There were so many low points in my childhood. One of my biggest memories was in high school when I scored 48 points in a basketball game on Friday night and 44 in a game on Saturday. After the game, when we got in the car, the only thing my dad said to me was, 'How did you miss those shots?' There was no love, no hugs in our house," Sydney said. Despise him as he did, Harry Sydney still had to polish his dad's military boots.

Harry learned discipline from his dad but not much else—unless you count the things he learned not to do. Some of his first memories in life are of his father physically abusing his mother, who was an alcoholic. For years, Harry went to sleep with his head under his pillow so that he wouldn't hear his dad hitting his mom.

Finally, when he was a freshman in high school and he began to lift weights and fill out physically, Harry no longer was afraid of his dad. His mother shot his dad in the leg one night and Harry was there to back her up. "I told him if he ever hit Mom again, I'd kill him. I wasn't scared anymore. I made him stop," Sydney said.

When Sydney blossomed as a football player in high school and got a scholarship to Kansas, he was gone. "I wanted to get away," he recalled. "I had a suitcase and $50. I said, 'Mom, don't send me any money. I'll make it on my own.'"

Sydney grew up with a lot of anger, made mistakes, blamed his dad, and somehow succeeded. Like the men he's trying to help, he finally got his priorities straight after his divorce at age 35 in Green Bay. "I was becoming my dad. I made a lot of bad choices. I was a man of stuff and not of substance. Fortunately, I met Madonna, who has helped me become the person I am," Sydney said of his second wife.

He has reconciled with his father. "I've stopped blaming him for things in my life."

Sometimes, when he works with people like Brian Barton, Sydney is thankful for the difficult times he's faced. He can relate to their troubles.

Barton grew up four blocks from Lambeau Field in Green Bay and went to games as a kid. He got married and eventually moved to Kansas to work as a corporate pilot. Then he began making mistakes. He went through a divorce, had a troubled relationship with his daughter, and saw his weight balloon to more than 400 pounds. At close to 50 years old, he then lost his $80,000-a-year job. He returned to Green Bay, where he began living off unemployment, drinking heavily, and living in a run-down hotel.

"I wasn't suicidal, but I didn't care if I lived or died. I didn't have any desire to fly an airplane again. I was waiting for the end to come, I guess," Barton told me on the telephone.

He was running out of unemployment money when he heard an ad for My Brother's Keeper. Barton called, and Madonna Sydney told him to come in even though he didn't have any money.

"It changed my entire life," Barton said. "Harry didn't feel sorry for me. I thought he was going to take care of me and find me a job. It wasn't like that at all. He said, 'What do you need to do to become the man you want to be? You can't do anything about the past. Take what you've got now and go forward,'" Barton said.

"It was almost like getting splashed in the face with cold water. He told me my situation wasn't a result of someone else. It was about the choices I made in life. He went back and proved it to me. Then I realized I could change my life by making good decisions. He gave me homework assignments. I counted the minutes until I could go back and see him."

Within three months of seeing Sydney, Barton had a job and began to exercise. He lost 70 pounds. He then looked for work as a pilot again. Within a year, he was flying an airplane for a company out west and had patched up his relationship with his ex-wife and daughter. "I can't say enough about what Harry did for me," Barton said.

While we sat in his office, Sydney showed me letters from people he has helped. One was from a man who had been sent to prison in Wisconsin at age 38. Now he was out of prison, had a job, and was a deacon in his church. It was a letter of thanks. "I want to thank you for helping me realize my goals. I've learned to walk with my head held high in my community. Thank you for helping me believe in my abilities and talents. Thank you for helping me keep my goals and dreams alive. I am a man of integrity," the man wrote to Sydney.

Harry Sydney played pro football for less than a decade. But despite the Super Bowl rings, the trophies, jerseys, photos, and stories that testify to football glory, he hopes to be helping people many more years than he played football. His trophies now are the letters and the words of thanks he receives from people whose lives are on the right track, perhaps for the first time.

"The Super Bowl rings are great," he said. "That's what I did, but it's not who I am. To go to the Juvenile Detention Center and to talk with 13- and 14-year-old kids to get them to think about themselves.... Life is about what you can do to help other people."

WHAT HAPPENED TO THE HEROES: THE 1996 GREEN BAY PACKERS

A pro football career is a life within a life. After months and sometimes years of anticipation, it is given birth via a draft pick or a free-agent contract. A team becomes a player's family and its coaches his de facto parents. Meals, housing, clothing, nurturing, family trips, and education are provided with the tacit expectation that the progeny will make something of himself when his abilities are tested. There are no guarantees of individual or family well being. Injury and sickness, good and bad times are to be expected. Only one thing is certain—sooner or later, it will all come to an end. The fatal blow can be quick and painful, such as a career-ending injury. Or it can be painless, such as the arrival of a more favored son or the long, slow, inevitable decline of athletic ability.

Ten years after the Green Bay Packers won Super Bowl XXXI in New Orleans, only a handful of those players still were on NFL rosters heading into the 2006 season. They included Brett Favre, Mike Flanagan, William Henderson, Marco Rivera, Craig Hentrich, and Adam Timmerman. Favre, Flanagan, and Henderson were members of the Packers, Rivera played for Dallas, Hentrich for Tennessee, and Timmerman for St. Louis in 2005. In 2006 or soon thereafter, they will follow their former teammates to the sidelines, and another chapter in Packers history will be closed.

The 1996 Packers were a special team, according to Bob Valesente, defensive backs coach that season. "The offense played extremely well with Brett, and the running game came on strong at the end of the year. The defense was about as strong of a defense as there was in the NFL. We were strong on both sides of the ball, and we were a speed team," said Valesente, who in 2006 was retired and living in Hilton Head, South Carolina.

That team had more than physical skills, however, Valesente said. "We had the four Cs—chemistry, character, commitment, and competitiveness. This team had all those intangibles going for it," he said.

Members of the 1996 team slowly drifted apart over the next few years as management let a variety of key players go via trades, cuts, and free-agent departures. Other players, such as Keith Jackson, Sean Jones, Reggie White, and Robert Brooks, retired. Injuries also played a role. Mike Holmgren left to coach Seattle, taking with him many of the Packers' assistant coaches. Much-admired defensive coordinator Fritz Shurmur died in 1999. In 2000, General Manager Ron Wolf left and put Mike Sherman in charge as coach and general manager. Although the Packers continued to win division titles and make the playoffs in the early 2000s, the magic of the 1990s gradually faded from view, along with the players and coaches who had made it happen.

1996 Players

Arthur, Mike. *Center.* Played in the first five games of 1996 as a substitute, went on injured reserve in week six, and was let go after week 12. It was the end of his six-year career, the last two with the Packers.

Beebe, Don. *Wide receiver.* Saw action as a substitute in the Super Bowl but did not catch a pass. After fighting injuries in 1997 and being left off the active list for the 1998 Super Bowl, he retired. He then started House of Speed athletic training service in Sugar Grove, Illinois. In 2004 and 2005, he also coached the Aurora Christian High School football team in Aurora, Illinois. He played nine NFL seasons, two in Green Bay, and caught 219 passes. He caught 23 touchdown passes, including a career-long 80-yarder against Minnesota in 1996. He also returned one kickoff for a touchdown in his career, a 90-yarder in Green Bay against Chicago in 1996.

Bennett, Edgar. *Halfback.* In the Super Bowl, he rushed 17 times for 40 yards and caught one pass for four yards. After missing the 1997 season with an injury, he signed with the Chicago Bears in 1998, rushing for 611 yards. He gained just 28 yards in six carries in 1999 and retired. In 2001, he became the Packers director of player programs. In 2005, he was named Packers running backs coach. In 2006, he was rehired as running backs coach by new head coach Mike McCarthy. Bennett rushed for 3,992 yards in a seven-year career, including 1,067 in 1995. In 2005, he ranked ninth all-time in Packers history with 3,353 yards.

Bostic, James. *Running back.* A second-year player, he was on injured reserve in 1996 and did not return to the Packers in 1997. He played for Philadelphia in 1998 and 1999 before retiring. In his career, he rushed five times for 19 yards and caught five passes for eight yards. He did not score a touchdown.

Brooks, Bucky. *Cornerback.* Was with the team through week nine, seeing action as a substitute in two games. He also played three games in 1997 with the Packers. He finished his four-year career in 1998 in Oakland.

Brooks, Robert. *Wide receiver.* Was on injured reserve during the Super Bowl as a result of knee surgery in October of 1996. He tore two ligaments and a tendon in his right knee on the first play of a Monday night game on October 14, 1996, against San Francisco. In 1997, he was named NFL Comeback Player of the Year with 1,010 yards receiving. In early 1998, he signed a five-year, $15.1 million contract. However, in August of 1999 he retired because of chronic pain in his knee. In 2000, Brooks tried to play again. He signed with Denver but caught just three passes in four games and retired again. In 2005, Brooks was a businessman and the minister of Capstone Cathedral in Phoenix. In his eight-year career, he caught 309 passes and scored 35 touchdowns. He had 32 career touchdowns receiving, including a Packers record 99-yarder against the Chicago Bears in 1995. He also returned three kicks for touchdowns in his career. In 1995, he had 1,497 yards receiving, a franchise record.

Brown, Gary. *Tackle.* Was inactive for the Super Bowl after playing five games at left tackle during the regular season. He was with the Packers from 1994 to 1996 and then retired. He played in a total of 25 games.

Brown, Gilbert. *Nose tackle.* In the Super Bowl, he had five tackles. He remained with the Packers through 1999, was not re-signed in 2000, improved his physical condition and returned to the team from 2001 to 2003, then retired after the Packers released him in March of 2003. Brown, nicknamed "The Gravedigger," was living in the Detroit area in 2005 and visited Green Bay often. He played 10 seasons, all in Green Bay, after the Minnesota Vikings cut him in 1993. The Packers claimed him on waivers. He had seven career sacks. At 350 pounds, he was considered one of the best nose tackles in the game and one of the best run-stoppers. "I don't think there was a nose tackle that could compete with him," teammate Marco Rivera said. In his final season as a Packer, Brown received the team's Ed Block Courage Award, voted by teammates for "commitment to the principles of courage and sportsmanship."

Butler, LeRoy. *Safety.* In the Super Bowl, he had seven tackles, all solo, including a sack to cap one of his best seasons. In 1996, he totaled 6 $1/2$ sacks, five interceptions, and 92 tackles. He remained with the Packers five more seasons, until he suffered a broken shoulder blade in November of 2001. Still struggling with the injury, he retired on July 18, 2002. In 2005, he was vice president of JJK Sports Entertainment and head of the LeRoy Butler Foundation for Breast Cancer, both in Jacksonville, Florida. He was in Wisconsin often in 2005 and 2006 to raise money for his foundation. He raised $25,000 in one weekend for breast cancer research. (His immediate family has not been affected by breast cancer.) He also wrote a book, *The LeRoy Butler Story: From Wheelchair to the Lambeau Leap.* Proceeds from his book have gone to his foundation. By 2006, he had raised several million dollars for breast cancer research and for an underprivileged youth center in Jacksonville. In 12 NFL seasons, all with the Packers, he had 20 sacks and 38 interceptions and was one of the team's best playmakers and most consistent performers in the mid-1990s.

Carpenter, Rob. *Wide receiver.* Was on injured reserve throughout 1996, including the Super Bowl. He did not return in 1997 and retired. Carpenter played for New

England in 1991, the New York Jets from 1992 to 1994, and Philadelphia in 1995. In five seasons, he caught 51 passes and scored one touchdown.

Chmura, Mark. *Tight end.* Had two catches for 13 yards in the Super Bowl. In September of 1999, he suffered a neck injury and subsequently retired. He was cut by the Packers in April of 2000 after being charged with sexual assault after a party near Milwaukee. He stood trial and was acquitted in February of 2001. Later, he pleaded no contest to being a part of underage drinking at the party, which involved teenage girls after a prom. In 2004, he apologized publicly for his actions at the party and took a job as co-host of "The Football Show" on WAUK-AM radio in Milwaukee. He also was working as a legal assistant for his defense attorney, Gerald Boyle, and pursuing a law degree. In 2005, "The Football Show" was broadcast on Sunday mornings. Chmura and co-host Bill Johnson offered insight and analysis about pro and college football, including the Packers. In seven NFL seasons, all with Green Bay, Chmura had 188 receptions and scored 17 touchdowns.

Clavelle, Shannon. *Defensive end.* Was inactive for the Super Bowl after seeing action in eight games in 1996. He played in six games in 1997, then was cut in October. His career consisted of 15 games with the Packers from 1995 to 1997.

Cox, Ron. *Linebacker.* In the Super Bowl, he had four tackles. He started after George Koonce was injured in the first round of the playoffs. Signed to a $1.3 million a year free-agent contract in 1996, Cox was placed on waivers in 1997 and claimed by Chicago, where he finished his career in 1997. Cox also played with the Bears from 1990-95. In eight NFL seasons, Cox had eight sacks and one interception.

Darkins, Chris. *Running back.* Was on injured reserve in 1996, including the Super Bowl. He returned to the Packers in 1997, playing in three games—the only games of his career—and returning four kickoffs for a 17-yard average.

Dellenbach, Jeff. *Center.* Signed late in the 1996 season, Dellenbach played as a reserve in the Super Bowl. A native of Wausau, he remained with the Packers through 1998. After playing with Philadelphia in 1999, he retired. In 15 NFL seasons, the first 10 with Miami and two with New England, he played in 211 games.

Dorsett, Matthew. *Running back.* Was on injured reserve in 1996, including the Super Bowl, and did not return in 1997. In his career, he played in one NFL game, a 1995 game with the Packers.

Dotson, Earl. *Offensive tackle.* Started every game at right tackle in 1996, including the Super Bowl. He remained with the Packers through 2002, his final season in the NFL. In 2006, he was living in his home state of Texas. Dotson played 10 seasons in the NFL, all with the Packers.

Dotson, Santana. *Defensive tackle.* In the Super Bowl, he had four tackles, including a sack. He left the Packers after the 2001 season and signed with the Washington Redskins. He ruptured his Achilles tendon before the 2002 season began and did not play again. In 2006, Dotson was living in Houston, where he was a businessman and oversaw the Santana Dotson Foundation. Founded in 1995, the foundation's goal is to provide financial aid to underprivileged, inner-city Houston youth to help them get a college education. He held an annual fundraiser in Milwaukee. Dotson played 10 years in the NFL, the first four with Tampa Bay, and had 49 career sacks.

PHOTO COURTESY EAU CLAIRE LEADER-TELEGRAM.

Defensive tackle Santana Dotson was a key member of the 1996 team that went on to win the Super Bowl. Dotson played with the Packers through 2001 and retired in 2002.

Dowden, Corey. *Cornerback.* Played as a substitute the first nine games of 1996 before being waived. He played two games with Chicago in 1997 and retired, ending a three-year career.

Evans, Doug. *Cornerback.* Had an interception and four tackles in the Super Bowl. He signed a five-year contract with the Carolina Panthers in 1998 worth $22.5 million. He played with Carolina through 2001, spent 2002 in Seattle, and parts of 2003 with Seattle and Detroit before retiring. He played 11 seasons, the first five in Green Bay, and totaled 28 interceptions.

PHOTO COURTESY EAU CLAIRE LEADER-TELEGRAM.

Quarterback Brett Favre was one of just a handful of players from the 1996 championship team who still were playing in 2005.

Favre, Brett. *Quarterback.* In the Super Bowl, he completed 14 of 27 passes for 246 yards with two touchdowns and no interceptions. He also rushed four times for 12 yards, including a two-yard touchdown run. He remained with the Packers as the starting quarterback through 2005. Early in 2006, he pondered retirement, then announced in April that he would return for another season. Favre already had started the Brett Favre Fourward Foundation to help disadvantaged children in Wisconsin and Mississippi. His wife, Deanna, a breast cancer survivor, heads the Deanna Favre HOPE Foundation to support breast cancer research and education. One of the top-ranking quarterbacks in NFL history, Favre was destined for the Pro Football Hall of Fame.

Flanagan, Mike. *Center.* A rookie, he was on injured reserve the entire 1996 season, including the playoffs. He remained with the Packers through 2005, when he was slowed by an injury.

Freeman, Antonio. *Wide receiver.* He caught three passes for 105 yards in the Super Bowl, including an 81-yard reception for a touchdown. In 1999, Freeman became the NFL's highest paid receiver when he signed a seven-year contract for $42 million. He remained with the Packers through 2001, played with Philadelphia in 2002, and finished his career as a Packer in 2003. In 2006, he was living in the Miami area. In nine NFL seasons, eight of them with Green Bay, he caught 477 passes and scored 64 touchdowns.

Harris, Bernardo. *Linebacker.* In the Super Bowl, he had two special-teams tackles. He remained with Green Bay through 2001. In 2002, he signed a one-year contract with the Baltimore Ravens. He played in 13 games for the Ravens and then retired. Harris played eight NFL seasons, seven with Green Bay. He totaled nine sacks and five interceptions.

Hayes, Chris. *Safety.* A practice squad player for most of the 1996 season, he saw action in the final two regular-season games, the playoffs, and the Super Bowl. He played for the New York Jets from 1997 to 2001 and with the New England Patriots in 2002. In seven NFL seasons, including one with the Packers, Hayes had one career interception.

Henderson, William. *Fullback.* In the Super Bowl, he caught two passes for 14 yards and rushed once for two yards. He played in all 16 games in 1996, starting 11, and started throughout the playoffs. He remained with the Packers through 2005, and in 2006 he signed a new two-year contract. He started eight games in 2005, rushed once for −5 yards, and caught 30 passes. After 11 NFL seasons, all with the Packers, he had 426 career rushing yards and 308 career pass receptions.

Hentrich, Craig. *Punter.* In the Super Bowl, he kicked seven times for a 42.7-yard average, including one punt of 58 yards. In 1998, he signed a free-agent contract with Tennessee, where he remained through 2005. After leaving the Packers, he led the NFL with a 47.2-yard punting average in 1998. In his 12 years in the NFL, Hentrich had a career punting average of 42.9 yards.

Holland, Darius. *Defensive tackle.* Played as a substitute in every game for the Packers in 1996. He did not have a tackle in the Super Bowl. He left the Packers after 1997 and played for Detroit and Kansas City in 1998, Cleveland in 1999 and 2000, Minnesota in 2002, and Denver in 2003. He was with Denver in 2004 but did not play. After nine NFL seasons, the first three with the Packers, he had four career sacks.

Hollinquest, Lamont. *Linebacker.* In the Super Bowl, he had one special-teams tackle. After playing his first two seasons with Washington, he was with the Packers from 1996 to 1998. He signed a free-agent contract with Kansas City in 1999 but was cut early in training camp and returned to the Packers. He would have missed the first four games of the 1998 season for violating the league's substance abuse policy, but the Packers cut him prior to the regular season, ending his career. Hollinquest did not say what substance he used. He played five NFL seasons and was credited with one-half of one sack.

Howard, Desmond. *Wide receiver/kick returner.* In the Super Bowl, he returned six punts for 90 yards, including one for 34 yards. He also returned four kicks for 154 yards, including a 99-yard touchdown to open the third quarter. He was named Super Bowl MVP. After 1996, he signed a free-agent contract with Oakland, where he played two years. He played parts of 1999 with Detroit and then Green Bay (eight games), and finished his career with Detroit from 2000 to 2002. In 2005, Howard was an announcer for ESPN college football broadcasts. He also was chosen to appear on the cover of the 2006 Electronic Arts—also known as EA Sports—video game named "NCAA Football '06" featuring the "Race for the Heisman." Howard was the 1991 Heisman Trophy winner at the University of Michigan. In 11 NFL seasons, he totaled 123 catches, an 11.9-yard punt return average, and 22.2-yard kick return average. He returned eight punts for touchdowns, three of them in his lone season with the Packers.

Jacke, Chris. *Place-kicker.* In the Super Bowl, he made 31- and 37-yard field goals and missed a 47-yard attempt. In 1997, Jacke and Packers management had a falling out. He was not re-signed and was not invited to accompany the team to the White House in June. Jacke also was not invited to the team party when players received their Super Bowl rings. When asked why Jacke had been excluded from the team celebrations, President Bob Harlan had no comment. In 1997, Jacke signed with Pittsburgh but injured his hip and was cut without appearing in a game. He then was signed by Washington and played one game in 1997, attempting no field goals. He finished his career in Arizona in 1998 and 1999. In 2000, Jacke was involved in a fight with his estranged wife, Tracey, at a Green Bay bar. Police said Tracey Jacke hit Chris Jacke, and she was put in jail overnight. In February of 2002, Chris Jacke pleaded no contest to a disorderly conduct charge involving a domestic abuse incident in Brown County. In 2005, he remained in Green Bay. In 11 NFL seasons, the first eight in Green Bay, he made 202 of 265 field-goal attempts and 338 of 343 extra-point attempts. He left the Packers as the team's second leading scorer of all time with 820 points, three behind Don Hutson. By 2004, kicker Ryan Longwell, Jacke's replacement, had surpassed both of them.

Jackson, Keith. *Tight end.* In the Super Bowl, he had one catch for 10 yards as Mark Chmura's backup. He retired after the 1996 season. He played from 1988 to 1991 in Philadelphia and 1992 to 1994 for Miami before signing with Green Bay in 1995. In nine seasons, Jackson caught 441 passes for 49 touchdowns.

Jervey, Travis. *Running back.* Played in every game in 1996 and made two special-teams tackles in the Super Bowl. In 1997, he made the Pro Bowl as a special-teams player. He remained with the Packers through 1998. In 1999, he signed a four-year contract for $6 million with San Francisco. In 1999 and 2000, he rushed for just 49 yards and one touchdown for the 49ers, partially because of injuries. He also was suspended for four games by the NFL for using steroids. After being waived by the 49ers, he played for Atlanta from 2001 to 2003 before retiring. He then moved to Costa Rica after buying land there. In nine NFL seasons, Jervey rushed for 503 yards and two touchdowns, one as a Packer. He caught 10 passes. He also returned 36 kickoffs for a 23.4-yard average.

Jones, Calvin. *Running back.* In his third year in the NFL and first season in Green Bay, he played in one regular season game and was a substitute in both the NFC championship game and the Super Bowl. He was not re-signed by the Packers in 1997 and retired. In three NFL seasons, he rushed for 112 yards and no touchdowns. He also caught two passes.

Jones, Sean. *Defensive end.* In the Super Bowl, he had three tackles. He was the starting right defensive end throughout 1996. After the Super Bowl, he was not re-signed by the Packers and retired. In 2003, Jones was working as a sports agent when he was found guilty of violating NFL Players Association regulations. He was suspended from representing NFL players until February of 2005. In 2005, he was working in the

Oakland Raiders' personnel department. He played his first four seasons for the Raiders, beginning in 1984, and the next six with the Houston Oilers. In 13 NFL seasons, the last three with Green Bay, Jones had 113 career sacks.

Knapp, Lindsay. *Guard/tackle.* Did not play in the Super Bowl. Knapp played for Kansas City in 1994 and Green Bay in 1996. He was cut by the Packers in August of 1997 and retired.

Koonce, George. *Linebacker.* A starter throughout the 1996 season at middle linebacker, Koonce injured his knee in the first playoff game against San Francisco and subsequently missed the Super Bowl. He remained with the Packers through the 1999 season then signed with the Seattle Seahawks, where he played the 2000 season and subsequently retired. In 2005, he was working at East Carolina University, his alma mater, as an assistant to the athletic director. He also owned Koonce Properties, an apartment and home rental business, and was working toward a master's degree in sports management. In nine NFL seasons, the first eight with Green Bay, Koonce had nine sacks and five interceptions.

Kuberski, Bob. *Defensive tackle.* Played in one game in 1996 but was inactive for the Super Bowl. He left the Packers after the 1999 season. He played with New England in 1999. In five NFL seasons, the first four in Green Bay, he had two career sacks.

Levens, Dorsey. *Fullback.* In the Super Bowl, he rushed 14 times for 61 yards and caught three passes for 23 yards. He remained with the Packers through 2001. He played for Philadelphia in 2002, the New York Giants in 2003, and the Eagles again in 2004. In 1998, he started the Dorsey Levens Foundation in Syracuse, New York, to help inner-city youth. In 11 NFL seasons, he totaled 4,955 yards rushing and scored 36 touchdowns. He also caught 36 passes, 17 for touchdowns. He rushed for 1,435 yards in 1997 for the Packers and also topped 1,000 yards in 1999.

Matthews, Eric. *Wide receiver.* Was on the practice squad in 1996. He did not return to the Packers in 1997 and retired without playing in an NFL game.

Mayes, Derrick. *Wide receiver.* A rookie in 1996, he played in seven games and caught six passes. He was inactive for the playoffs, including the Super Bowl. Mayes was traded to Seattle in 1999, where he finished his career in 2000. In 2006, he was living in Los Angeles and New York, and working in television and film production. In five NFL seasons, he had 145 receptions and scored 16 touchdowns.

McGuire, Gene. *Center.* Joined the team in week six and saw action as a substitute for the next eight games before being cut, ending his career. Prior to 1996, he played in 1993, seeing action in nine games with Chicago.

McKenzie, Keith. *Linebacker.* In the Super Bowl, he had two special-teams tackles. He played with the Packers through 1999, when he went to the Miami Dolphins. He was with Cleveland from 2000 to 2001, Chicago and Green Bay in 2002, and finished his career in Buffalo in 2003. In eight NFL seasons as a linebacker and defensive end, McKenzie had 29 sacks and one interception.

McMahon, Jim. *Quarterback.* A backup to Brett Favre all season, McMahon did not play in the Super Bowl. It was the final game of his 15-year NFL career, the last two of which were with Green Bay. He completed four of five pass attempts as a Packer. McMahon, who led Chicago to a Super Bowl victory during the 1985 season, threw for 18,148 yards and 100 touchdowns in his career. He also had 90 passes intercepted.

Michels, John. *Offensive tackle.* After playing most of the season at left tackle, Michels, a rookie, was replaced in the starting lineup at the end of the regular season and in the playoffs by veteran Bruce Wilkerson. Michels played in the Super Bowl as a substitute. He played in nine games for the Packers in 1997, his final season in the NFL.

Mickens, Terry. *Wide receiver.* In the Super Bowl, he had one special-teams tackle. He was a Packer from 1994 through 1997 and finished his career with Oakland from 1998 to 1999. In six NFL seasons, he had 70 catches and scored four touchdowns.

Miller, Jeff. *Tackle.* Was on injured reserve through week 10 before being cut, ending his career. He did not play in an NFL game.

Morgan, Anthony. *Wide receiver.* Joined the team in week 10 and played as a reserve in three games, with no catches. He then was let go, ending his career. He played for Chicago from 1991 to 1993 and the Packers from 1993 to 1996. He played in every game with Green Bay in 1994 and 1995, catching 59 passes and scoring eight touchdowns. He had 87 career receptions and 12 career touchdowns.

Mullen, Roderick. *Safety.* Played as a substitute in the Super Bowl. After playing for the Packers from 1995 to 1997, he played in 15 games for Carolina in 1998. In four NFL seasons, he had one career interception.

Newsome, Craig. *Cornerback.* Had six tackles and an interception in the Super Bowl. In 1997, he suffered a major knee injury early in the season. In 1999, he was traded to San Francisco. He was out of football in 2000 when he ran into legal trouble involving prescription drugs in La Crosse, Wisconsin. He pleaded guilty to obtaining a controlled substance by fraud, a felony, and being party to a crime of possessing prescription drugs, a misdemeanor. On September 18, 2003, he was arrested for drunk driving and causing an injury while driving drunk in Grand Chute, Wisconsin. He pleaded guilty to the misdemeanor on April 30, 2004. At the time, he was living in Scottsdale, Arizona. Newsome played five NFL seasons, the first four with Green Bay, and had four career interceptions.

Owens, Buster. *Cornerback.* Was on the practice squad in 1996 and did not return to the Packers in 1997. He retired without playing in an NFL game.

Pederson, Doug. *Quarterback.* He played in one game in 1996 and suited up for one more but was the inactive third quarterback the rest of the season, including the playoffs. He played for Philadelphia in 1999 and Cleveland in 2000. Pederson finished his career in Green Bay from 2001 to 2004 as a backup to Brett Favre. In 10 NFL seasons, seven in Green Bay, he completed 286 of 522 pass attempts (55 percent) for 2,762 yards, 12 touchdowns, and 19 interceptions.

Prior, Mike. *Safety.* In the Super Bowl, he intercepted a Drew Bledsoe pass in the second quarter and returned it eight yards. The Packers then drove 74 yards, scoring on a 2-yard Brett Favre run to take a 27-14 halftime lead. Prior played with the Packers through 1998. In 2005, he was named director of youth football programs, including clinics and camps, for the Indianapolis Colts. Prior played for the Colts from 1987 to 1992, before joining the Packers. In 13 NFL seasons, he had 35 interceptions.

Rison, Andre. *Wide receiver.* Caught a 54-yard touchdown pass from Brett Favre in the first quarter to open the scoring in Super Bowl XXXI. He finished the game with two catches for 77 yards. Rison was not re-signed by the Packers in 1997. Before signing with Green Bay, he played with Indianapolis, Atlanta, Cleveland, and Jacksonville, starting in 1989. He played for Kansas City from 1997 to 1999 and Oakland in 2000. In December of 2004, he was sentenced to jail in Georgia for not paying child support. He played for the Toronto Argonauts of the Canadian Football League in 2004, catching 14 passes and scoring one touchdown. In 2005, he was living in Miami Beach, Florida, and working as a nightclub promoter. In 12 NFL seasons "Bad Moon" Rison had 743 receptions and 84 touchdowns. He played a total of five regular season games for the Packers.

Rivera, Marco. *Guard.* A rookie, he made the Packers' final roster but was inactive for all 16 games and the playoffs. After remaining with the Packers through 2004, he signed a free-agent contract with the Dallas Cowboys in 2005. He started and played in 14 games with Dallas that season.

Robinson, Eugene. *Safety.* In the Super Bowl, he led the Packers with nine tackles. The Packers did not re-sign him after the 1997 season, and he played for the Atlanta Falcons in 1998 and 1999. He finished his career in 2000 with the Carolina Panthers. With Atlanta in 1998, he played in his third consecutive Super Bowl. The night before the game in Miami, Robinson was arrested for soliciting an undercover police officer for sex. After retiring, he turned down an offer to be an assistant coach with the Minnesota Vikings. From 2002 to 2005, Robinson was a radio announcer for Carolina Panthers broadcasts. In 16 NFL seasons (11 with Seattle), Robinson had 57 career interceptions, 10th best in NFL history. He played in 250 games, missing only six in his career.

Robinson, Michael. *Cornerback.* Played in six games in 1996 but was inactive for the Super Bowl. He was not re-signed by the Packers in 1997 and retired. It was his only season in the NFL.

Ruettgers, Ken. *Left tackle.* Retired during the 1996 regular season because of a knee injury. In 2005, he was director of *GamesOver.org*, which helps educate and counsel professional athletes who are retired or planning to retire. He played 12 NFL seasons and 156 games, all for Green Bay.

Satterfield, Brian. *Fullback.* Played as a reserve in the season opener and then was on injured reserve through week 14 before being waived. He did not play in another NFL game.

Schroeder, Bill. *Wide receiver.* A practice squad player in 1996, Schroeder was a member of the Packers from 1997 to 2001. He played for Detroit in 2002 and 2003, and Tampa Bay in 2004 for seven games before retiring. In eight NFL seasons, he totaled 304 receptions and 28 touchdowns. In 2006, he, his wife and two young children were living in Green Bay, where he was working in performance enhancement/sports medicine for a health care provider.

Scott, Walter. *Defensive end.* He was on the practice squad the last seven games of the 1996 season and the playoffs. He did not return to the Packers in 1997 and retired. He played in one NFL game, with New England in 1996.

Sedoris, Chris. *Center/guard.* Was on the practice squad through week five before being let go. He was signed by Washington, where he played eight games, the only games of his career.

Simmons, Wayne. *Linebacker.* In the Super Bowl, he had four tackles. He was traded to the Kansas City Chiefs in 1997. The Chiefs cut him during the 1998 season, and he played the rest of the season with the Buffalo Bills, who then waived him. He retired, returned to Kansas City, and started a nightclub. Simmons died on August 23, 2002, in a single-vehicle car crash near Kansas City. He was 32. In six NFL seasons, he had 11 sacks and three interceptions.

Smith, Kevin. *Fullback.* Joined the team the second week of the season, played as a reserve against Philadelphia—with no carries or receptions—then was let go, ending his career. He also played 14 games with the Los Angeles Raiders from 1992 to 1994, running once for two yards and catching one pass for eight yards.

Sturgis, Oscar. *Defensive end.* Was with the team for one game in December against Denver, was not active, and was let go the next week, ending his career. He played in one NFL game, with Dallas in 1995.

Taylor, Aaron. *Guard.* Started every game at left guard for the Packers in 1996, including the Super Bowl. In 1998, he left the Packers for San Diego, where he played two years and retired. In 2005, Taylor was a studio analyst for college football on ABC and living in New York City. He also was taking graduate courses in San Diego toward a teaching degree. Taylor played five NFL seasons, three in Green Bay.

Thomason, Jeff. *Tight end.* In the Super Bowl, he had one special-teams tackle. He remained with the Packers through 1999. Thomason played for the Philadelphia Eagles from 2000 to 2002, catching 25 passes and scoring seven touchdowns. In 10 NFL seasons, five with Green Bay, he had 67 catches and scored 10 touchdowns.

Timmerman, Adam. *Guard.* Started every game at right guard in 1996, his second year after being drafted in the seventh round in 1995 by the Packers. He remained with Green Bay through the 1998 season. In 1999, he signed a free-agent contract with the St. Louis Rams. In 2005, he remained with the Rams. From 1996 through 2005, Timmerman did not miss a game and missed only one start.

Wachholtz, Kyle. *Quarterback.* Was on the Packers' practice squad in 1996 and in 1997. He tried to make it as a tight end in training camp of 1998 before being cut. He did not play a game in the NFL.

White, Reggie. *Defensive end.* Set a Super Bowl record with three sacks, all in the fourth quarter. He retired with the Packers after the 1998 season but returned to play in 2000 with Carolina before retiring again. He was the NFL's all-time sack leader when he retired. On December 26, 2004, he died of respiratory failure at his home near Huntersville, North Carolina. He was 43. On September 18, 2005, his number, 92, was retired by the Packers at halftime of the home opener against the Cleveland Browns. In 2006, White was nominated for the Pro Football Hall of Fame and was all but certain to be elected. In his 15-year NFL career, six with Green Bay, White played in 232 games and had 198 sacks. He also had three interceptions.

Wilkerson, Bruce. *Tackle/guard.* A key free agent who signed with the Packers in 1996, he played in 14 regular season games, starting two. He started every playoff game at left tackle, replacing John Michels. He retired after the 1997 season. He returned to his home state, Tennessee, where he worked for Alcoa in Knoxville. He played 11 NFL seasons, the last two with Green Bay.

Wilkins, Gabe. *Defensive end.* Started one game in 1996 and played in every game. He had one tackle in the Super Bowl. In 1998, he signed a five-year deal worth $20 million with San Francisco. After recording just one sack in two seasons, he was waived by the 49ers in June of 2000 and retired. Wilkins played six NFL seasons and had 13 sacks.

Williams, Brian. *Linebacker.* Had three tackles and intercepted a Drew Bledsoe pass in the Super Bowl. He played for the Packers from 1995 to 2000. He was with New Orleans and Detroit in 2001 and Detroit in 2002. In 2006, he was involved in real estate and housing development projects in the Dallas area. In eight NFL seasons, he had four interceptions and six sacks.

Williams, Ty. *Cornerback.* A reserve who played in every game in 1996 as a dime defensive back and special-teams player, Williams had one tackle in the Super Bowl. He remained with the Packers through the 2002 season. He played in six games with Atlanta in 2003 and three games with Dallas in 2004. In nine NFL seasons, the first seven in Green Bay, he had 19 interceptions.

Winters, Frank. *Center.* Started every game in 1996 and in the playoffs. He remained with the Packers through the 2002 season, when he retired. Winters played in Cleveland from 1988 to 1989, with the New York Giants in 1990 and with Kansas City from 1990 to 1991 before signing with the Packers. He played 16 NFL seasons, the last 11 in Green Bay. In 2006, he was living in Overland Park, Kansas.

1996 Coaches

Brooks, Larry. *Defensive line.* Held that position with the Packers from 1994 to 1998. In 2005, he coached the defensive line for Detroit. In 2006, he was hired to coach the defensive line for the Arizona Cardinals.

Cromwell, Nolan. *Special teams.* Coached the Packers' special teams from 1992 to 1997 and the receivers in 1998. In 1999, he followed Coach Mike Holmgren to Seattle and became the Seahawks' wide receivers coach. He remained wide receivers coach in 2005.

Haskell, Gil. *Wide receivers.* Started with the Packers as running backs coach from 1992 to 1994. He coached wide receivers from 1995 to 1997, then became offensive coordinator with the Carolina Panthers in 1998 and 1999. He was named the Seattle Seahawks' offensive coordinator in 2000 and remained in that position in 2005.

Holland, Johnny. *Defensive assistant/quality control.* Held that job from 1995 to1997. He coached the special teams in 1998 and linebackers in 1999. In 2000, he was special-teams assistant and assistant strength and conditioning coach with Seattle. In 2001 and 2002, he was the Seahawks' linebackers coach. From 2003 to 2005, he was a defensive assistant with the Detroit Lions. Holland was a standout linebacker for the Packers from 1987 to 1993. He joined the Packers Hall of Fame in 2001.

Holmgren, Mike. *Head coach.* The Packers' 1996 Super Bowl season was his fifth year in Green Bay. After the 1998 season, he left to become head coach of the Seattle Seahawks. In 2005, the Seahawks had the best record in the NFC at 13-3 and reached the Super Bowl, losing to Pittsburgh. After seven seasons in Green Bay, Holmgren had a 75-37 regular season record and an 8-5 playoff record, including one Super Bowl title and one Super Bowl loss. After seven seasons in Seattle, he had a 63-49 record, a 2-4 playoff record, and one Super Bowl loss.

Johnston, Kent. *Strength and conditioning.* Remained in Green Bay in that capacity from 1992 to 1998. In 2005, he was strength and conditioning coach at the University of Alabama.

Lewis, Sherm. *Offensive coordinator.* Joined the Packers as offensive coordinator in 1992 and left after the 1999 season. After a stint with the Minnesota Vikings, he became offensive coordinator in Detroit, retiring after the 2005 season.

Lind, Jim. *Linebackers.* A defensive assistant with the Packers from 1992 to 1994 and linebackers coach from 1995 to 1998, he left for Seattle with Mike Holmgren in 1999. When Fritz Shurmur died in 1999, Lind was the Seahawks' defensive coordinator. In 2005, he coached the Seahawks' tight ends.

Lovat, Tom. *Offensive line.* Arriving in 1992, he remained with the Packers through 1998, when he left for Seattle with Mike Holmgren. He coached the Seahawks' offensive line from 1999 to 2004 and then retired. He and his wife moved to Grand

Chute, Wisconsin. In 2006, he worked on a part-time basis for sports agents, helping offensive linemen prepare for the NFL scouting combine. Lovat coached 24 years in the NFL, beginning in 1980 in Green Bay under Bart Starr. Lovat's son, Mark, was an assistant strength and conditioning coach with the Packers beginning in 1999 and was retained by new Coach Mike McCarthy in 2006.

Mornhinweg, Marty. *Quarterbacks.* Left the Packers after the 1996 season to become offensive coordinator in San Francisco, a job he held through 2000. In 2001, he was named head coach of the Detroit Lions. He was fired after the 2002 season when his teams went 5-27. In 2003, he was senior assistant coach with Philadelphia. In 2004, he was assistant head coach/offensive coordinator for the Eagles, a job he held going into the 2006 season.

Reid, Andy. *Tight ends/offensive line assistant.* After holding that job from 1992 to 1996, Reid became the Packers quarterbacks coach in 1997. In 1999, he was named head coach of the Philadelphia Eagles. He was NFL coach of the year in 2000 and 2002. In 2006, he remained coach of the Eagles. In seven seasons, he had a 77-47 record. He led the Eagles to playoff appearances from 2000 to 2004, reaching the NFC championship game four times and the Super Bowl once.

Shurmur, Fritz. *Defensive coordinator.* In January of 1999, he left the Packers to join Mike Holmgren in Seattle. He was diagnosed with liver and esophageal cancer that spring and died in August of 1999 at his home in Suamico, Wisconsin. He was 67. Shurmur coached in the NFL for 24 years and wrote four books about defense. A favorite with players in Green Bay, he is considered one of the great defensive coordinators in NFL history. Predicated on attacking and confusing the offense, Shurmur's innovative 1996 Packers defense set a league record by giving up just 19 touchdowns during the regular season. In 2005, Shurmur's nephew, Pat Shurmur, was quarterbacks coach for Philadelphia.

Sydney, Harry. *Running backs.* Coached Packers running backs from 1995 through the 1999 season, after spending 1994 as a general assistant coach. In 2000, he was not re-hired by new Coach Mike Sherman. Sydney stayed in Green Bay and started My Brother's Keeper Inc., a counseling service for boys and men.

Valesente, Bob. *Defensive backs.* Was linebackers coach from 1992 to 1994 and defensive backs coach from 1995 to 1998. He then left to become an assistant with Carolina in 1999. From 2000 to 2002, he was the defensive coordinator for the Frankfurt Galaxy in NFL Europe and then retired. In 2005, he was living in Hilton Head, South Carolina.

1996 Front Office

Harlan, Bob. *President.* In 2005, he remained president of the Packers.

Reinfeldt, Mike. *Chief financial officer.* In 2005, he was vice president of football administration for the Seattle Seahawks.

Thompson, Ted. *Director of player personnel.* Remained in that position through 1999. From 2000 to 2004, he was vice president of football operations for the Seattle Seahawks. In 2005, he was named general manager of the Green Bay Packers. After the 2005 season, Thompson fired Mike Sherman as coach and replaced him with Mike McCarthy.

Wolf, Ron. *General manager.* Retired from the Packers and football in 2002.

PART TWO:
BEFORE THE
NEW GLORY YEARS

STILL MAGICAL
Don Majkowski (5, 7)

College: Virginia
Position: Quarterback, 1987–92
Highlight: Passed for 4,318 yards in 1989, third best in team history, and was named to the Pro Bowl.
After football: Atlanta real estate investor, Packers broadcaster, print analyst.

Suddenly, there he was, emerging from behind a plastic beer promotion banner and taking the stage. Wearing snug jeans and a black T-shirt, he strode confidently to a table at Dale's Weston Lanes, a bowling alley, bar, and restaurant near Wausau, Wisconsin. To the cheers of several dozen Packers fans clad in green and gold in a dimly lit hall, he pulled up to a microphone and began to talk. It was time for the News Line 9 Monday Night Pack Attack, and he was ready to dissect the previous day's game and sign some autographs.

Don Majkowski was making a comeback. For the player nicknamed "Majik Man" by Packers fans, the ability to disappear from Green Bay and then reappear years later should have been no surprise.

While Majkowski talked Packers at the bowling alley, two of his business associates were sitting nearby on bar stools and sipping drinks. They explained what had been happening in the world of the Majik Man, the quarterback who gave the Packers and their fans hope, if only briefly, that their team was not dead after nearly two decades of mediocrity.

In late 2004 and 2005, he was a busy man. He was interviewed by the *Chicago Tribune* on the 15th anniversary of the famous 1989 Bears replay game; made a brief appearance as a sideline guest on *Monday Night Football*; provided analysis to radio and TV stations in Milwaukee and Green Bay; wrote a weekly column for the *Packer Report* news weekly; wrote a weekly column and answered fans' questions for the official Packers Web site; and started a Web site of his own, the Majik Network.

His media work was just part of the circus that still surrounded Majkowski. In 2005, he was inducted into the Packers Hall of Fame, posed for a new poster and attended various autograph signings before games, including one outside Brett Favre's Steakhouse that lasted for one and one-half hours—about a good half of football.

Majkowski, at age 40, was a regular in Green Bay and Packerland again. While it remained to be seen how successful he would be—his goal was to get a seat in a network television broadcast booth on Sundays—he wasn't holding back from fans and the media. Visiting the bowling alley was just a start, one of many afternoons and evenings of learning how to talk a good game. He sounded ready for a starring role as he entertained the Weston Lanes crowd and TV viewers with studied, smooth responses to questions, proving that he still could more than hold his own on center stage.

Packers fans hadn't forgotten him, even though it had been 15 years since his most magical moment, the 1989 game that Packers and Bears fans refer to simply as the "Instant Replay Game," and even though he had been out of football for nearly a decade.

At Weston Lanes, fans wore Ahman Green, Brett Favre, and Vonnie Holliday jerseys, one of them with the slogan "And The Bears Still Suck" on the back. Dan Helding, 30, of Schofield, was back to see Majkowski for the second time in a few weeks. The first time, Majkowski signed his copy of an old Nintendo video football game in which the Majik Man was a featured player. "He didn't even know what I was talking about," Helding said of the game. "He was the big guy back then."

Debbie Norum, 42, eating a sausage-and-mushroom pizza with her husband, Tore, said she didn't remember Majkowski's number—it originally was 5 but he changed it to 7 out of respect to Packers great Paul Hornung who had worn 5. Hornung was the flash and heartthrob of the Packers in the golden 1960s, and Majik shared more than just a number with him. "I do remember that he was good looking," Norum said of Majkowski, recalling his days as the Packers poster boy, a golden, curly mullet hanging down to his collar.

After he left Weston Lanes, Majkowski drove across Wausau to Buffalo Wild Wings, a bar and restaurant, to do a radio show. He was a hit there, as well. One woman asked Majkowski to sign her "Majik Man" poster, which hangs in her bedroom despite protests from her husband. Another woman asked him to sign an "It's Majik Time" poster—a shot of Majkowski in a magician's outfit at Lambeau Field. She asked him to sign, "To Adrian, from your boyfriend." He obliged, flashing a warm smile and displaying some of the charm that made him a fan favorite, especially with women.

As he signed items at the restaurant, his business partners at the Majik Network, Tom Andrews and Michael Beightol, laughed as they shared the story about the woman who approached Majkowski at a signing and told him what had happened to her on November 5, 1989, the day that Majkowski's late touchdown pass survived a replay review and gave the Packers an upset win over the Bears at Lambeau Field. When the official announced that Majkowski had not stepped over the line of scrimmage after throwing 14 yards to Sterling Sharpe, the woman at the autograph signing said she jumped out of her chair to celebrate.

She was eight-and-a-half months pregnant and the excitement proved too much for her. She went into labor and gave birth, the same day that the Packers' 14-13 win ended Chicago's eight-game winning streak in the oldest NFL rivalry. Majkowski signed the woman's piece of memorabilia, "Never forget Nov. 5, 1989. We both delivered."

The magic began in the 10th round of the 1987 draft, when the Packers picked Majkowski. The draft was 12 rounds that year. He was the 255th player chosen, an afterthought. Few 10th-round draft picks end up playing in the NFL.

The first player chosen that year also was a quarterback, Vinny Testaverde, who had a long NFL career. However, many quarterbacks picked before Majkowski, including first-rounders Kelly Stouffer and Chris Miller, along with later-round picks Sammy Garza, Doug Hudson, and Ken Lambiotte, never established themselves.

PHOTO COURTESY EAU CLAIRE LEADER-TELEGRAM.

Quarterback Don Majkowski looks to the sidelines for instructions during the 1991 season.

Majkowski looked like he might be a bargain. He certainly felt like one, having signed for just $71,500. Before the draft, he thought of himself as more than a 12th-round pick. After all, he had been an athletic star all his life. In western New York, he starred in football, basketball, and baseball in high school. He also could high jump 6-foot-11. He received a scholarship to play football at the University of Virginia and was the Cavaliers' starter at quarterback by his sophomore year. He finished his career as the school's all-time passing and total offense leader, using his all-around athleticism to run the option offense. He could have done more, had he not missed part of his senior year with an injury, which scared off most NFL teams in the draft.

He eventually made Packers Coach Forrest Gregg look like a genius when he strolled into camp. Majkowski may have been a 12th-round pick, but he had first-round athletic ability and the cocksure attitude that head coaches love to see in their leaders. "I always thought I was a better quarterback than I was given credit for [in the draft]," he said. "I was a better all-around athlete than any other quarterback in the NFL, including John Elway. I had a lot of confidence in my ability. It was just a matter of time until I got an opportunity."

For a while, he was a no-name. Some people didn't know how to pronounce his last name, not realizing the "j" was silent. It came out "Majikowski," and his nickname was born.

Majkowski raised eyebrows with his play and his attitude. In an August 1987 scrimmage, he completed 17 of 28 passes for 291 yards and was called one of the pleasant surprises of camp. With veteran quarterback Randy Wright unsigned going into camp, Majkowski was seeing playing time with David Woodley, Chuck Fusina, and Robbie Bosco, and there was talk that the Packers might try to pick up veteran free agent Ron Jaworski.

Majkowski made the team and became Wright's backup. Although the season was shortened by a player strike, he still played in seven games and started five when Wright battled injuries. Majkowski started the second week and helped the Packers tie Denver, the defending AFC champion, 17-17, in the rain. Six weeks later, he became the first Packers rookie quarterback to throw for more than 300 yards in a game.

Majkowski's stock rose in 1988 under new coach Lindy Infante after the departure of Forrest Gregg.He saw more playing time, starting nine times when Wright was again injured. He opened more eyes with a 34-14 win over Minnesota, completing 19 of 32 passes for 243 yards and using his ability to scramble to keep the Vikings defense out of sync.

He was proving to be a winner. The Packers were 4-2-1 when Majkowski started but were winless in Wright's last five starts.

Finally, in 1989, Infante let the veteran Wright go in the final preseason cut and made Majkowski his man. Anthony Dilweg was the backup and Blair Kiel the third QB. Wright complimented Majkowski but also took a parting shot at him. He said

Majkowski was more gifted than the 16 quarterbacks he had seen in Green Bay in six years but that he didn't prepare enough mentally.

The comments hurt Majkowski but only a little. By 1989, as the starting quarterback for an NFL team, his swagger was in full motion. His confidence caught the attention of one teammate, lineman Billy Ard. "I said, 'Who the hell is this guy, walking around cool and cocky?' Someone said he was a quarterback. I said, 'Geez, how many 300-yard games did he throw for last year?' You see this guy walking around and say, 'Hey, is this guy a jerk or something?' He's very confident. Then you get to know the guy. You get to appreciate that," Ard told a reporter in 1989.

Offensive lineman Ken Ruettgers called Majkowski a "phenomenal" athlete, one who was fully aware of his abilities. "He plays like a prima donna but he definitely is not a prima donna. He's more of a positive kind of guy," Ruettgers said in 1989. "He's real calm in the huddle. There were times earlier this year when fans booed him and he came into the huddle smiling, almost laughing. And by the end of the game, they were back on his side, cheering him."

Ard and Ruettgers had seen what Majkowski could do. In the second game in 1989, the Packers trailed New Orleans, 24-7, at halftime. Majkowski started the second half by completing 18 straight passes, tying Lynn Dickey's team record. Majkowski threw three second-half touchdown passes as the Packers rallied for a 35-34 win. For the game, he completed 25 of 32 passes for 354 yards.

It was the start of a magical season. "Majik" led the Packers to five come-from-behind wins in the fourth quarter that year, and he almost pulled off another one. The week after the New Orleans reversal, the Packers trailed the Los Angeles Rams, 38-7, at halftime and lost, 41-38. A lost fumble by Packers back Brent Fullwood at the Rams' 1-yard line in the final minutes cost the Packers the win.

Majkowski's 2005 reincarnation as a media personality seemed to be a good fit. When he was a Packer, he always made headlines, partly because he was the focal point of the team but also because the media seemed drawn to him and the air of confidence he exuded. It didn't hurt either that he was—and still is—admired by female fans and played with a flair for the dramatic, not unlike Joe Namath. Majkowski didn't come close to winning a Super Bowl, as Namath did, but they both passed for more than 4,000 yards in a season and seemed to play their best in big games.

The 1989 Bears game was Majkowski's Broadway moment in the NFL. Ranked as one of the most memorable games in Lambeau Field history, it has been considered by some a turning point in the revival of a franchise that hadn't been a Super Bowl challenger since the 1960s.

It certainly was a big win in 1989. The victory on November 5 improved the

Packers' record to 5-4. With that momentum, they went on to win five of their last seven games. Although the 10-6 Packers didn't make the playoffs that year and wouldn't until 1993 when Majkowski already was gone, he believes the 1989 season and the replay game gave the organization and fans reason to believe in the future and to expect a winner again.

Majkowski was right in the middle of it all, scrambling to his right before hitting Sterling Sharpe in the back of the end zone with only a few seconds left in the game. Official Jim Quirk threw a flag, believing Majkowski was over the line of scrimmage when he threw. After a review of the play, official Bill Parkinson overruled Quirk, to the disbelief of Bears fans and Coach Mike Ditka.

During the delay, as officials reviewed the videotapes, Bears linebacker Mike Singletary came over to Majkowski and said, "Great game, but you still didn't beat us."

After officials ruled that Majkowski did not cross the line—he believes they got it right, that he was comfortably behind the line of scrimmage—he turned to Singletary. "I winked at him," Majkowski said. It takes a little nerve for a young, still somewhat unproven quarterback to wink at one of the best linebackers in the NFL, a player who was one of the big reasons the Bears won the Super Bowl in 1986.

The replay game has defined Majkowski. Of course, he had more than one big game with the Packers, but he seems to understand its importance and never grows tired of fans who want to talk about it, right down to the woman who wore a Bears jersey at one of his memorabilia signings and waited in line just to tell him, "You were over the line."

"People really appreciated the fact that I was part of the era that brought the team back to respectability. I brought a totally different style to Packerland. We got the Packers back on the map," Majkowski said. "Finally, there was something to cheer about when you turned on the TV on Sunday."

The dramatic win put Infante's surging team and the emerging star Majkowski in the national spotlight as sports shows dissected the controversial ending. Majkowski was a guest at halftime of the next broadcast of *Monday Night Football* and on a national pregame show the next Sunday. As the Packers inched closer to the playoffs, *Sports Illustrated* ran a six-page feature, entitled "The Majik Show." Majkowski and linebacker Tim Harris were on *Good Morning* on CBS, Infante and Majkowski were on NBC's *Today*, and *USA Today* ran a feature on the team on its sports cover. People were beginning to call the Packers "America's Team."

The Pack seemed to be back; people were beginning to believe in Infante's system and there was excitement in Green Bay for the first time since the early 1980s. The Packers' 10-6 record in 1989 was their first winning season in 7 years and their best winning percentage in 17 years.

Majkowski clearly was one of the reasons for the team's revival. In 1989, Majkowski passed for 4,318 yards, third most in team history, and set team records with

599 pass attempts, 353 completions, six 300-yard games, and 13 straight games with a touchdown pass. He also threw for 27 touchdowns (with 20 interceptions) and became the first Packers quarterback to make the Pro Bowl since Bart Starr.

Majkowski said the team had marginal talent that year—seven of the wins were decided by a field goal or less—and credited Infante's offense for much of the team's success. Still, everyone thought that with a young quarterback, other players on the rise, and an offense-minded coach, the Packers would be a team of the future.

One of their 1989 wins seemed to indicate they were no fluke. On November 19, they defeated the reigning Super Bowl champion 49ers in San Francisco, 21-17. Majkowski ran for two of the Packers' touchdowns. At 6-foot-2½ and 203 pounds, he was one of the most mobile and athletic quarterbacks in the league. The 49ers' loss was their last one that season as they went on to win their second straight NFL title.

Players, especially Majkowski, believed in Infante's system. "I can't give him enough credit for the offensive genius that he was," Majkowski said. "He was so well-prepared that year. There were so many times I thought, 'This is too easy.' He'd call a play, the guy would be wide open, and I'd get the credit."

Everything clicked that year for Majkowski and the Packers, including team chemistry. He remembers most of the players on the team hanging out with each other, going out on Thursday nights to Nicky's bar in DePere or each other's houses. "A lot of the guys were great friends, and Lindy was a great guy to play for. He kept his professional distance, but he could mix it up with the guys," Majkowski said.

They were hanging out at linebacker Brian Noble's house—with an ABC camera crew present—on the final night of the 1989 regular season, hoping Cincinnati would beat Minnesota to put the Packers in the playoffs. The Vikings won. "It was a sad night. We had won six of [our last] seven games. We could have done some damage in the playoffs."

That Bears replay game and 1989 season represented everything Majkowski had worked for since college at Virginia, but with his confidence high those successes also played a major role in the events of the next few years as the Majik Man disappeared from Green Bay.

Almost as soon as the Packers came together as a team in 1989, they began to unravel. As training camp got under way in 1990, 11 veterans, including Majkowski, held out for more money after they had big years, upsetting the team's chemistry. It didn't help that Tony Mandarich had received $4.4 million for four years in 1989; when Mandarich didn't live up to expectations that year, everyone on the team thought they were underpaid.

With his contract up, Majkowski had plenty of bargaining power heading into 1990. Along with being voted to the Pro Bowl, he finished runner-up in the league's

MVP voting to San Francisco quarterback Joe Montana. He led the NFL in passing yards, attempts, and completions. He was getting national media attention, and fans could buy a "Leader of the Pack" glamour shot poster for $4.95 of him wearing a leather jacket, half-finger gloves, and jeans while sitting on a high-handle motorcycle.

Quarterback Don Majkowski looks for a receiver during the 1991 season. After a breakthrough year in 1989, when he made the Pro Bowl, Majkowski struggled with injuries from 1990 through 1992, his final season with the team.

He knew it was time to flex his muscles and cash in. He had made about $600,000, with incentives, in 1989. In 1990, he and agent Randy Vataha—himself a Packers wide receiver in 1977—used $22 million over six years as a starting point. "Very few quarterbacks made the Pro Bowl in their third year. I figure I'm just scratching the surface," he said in July of 1990. The Packers quickly said Majkowski and Vataha couldn't be serious. "There's no one in the league, in the world, who's going to pay him that," Packers Vice President Tom Braatz said at the time.

He had the support of his teammates—all 15 in an anonymous poll backed his holdout—but 96 percent of fans in an informal survey thought he was asking for too much. Up to 70 percent of fans thought the Packers could make it to the Super Bowl without him. One Green Bay fan, citing some "bonehead" Majkowski plays in 1989, wrote: "There's little doubt the Packers need Majkowski in 1990, but he clearly is not the super quarterback he and his agent are making him out to be. At least not yet."

The fan and administration disappointment ran deeper. Some fans and Packers officials weren't happy when he declined to play in the Pro Bowl after the 1989 season. He was suffering with tendonitis in his throwing shoulder and an injured knee, and had been nursing fractured ribs late in the season, getting shots to numb the pain. But because he was looking for a big new contract, he didn't divulge all that in the summer of 1990. Most people thought he refused the Pro Bowl honor because he was afraid of getting hurt during contract negotiations.

When his backup, Anthony Dilweg, had four passes intercepted and lost two fumbles in the team's final 1990 preseason game, the Packers got more serious about signing Majkowski, even though Infante said he was comfortable with Dilweg. In the season opener, Dilweg looked like a winner, completing 20 of 32 passes for 238 yards and three touchdowns in a 36-24 win over the Los Angeles Rams in Green Bay.

Then both sides got serious. After a 45-day holdout, Majkowski and the Packers finally settled on September 4 for $1.5 million for one year. Majkowski was 26 and a rich man, but he had been driving a Mercedes-Benz sedan even before he signed the new contract.

After the holdout, he promised he wouldn't get a big head and would work hard. He thanked everyone who got the deal done and looked ahead. "Now we can concentrate on winning the Super Bowl," he said.

He was back in the starting lineup by the third game of the season, but 1990 wasn't anything like 1989. In the wake of the holdouts, the whole team seemed in disarray. In his first game back, Majik threw for only 171 yards, scored no touchdowns, and had two passes picked off in a 17-3 loss to Kansas City. At Chicago two weeks later, he couldn't resurrect the magic of a year before. Under constant pressure from the Bears defense, he completed just 12 of 39 passes and threw two more interceptions in a 27-13 loss.

Majkowski looked solid in a couple of Packers wins, but had yet to regain his 1989 form when he went down for the season on November 18 in Phoenix in a play that changed his life. He was scrambling toward the sideline when defensive end Freddie Joe Nunn of the Cardinals caught him from behind. Nunn put a bear-hug on him, pinned his arms to his sides, and brought all of his and Majkowski's weight—about 500 pounds—down on Majkowski's throwing shoulder.

Majkowski immediately knew something serious had happened when he got to his feet. "There was burning pain, then the shoulder went numb and I couldn't even lift my arm," he recalled. He had suffered a torn rotator cuff in his right shoulder. He was out for the season, and so were the Packers. Without him, they lost their final five games to finish 6-10.

At first, a team surgeon said Majkowski had a bruised shoulder and gave him the OK to play late in the season. He returned to practice in four weeks but fell to his knees in pain when he attempted a pass. The Packers sought another medical opinion. Further diagnosis revealed a major, two-inch tear in a tendon leading to Majkowski's rotator cuff muscle. He had surgery done in San Diego by Dr. Gary Losse, who specialized in trying to fix athletes' million-dollar limbs and joints.

Majkowski, positive as always, was unfazed by the injury. The shoulder had given him problems even before Nunn's tackle, so he figured the surgery would clear up everything. "I know I'll be 100 percent," he said. He couldn't afford to be downcast. With his contract up again on February 1, 1991, he at least had to talk a good game so the Packers would re-sign him.

They did, and he and the Packers made a 100 percent effort during rehabilitation to get him back to his magical form of 1989. The Packers bought a rehabilitation machine from Losse, and for nine hours a day, for six weeks, Majkowski went through rehab in his Green Bay home. For an hour at a time, he sat at the machine while it slowly raised and lowered his arm to prevent scar tissue from building up and to maintain his mobility. After each session, six of them per day, his shoulder was wrapped in ice for a half-hour. He fought boredom, anger, and tears; for a time, lifting a one-pound weight caused more pain than he could bear. The inevitable question began to haunt him: Would he ever play football again?

Slowly, he got his shoulder and withered arm muscles back in shape and started throwing. He also got a $200,000 raise, signing for $1.7 million for 1991.

Majkowski was rusty in training camp that summer, and his inconsistency carried over to the regular season. Observers said he wasn't the same, but he and Infante said the team as a whole was playing poorly. However, Majkowski's throwing motion had changed since the injury, and his arm strength wasn't what it had been. His throws lacked their pre-injury zip. He no longer could throw well off balance or flat footed. "For all intents and purposes, my arm and my career were never the same again," he said as we talked in Wausau.

In 1991, he played only half the season again before going down with a hamstring injury. He threw just three touchdown passes, was on pace to throw for about a third fewer yards than in 1989, and had the worst quarterback rating of his career. His backup, former Bears QB Mike Tomczak, didn't fare much better as the Packers finished 4-12, costing Infante his job.

Despite his injury problems—and rumors that his arm strength had been sapped by the rotator cuff surgery—new Coach Mike Holmgren said he expected Majkowski to be the starter in 1992. Holmgren thought he would flourish in the West Coast offense, which didn't require a power thrower but someone who could make numerous quick, short, rhythmic throws. Majkowski, ever confident, was ready and willing. New General Manager Ron Wolf, however, had been around football for decades. He knew that Majkowski, with his injury history, wasn't likely to be the quarterback of the future for the Packers.

During the off-season, the Packers gave up a number one-draft pick to get an untested backup quarterback from Atlanta. No one knew much about Brett Favre, other than that he had a very powerful and healthy arm, and was a bit of a partier.

Majkowski, for one, wasn't worried about Favre taking his job when he got his first look at him in training camp. "I couldn't believe they had traded a first-round draft pick for him. He was not in shape, not really professional. I liked him as a person. He had a great arm, but he was a reckless thrower," Majkowski said.

Majkowski and Holmgren, however, got off to a rocky start early in the 1992 regular season. The Packers lost their opener, 23-20, to the Vikings then got blown out at Tampa Bay, 31-3. Holmgren pulled Majkowski at halftime of the Tampa Bay game, with the Packers trailing 17-0. Majkowski wasn't happy and said so to the media. "You try to be a leader on the team, and when things aren't going well you get pulled. I was real upset. I was [expletive] off, and I let him know it. If I wasn't, there would be something wrong," Majkowski said at the time.

He was 10 of 15 passing for 75 yards with an interception. Favre, in his Packers debut, wasn't much better, going 8 of 14 for 73 yards with an interception.

None of that mattered. By the next week, Majkowski was on his way to becoming a Packers trivia question: Who was the last starting quarterback for Green Bay before Brett Favre?

In the third game of the 1992 season, Majkowski went down again with an injury. This time, he hurt his ankle on the Packers' sixth offensive play when he was sacked by Cincinnati nose tackle Tim Krumrie, a Wisconsin native and former University of Wisconsin standout. In came Favre, who seemed almost out of control at times. He had four fumbles and was sacked five times.

Then, inexplicably, the tide changed. Favre went on to direct the most exciting

Packers win at Lambeau Field since the replay game of 1989. With 13 seconds to play, he hit substitute receiver Kitrick Taylor—who had just come in to replace the injured Sterling Sharpe—with a 40-yard rocket down the sideline for a touchdown and a 24-23 win. Favre's improbable 92-yard scoring drive took less than a minute. All 57,272 astonished fans were on their feet. It was Mike Holmgren's first win in Green Bay and the dawn of the Brett Favre era.

What Favre lacked in experience, he made up for in arm strength. With Majkowski out for the next few weeks, Favre eventually won the starting job and, despite many more weeks of on-the-job training, didn't lose it. He led the team to a 9-7 record.

Majkowski realized what was happening—Favre was in and he was out. At first, he was confused and angry. Then he accepted it and tried to mentor Favre, he said. "He was going through a learning process. I understood that. I never held anything against Brett. We were good friends. I'm amazed at how well he's turned out. It makes losing the quarterback job a little easier," Majkowski said in 2005, as Favre still held the job more than 12 years, 200 consecutive starts, three MVP trophies, and one Super Bowl win later.

Still, there was disappointment. Majkowski went from one of the highest-paid marquee players in the league in 1990 to a backup in less than two years, largely because of one shoulder injury. "I planned on being in Green Bay at least 10 years. I was just expecting some great things for a lot of years. I was pretty good, and I was coming into my own," he said, sipping a Coke more than a decade later.

By 1993, it was clear that Majkowski would not be considered for the starting job. He didn't want to be a backup, and the Packers didn't want to pay their backup $1.7 million. Besides, Majkowski had off-season surgery to remove scar tissue from the rotator cuff surgery and couldn't throw for six weeks.

He and the Packers agreed to part. He moved on, playing two years for the Indianapolis Colts and two for Detroit. Majkowski started eight games in Indianapolis one year but still had trouble with his throwing shoulder. "I was playing in pain every day. I was a good backup at that point," he said.

Majkowski retired after the 1996 season—the year the Packers won the Super Bowl under Favre. It might have been Majkowski directing the Packers to the NFL title, firing passes to Andre Rison and Antonio Freeman in the Superdome in New Orleans. He would have been in his 10th season, perhaps in the prime of his career. But then again, if Majkowski didn't suffer the shoulder injury in 1990, the Packers might never have traded for Favre.

Majkowski returned to Lambeau Field as a member of the Colts and the Lions. He received cheers and some boos from Packers fans, some of whom still thought he should have played in the Pro Bowl and shouldn't have held out in 1990. The magic between Majik and the Packers was gone.

Fifteen years later, Majkowski again was making Green Bay his stage. He flew to Green Bay for every home game in 2004 and 2005 from his home in Atlanta, hoping Titletown would help launch a second career, this time in television, as it had his first one. In Atlanta, he is a partner in a business, Hotlanta Home Buyers, a real estate investment firm.

Business had been good, he said. He and his wife, whom he met in Milwaukee, were happy and raising two children, but he missed the excitement of football. He had been the center of attention ever since his days as a multitalented high school athlete in Buffalo, and he wanted to experience it again. "I'm used to being the field general," he said.

When we finished talking in Wausau, I was sure of two things about Don Majkowski. One, he hadn't lost his confidence. Even though his athletic skills had diminished at age 40, he still believed he could do the job, even if the job he wanted was in a broadcast booth. Two, as Billy Ard said, you have to get to know the guy. Spend a few hours with him, and you can't help but like him and wish he was your friend. He's the cool kid on the block everyone wants to hang out with. As a Packer, he was flamboyant on the field but one of the guys who drank beer with his teammates off the field. I can imagine him holding court in the middle of the Packers huddle or at the center of a media horde in the locker room, capturing all the attention, or in that 1989 Bears game when he winked at Mike Singletary, and then thrust his helmet and arms in the air in victory.

What kind of guy is Majkowski? In 1990, when he suffered the severe shoulder injury that ultimately destroyed his career, the team doctor, E.S. Brusky, suggested at first in the media that the injury was in Majkowski's head, that he wasn't hurt as badly as he said. When doctors finally diagnosed Majkowski's torn rotator cuff tendon, Majkowski didn't hold a grudge against Brusky. He said Brusky just wanted to see the Packers win. Majkowski may have had so much confidence that people sometimes got the wrong impression of him, but he also had integrity.

A couple of months after we talked, in January of 2005, the Packers announced that they had named Majkowski to their hall of fame. He was inducted on July 23, 2005, in the Lambeau Field Atrium as Packers training camp was getting under way. Majkowski was excited about the honor, which he hadn't expected.

His selection stirred some debate. He was fifth in team history in passing with 10,870 yards and threw 56 touchdown passes. However, he also threw 56 interceptions, played only one full season and was 22-27-1 as a starting quarterback. One sports reporter said the Packers hall of fame had lowered its standards. However, in the 2005 Packers record book, Majkowski's name pops up many times: career passer rating (4th, 73.5); passes attempted, season (1st, 599); passes attempted, career

(5th, 1,607); passes attempted, game (2nd, 59); passes completed, season (3rd, 353); passes completed, career (4th, 889); passes completed, game (3rd, 34); consecutive passes complete (tied for 1st, 18); touchdown passes, game (tied for 2nd, 4); passing yards, season (3rd, 4,318); most 300-yard games (2nd, 6). He also held the team record for most passes attempted in a game without an interception (46, on September 30, 1990, against Detroit).

In addition, Majkowski held the distinction of being sacked more times in one season than any quarterback in Packers history (47 in 1989). No wonder he was hurting and declined to play in the Pro Bowl after that season. He was young, mobile, and a good runner, but Infante's offense required him to take seven-step drops before throwing and linemen had trouble holding their blocks that long.

Other Packers Hall of Fame quarterbacks include Bart Starr, Lynn Dickey, Zeke Bratkowski, Tobin Rote, Arnie Herber, and Cecil Isbell. Majkowski may not have had the staying power of many of them, but he had star power, was a playmaker, and usually made an impact when he stepped on the field—before he was injured.

Five days after he was inducted into the hall with Edgar Bennett, I called Majkowski to see how it felt. It was a week he'll never forget, he said. He arrived in Wisconsin 10 days before the induction, spending time in the Milwaukee area. He played in the U.S. Bank Championship pro-am golf tournament with Wisconsin native and Professional Golfers Association tour member Skip Kendall. Also in the pro-am were Packers Favre, Ryan Longwell, and Mark Tauscher. Up to 4,000 fans followed the Packers stars as they competed for charity. Favre and Jerry Kelly, another PGA tour pro from Wisconsin, won $20,000 for charity. Majkowski's son got to meet Favre and walk down the fairway with him, and during the event it was announced that Majkowski was going into the Packers hall. He was congratulated by PGA tour players. He was back in the spotlight.

It began to sink in. Majkowski was going down in Green Bay history. "It's such a huge honor," he said over the phone. "With all the rich history, all the great players who paved the way. To be included in that group is such an elite honor." His old coach, Infante, as well as teammates Jim Campen, Alan Veingrad, Ron Hallstrom, Brian Noble, Rich Moran, Ken Ruettgers, and others called to congratulate him.

Majkowski not only was back as an announcer and part of Packers history, he was back as a Titletown poster boy. A day after the golf tournament, he unveiled his latest poster, "After Further Review," featuring him in the 1989 Bears game.

Before the induction, he attended a corporate golf outing, had an autograph signing at Curly's Pub at Lambeau Field with his family and old teammate Paul Ott Carruth, and drove through town with his father. His dad asked him, "Have you thought about what it really means?" He reminded Don how he had battled through injuries in high school and college just to get to the NFL.

"I'm pretty proud I stuck with it," he said. "I loved the game so much I would have put my body through anything. That may sound sick, but I think most guys would say that. How many people in life get to live out their childhood dream? So I'm a lucky guy. I was a guy who showed up every week. I always gave it everything I had. I didn't have a lot of great years, but I played well when I was healthy and helped bring the Pack back to respectability."

The Majkowski and Bennett inductions took place before a sold-out crowd of about 1,200 in the Atrium. Majkowski's wife, Kelly, produced a 10-minute video highlight of his career that brought Majkowski to tears. Then, before his speech, in which he thanked the Packers and paid tribute to all the great players and coaches in "the greatest franchise in NFL history," he was introduced by his friend and business associate, Tom Andrews, a writer who has covered the Packers for 30 years.

Andrews finished his remarks with: "So what's Majik's legacy? Where is his place in Green Bay Packer history? Majik didn't get to play in a Super Bowl or even the playoffs. But I believe his value to the Packers can't be measured in statistics alone. Don and his teammates built a bridge from hard times back to respectability, and they ushered in the later teams that finally brought the Vince Lombardi trophy back to Green Bay. Don returned flash and style to Green Bay. He helped restore a never-say-die winning attitude. Don made us all believe again."

Pause.

"Ladies and gentlemen, I give you the Majik Man, Don Majkowski."

Standing ovation.

Don Majkowski was back in Lambeau Field. To stay.

THE GOOD GUY
Bryce Paup (95)

College: Northern Iowa

Position: Linebacker, 1990–94

Highlight: Had 18 ½ sacks in 1993 and 1994 and was named to the 1994 Pro Bowl.

After football: Businessman, motivational speaker, and founder of Good
  Samaritan, a Green Bay-area charity.

In the third game of the 1991 football season, Bryce Paup woke up sick to his stomach. The 0-2 Packers were scheduled to play the Tampa Bay Buccaneers on September 15 at Lambeau Field, but Paup was wondering whether he even would be able to play. He ate dinner at a friend's house the night before and something about the meal didn't agree with him. The weather wasn't helping; it was overcast, cloudy, and humid, with the temperature near 80 degrees.

However, as the morning and game preparations wore on, he improved a little, suited up, and prepared to back up Johnny Holland at linebacker. Paup didn't much feel like playing, but chances were he wouldn't play a lot anyway. It was Paup's second season in the NFL and he still didn't know where he fit with the Packers. He missed most of his rookie season with a hand injury and hadn't been given a clear chance to prove himself.

Still queasy, Paup was a little startled when Packers defensive coordinator Hank Bullough approached him in the locker room before the game and told him to be ready to play the rover package. Maybe Paup would see a little playing time against the Bucs. Maybe this would be the day he had been waiting for ever since he was drafted in the sixth round in 1990, beating the odds to make the Green Bay roster. He would be ready, he told Bullough.

Usually, Tim Harris was the Packers' roving linebacker. Blessed with speed and agility, Harris was allowed to move about or rove on defense before the ball was snapped, often darting past surprised defenders into the backfield to throw running backs and quarterbacks for losses. In 1989, Harris totaled 19½ sacks, second best in the NFL that season, to help the Packers to a 10-6 record. On this day, however, Harris wasn't around. He was home, continuing a contract dispute that one week later would result in him being traded to San Francisco for two second-round draft picks.

When the Packers took the field, Paup heard announcer Gary Knafelc, a 1950s and early 1960s Packers star receiver, name the starting lineups. Paup headed for his familiar spot on the sidelines. Once again, Holland, the talented fifth-year pro from Texas A&M, would be filling Harris' position. Holland already was on the field for the Packers' first defensive series when Bullough called to Paup, "Hey, get out there!

Send Johnny Holland back." A little dazed, Paup quickly put on his helmet and sprinted onto the field. It was the official start of his NFL career.

Paup couldn't believe what Bullough had done. "I thought, 'What, are you crazy?'" Not Bullough, although he looked a little crazy with his gap-tooth smile and flattened nose, the result of one too many poundings on the football field. Known as the "Doctor of Defense," Bullough had been coaching for more than 30 years with five NFL teams, one USFL team and one college team, Michigan State, his alma mater. A fifth-round Packers draft pick in 1955, he had been around long enough to recognize talent and when to use it. He turned the 1981 Cincinnati Bengals' defense into one of the best in the NFL en route to the Super Bowl.

Plus, Bullough knew what Paup could do. In the season opener two weeks earlier, Paup sacked Philadelphia quarterback Randall Cunningham, injuring Cunningham's knee and knocking him out for the season.

So Bullough called back 6-foot-2½, 235-pound Johnny Holland, a former all-American who had close to 500 career tackles, and sent out 6-foot-5, 247-pound Bryce Paup, who had one career tackle going into the season.

Bullough wasn't entirely taking a chance on Paup. He had told Paup after 1990 to return in 1991 with the goal of starting. With Bullough's advice, the often-intense Paup began to watch every move of another starting linebacker, Brian Noble. After Noble missed training camp because of a knee injury, Paup led the team in tackles with 21 in the 1991 exhibition season and for the first time had media approaching his cubicle in the locker room. Yet, when the season began, Noble was healthy and Paup remained a backup at left inside linebacker.

When the Tampa Bay game started, however, Paup was at right inside linebacker, Noble at left inside linebacker, Scott Stephen at left outside linebacker, and Tony Bennett at right outside linebacker. The starters on the defensive line were Matt Brock and Robert Brown at the ends, and Esera Tuaolo at nose tackle. In the secondary, Chuck Cecil and Jerry Holmes were the corners, along with Mark Murphy and LeRoy Butler at safety.

After Chris Jacke's kickoff went out of the end zone, the Buccaneers and quarterback Vinny Testaverde went to work on the Packers, quickly moving 53 yards to the Green Bay 27. After calling a timeout, Testaverde dropped back to pass, but Paup flew into action. He ran past Bucs guard Tom McHale and got his arms on Testaverde. Reserve end Shawn Patterson came from the other side, and Testaverde went down. Paup had half of a quarterback sack. Bennett sacked Testaverde on the next play, and the Bucs had to punt.

Paup's day already was turning out much better than he expected. In the second quarter, it got better. A Packers drive stalled at the Bucs' 43 after Don Majkowski was sacked and threw an incomplete pass. Green Bay punter Paul McJulien then pinned the Bucs back with a 42-yard kick that was downed at the Tampa Bay

1-yard-line by tight end Jackie Harris. On second down from their two, the Bucs called a pass play. Testaverde dropped seven steps, into the end zone, and looked for a receiver. Paup rushed into the backfield, slipped the block of fullback Robert Wilson, and brought down Testaverde for a sack and a safety. The Packers led, 2-0.

By the third quarter, it was obvious the defenses had control of the game, and Paup was one of the reasons why. Late in the third quarter, with the Packers leading, 5-3, the Bucs got the ball at their 20. On second down, the Green Bay defense called a stunt. Packers reserve defensive end Lester Archambeau pulled around to block Bucs center Tony Mayberry. With an open lane, Paup rushed the middle, again shed Wilson's block, and took down Testaverde.

Paup wasn't done. On the next play, third down and 16 yards, Testaverde stood in the shotgun formation. From his position on the right side of the defense, Paup rushed the outside of the Tampa Bay offensive line. There he met highly regarded rookie tackle Charles McRae, the seventh player picked in the 1991 NFL draft. Paup was a lowly sixth-round draft pick, the 159th player chosen in the 1990 draft. He was making $245,000 a year; McRae was making about $1 million a year. Paup said goodbye to McRae and sacked Testaverde again.

Paup's back-to-back plays, totaling 18 yards in losses, pushed the Bucs back to their 5-yard line. They also gave Paup $3\frac{1}{2}$ sacks for the game, including the safety, and sent people in the stands and the press box looking through their programs to refresh their memories. Who exactly is Bryce Paup?

Midway through the fourth quarter, they heard the name one more time. On a third-and-18 play from his own 31-yard-line, an obvious passing situation, Testaverde again stood in the shotgun. He never got the pass off as the relentless Paup avoided Wilson's block again and toppled the veteran quarterback for the fifth time of the day.

Paup, who shared some time on the field with Holland, finished the game with $4\frac{1}{2}$ sacks and a safety for 31 yards in losses.

It was a happy day all the way around. The Packers trailed, 13-5, late in the fourth quarter then drove 76 yards to score on an eight-yard pass from Majkowski to running back Vince Workman to make it 13-12 with about two minutes to play. The Packers defense held, thanks to a tackle by Paup and a 10-yard loss on a sack by rookie nose tackle Esera Tuaolo.

Then Majkowski drove them downfield again, and Chris Jacke kicked a 22-yard field goal with 22 seconds to play. The Packers won, 15-13.

After the game, Paup was feeling much better about himself and his chances to play in the NFL. His upset stomach earlier in the day was all but forgotten. "This is something I'll remember forever," he told reporters. "I'm just trying to show the coaches I'm not a flash in the pan."

Paup's $4\frac{1}{2}$ sacks were the most by a Packer in a game since Ezra Johnson tied the team record with 5 in 1978.

The coaches were impressed with more than Paup's sack total; they loved his effort. On one play against Tampa Bay, Paup was taken down to his knees on a block by Bucs tackle Paul Gruber. Paup got up quickly, pursued the play, and caught speedy ball carrier Gary Anderson to prevent a long gain. "My parents taught me how to work hard," Paup said.

When he went home on Sunday night, September 15, 1991, he had to be wondering what had just happened. "It sure built the ego," he said of the attention after the game, but he knew better than to let that part of NFL life get the best of him. All he had to do was think of his humble roots, his hard-working parents and neighbors back in rural Iowa, where livelihoods were on the line each farming season. Or his sister, who was born mentally retarded as a result of birth complications.

Like many higher-round draft picks, Paup had big dreams but he also had doubts. He was a big, athletic kid growing up near Scranton, Iowa. He told people that someday he wanted to play pro football, but the odds weren't encouraging.

Scranton is a town of about 750 people surrounded by farms in west-central Iowa. Geographically, it's somewhat of a no-man's land, a small town next to the North Raccoon River surrounded by dozens of other small towns. The big city, Des Moines, was more than an hour's drive away, but the really big cities, Chicago, St. Louis, or Minneapolis, were many hours away.

Without a pro football team of their own, Iowans are a mixed lot when it comes to following NFL teams. They can be divided between the Minnesota Vikings, St. Louis Rams, Chicago Bears, Denver Broncos, and Kansas City Chiefs. Many, however, prefer the Packers because Green Bay is the closest thing in the NFL to a small Iowa town. Paup, however, grew up a Dallas Cowboys fan.

Born on February 29, 1968, Paup went to high school in Scranton. His senior class had 19 students, and his football team at times had just 12 players. The coach didn't worry much about getting penalized for having too many players on the field. But they were a winning team, and Paup was one of the stars.

The Paups lived more than six miles out of town in farm country. He ran the gravel roads to get in shape for football and dreamed about the NFL, but realistically he expected to work the fields one day like his dad. "That's all I wanted to do. I wanted to play in the NFL, but farming was something I'd pursue if it hadn't worked out," he said as he sipped a glass of water at a Green Bay restaurant in 2005.

College football coaches didn't know much about Paup, so he went to them. His girlfriend convinced an assistant coach at the University of Northern Iowa to look at tapes of Paup playing in high school. The coach liked what he saw, and the college, in Cedar Falls in northeastern Iowa, offered him a scholarship. The UNI Panthers, a Division I-AA school, weren't as big a name as the Division I University of Iowa Haekeyes and Iowa State Cyclones, but they were the next best thing in Iowa. (Later, in the mid-1990s, UNI produced Kurt Warner, who went on to star at quarterback for the St. Louis Rams.)

Paup lettered his first year at UNI, 1986, and then became a fixture in the starting lineup at linebacker, defensive end, or nose tackle. He played so well that NFL scouts who stopped by Cedar Falls began to ask about him rather than other players they had come to scout.

Linebacker Bryce Paup pauses for a drink of water during a 1992 game. Paup was the NFL's defensive player of the year in 1995, the year he left the Packers to play for the Buffalo Bills.

In his senior year, Paup was third-team I-AA all-American after leading UNI with 115 tackles. "My position coaches told me if I stayed healthy, I'd have a shot at playing in the NFL," he said.

His chances improved when he got picked to play in the Senior Bowl, an all-star game for the nation's senior best players. He liked the star treatment. "The Senior Bowl put a fire in me. I wanted to make the NFL," Paup told me.

When he reached Green Bay, Paup didn't know quite what to expect. He never had been to an NFL game or inside an NFL stadium. Paup was projected to play linebacker, but the Packers had picked two other linebackers in front of him, Tony Bennett in the first round out of Mississippi and Bobby Houston in the third round from North Carolina State. He wasn't overly confident about his chances.

Plus, the Packers already had a solid linebacking unit with veterans Harris, Holland, and Noble. "They had 10 guys who were decent players [at linebacker]," Paup said. "I remember the first minicamp, I counted all the linebackers and I couldn't believe it. I'll never forget when Hank Bullough said, 'Don't start counting numbers. When you do, you'll cut yourself. You'll start making mistakes.'"

So Paup, the youngest of four children, did what his father taught him on the farm: He worked. "I knew how to work, how to put in hours and stick with it," said Paup, who grew up baling hay, spraying and detasseling corn, and doing all the other kinds of manual labor that farmers do every day.

In Green Bay, he dug into the dirt and grass on the Oneida Street practice field and held his ground. He not only wanted to make the NFL, he needed to. He had gotten married, and his wife, Denise, had quit her job when they moved to Green Bay. Their fathers worked on farms together. They started dating when he was a senior in high school and she was a freshman at Northern Iowa. They needed the money; it would be back to Iowa, most likely, if he didn't make the Packers roster.

During the 1990 training camp, one with high expectations after the Packers had gone 10-6 the year before and just missed the playoffs, Paup gradually realized he had the size, speed, and agility to play in the NFL. After a scrimmage against Cleveland, when he made several key plays, teammates told him he had a shot at making the team. "I had the idea that, 'Hey, this is not so far out of reach,'" Paup said. The Packers thought so, too. They liked his explosiveness off the snap, his competitiveness, and his work habits.

When he injured his wrist, Green Bay put him on injured reserve rather than cut him. He spent most of the 1990 season watching his first pro football games. He liked the seat—right along the Packers sideline.

Despite his $4\frac{1}{2}$ sacks against Tampa Bay early in 1991, Paup didn't start again that season. He played in 12 games and finished with $7\frac{1}{2}$ sacks and 28 total tackles.

So when Mike Holmgren became coach in 1992 and evaluated everyone on the team, Paup didn't know where he stood. "He cut a lot of people who were good. It scared the heck out of me. Every Monday, there were two or three new players in the locker room. I was just praying every Monday my name still was up in the locker room," Paup said.

The list of linebackers in 1992 included Bennett, Holland, Burnell Dent, Noble, Scott Stephen and first-year players George Koonce, a free agent, and Mark D'Onofrio, a second-round draft pick from Penn State. Paup not only survived the scrutiny of Holmgren's first training camp, he wound up playing in all 16 games—starting for a time at outside linebacker—and recording 6$\frac{1}{2}$ sacks. All that came after he held out for 19 days to get a three-year contract worth $380,000 a year.

In 1993 and 1994, Paup added another 18$\frac{1}{2}$ sacks—just 2$\frac{1}{2}$ fewer than Reggie White in that span—as he became one of the best pass-rushers in the NFL. His ability to play all linebacker positions and defensive end and rush the passer made him a valuable member of the defense. Noble retired after 1993 with more knee problems, and with Paup's success the Packers let the former number-one draft pick, Bennett, leave as a free agent.

Paup was making headlines, such as "Talented Iowan making hay," and getting compliments from his coaches. He had come a long way in just a couple of years. Observers said his success was a combination of ability, instinct, and hard work. Others said it was his mental approach to the game. His new defensive line coach, Greg Blache, said, "I'm darned glad to have Bryce, and I know a lot of coaches around the league would love to have Bryce. He's not flashy. He doesn't say a word. He just brings his lunch pail and gets the job done. There's never been a snap where you could say Bryce was not giving 100 percent."

Paup's linebackers coach, Bob Valesente, credited his hard work, saying he made huge strides between 1992 and 1993 with his coverage and footwork skills. His head coach, Holmgren, simply called Paup the "total package."

Valesente essentially agreed with Holmgren's assessment. "As a pass rusher, he had as quick a move off the edge as anybody I'd ever seen. Bryce was willing to work extremely hard on his skills. He was very strong, very physical, but he wasn't a blazer. He was very smart at using the proper angles and filling the run. He could play all three linebacker positions—inside, outside, in the 4-3—and play them well. He was a great guy to work with."

Paup believed that it was even harder to stay in the NFL than it was to get there; he worked so hard and put in so much extra time that at times he had to tell himself to relax. He often could be found alone watching film after practice when other players had left. On weeknights, after a full day at practice, he would spend time with his family, watch video of opponents for up to two hours, and then study his playbook before going to bed at 1 A.M.

By the end of the 1994 season, Paup not only was entrenched as a Packers starter but was playing so well that he was being mentioned as a possible Pro Bowl pick, his next career goal. He had been National Football Conference player of the week twice that season and was one of the team leaders in interceptions.

One of those NFC honors came after a Monday night game in which he intercepted two passes, had a sack, and made six tackles in a win at Chicago. At age 26, when some of his friends from high school football actually were making hay in Iowa, Paup was making plays all over the field in the NFL.

With two games to play in the 1994 season, Paup was named a starter—along with teammate Reggie White—in the Pro Bowl. Wide receiver Sterling Sharpe, despite being on his way to an NFL-record 112 catches, was named as a reserve. Quarterback Brett Favre wasn't picked. Paup became only the second Packers linebacker to get the honor since Fred Carr in 1975. His coaches and teammates said he deserved it. Paup said he was shocked. His statistics that year, however, told the story: $9\frac{1}{2}$ sacks, 4 interceptions, 100 tackles, and 3 forced fumbles. He started 16 regular season and two playoff games.

The Pro Bowl honor came either at a perfect time or at the worst time for Paup, depending on how his career is evaluated. With his contract up and his name in lights, Paup was a free agent and looking for a big contract. Secretly, he was hoping to stay in Green Bay, where he had decided to raise his family, contract or no contract. He wasn't pleased that the Packers virtually took advantage of his many skills by making him learn multiple positions, but he wasn't complaining.

However, his agent, Jack Wirth, landed him an offer of $7.6 million for three years with the Buffalo Bills. It would be a nice raise: Paup was making $431,000 a year with the Packers. The Bills liked Paup's versatility and ability to make the big play. He forced nine fumbles and had four interceptions as a Packer. At least five other teams expressed an interest in Paup, but he had a connection with the Bills. Wirth also worked for Bills star receiver Andre Reed.

The Bills were one of the elite teams in the NFL, having appeared in four straight Super Bowls although they lost each one. They had some of the most famous players in the game, including quarterback Jim Kelly, running back Thurman Thomas, defensive end Bruce Smith, linebacker Cornelius Bennett, and Reed.

Paup came back to the Packers, expecting them to bargain and hopefully approach the salary the Bills were offering. The Packers simply said they couldn't come close to matching the Bills. Paup, named Packers co-defensive player of the year with White, was surprised and said he had no choice but to sign with Buffalo. "I'm not sure what happened," Paup said.

The Packers had signed Reggie White to a huge free-agent contract in 1993 and said they had salary cap restrictions. However, the Packers were $1.1 million below the salary cap in 1995 so their argument that they couldn't afford Paup seemed hollow. He was disappointed the Packers wouldn't try to hang onto a player who worked hard, was a positive influence in the locker room, and was involved in the community. "You'd think they'd want that in the locker room. At that time, it didn't seem to matter," Paup said.

Packers General Manager Ron Wolf may have let Paup go for several reasons. One, he likely thought of Paup as a pass rushing specialist—even though Paup had improved in all areas—and didn't want to pay a specialist that much money. Wolf also thought that Paup let Dallas tight end Jay Novacek catch too many passes in the 1993 and 1994 playoffs, and may have come to the conclusion that Paup didn't rise to the occasion in big games.

Also, Paup played so well that 1993 number-one draft pick Wayne Simmons didn't have a chance to play regularly. Wolf and Holmgren figured that Simmons, whom they were paying $1 million a year, could replace Paup. Wolf came to Green Bay in 1992 with Paup already on the roster. Wolf had a tendency to build a team around his own draft picks.

Simmons wound up playing well the next three seasons and helped the Packers win the Super Bowl; but, if it was any consolation, Wolf several years later said it was a "miscalculation" on his part to let Paup go, adding that it was his biggest personnel mistake while building the Super Bowl-bound Packers. "We misevaluated [Paup]. It was our error. We were stupid," Wolf told the *Milwaukee Journal Sentinel* in 1995.

Wolf realized his mistake that year when Paup again made the Pro Bowl with Buffalo but went far beyond everyone's expectations—including Paup's own—when he was named NFL linebacker of the year, AFC most valuable player, and the Associated Press NFL defensive player of the year. Paup could do no wrong in 1995. He had $17^{1}/_{2}$ sacks and led the Bills with 126 tackles. In his third game with the Bills, he had 14 tackles, three sacks, and forced two fumbles. He had blossomed into an NFL star. He had arrived.

In contrast, in 1995, without Paup, Green Bay's three starting linebackers had a total of just five sacks.

Everything Paup had been working for fell into place that year, partly because Coach Marv Levy and the Bills recognized his skills and where to use them. Instead of starting four positions, as he had in Green Bay in 1994, Paup stayed in one slot in the Buffalo defense and took off behind and alongside players like Smith and Bennett.

Paup benefited from the Bills' experience, but he also had the skills to make the plays when they developed. "They gave me great freedom to play with people's minds before the snap," Paup said. The Bills made the playoffs again at 10-6, but their Super Bowl run was over.

Paup made two more Pro Bowls—extending his streak to four straight—in 1996 and 1997, but didn't have the same success as in 1995. A torn groin muscle limited him in 1996 to 12 games and six sacks. He played through pain for seven weeks. His teammate, Smith, however, had 13$^1/_2$ sacks and was NFL defensive player of the year that season. Paup came back in 1997 with 9$^1/_2$ sacks.

He was a free agent again after 1997 and he got another big offer—$22 million for five years to play in Jacksonville. The deal made him the second highest-paid linebacker in the NFL.

He soon realized that money doesn't count for much when you're not happy. The Jaguars played him out of position, sometimes expecting him to drop back and cover receivers 20 yards downfield. He dreaded going to work each day. He had just 6$^1/_2$ sacks in 1998. In 1999, he tore a pectoral muscle lifting weights before the season, tried to return too soon, and wound up with just one sack. The Jaguars let him go.

Paup next signed with Minnesota for about $500,000 in 2000. Vikings Coach Dennis Green put him at defensive end and said he expected Paup to have 10 or more sacks. However, a right leg fracture caused Paup to miss six weeks. He finished with just two sacks in 10 games for the Vikings and retired.

In the end, Paup played 11 seasons and 148 games in the NFL, sacked quarterbacks 75 times, intercepted 6 passes, scored a touchdown, and made it to the playoffs seven times. In the process, he made millions of dollars in salary, not counting endorsements.

If Paup didn't have the Pro Bowl year in 1994, when he was a free agent, would he have stayed in Green Bay and had a longer, more productive NFL career? With him in the lineup, would the Packers and their banged-up defense been able to stop Denver's Terrell Davis in their second Super Bowl?

While he was a Packer, Paup and his wife used to have fun while they made someone else feel good at Christmas. As helpers with the Salvation Army, they would buy gifts for a needy family, ring the doorbell, drop the presents on the porch, and run.

Paup was one of the true Packers good guys. If he wasn't helping a needy family, he was helping a child with the Make-A-Wish foundation, visiting children's hospitals or taking part in a telethon to benefit the blind or people with cerebral palsy.

He also was there to set an example or be a witness for his faith. Paup usually sat in the hotel room when the team was on the road, going over plays or calling his family while some foot-loose teammates were out on the town and pushing the limit on curfew. He backed up big-hearted Reggie White when White took a stand for his Christian beliefs in the Packers' locker room, where players could be known to play the devil's advocate. He was a little like Reggie—an intense Christian who specialized in sacking quarterbacks—but not nearly the extrovert. In the 1996 movie *Reggie's Prayer*, loosely based on White's life and starring White, Paup had a cameo role, along with Mike Holmgren and Brett Favre.

Paup was a good guy because he believed in all the good things he did. He didn't do them just because his agent said it would boost his image and get him an endorsement deal. He did them because he was raised to do the right thing, and Paup was nothing if not true to his small-town Iowa roots. The proof came when his NFL career was over in 2000. He went back to his small-town NFL home to stay. A multimillionaire, he could have lived anywhere and done anything with his life. However, he picked Green Bay to settle down and raise his family.

And he kept doing the things he used to do when he was a player. Paup began to make the rounds as a motivational speaker in smaller towns, churches, and schools to talk about doing the right things in life. In 2005, the *Sheboygan Press* printed a notice: "Former Green Bay Packers linebacker Bryce Paup will be the guest speaker at the Friedens Men's Ministry chili supper at 6 P.M. at Friedens Evangelical Church, Port Washington." A little fellowship, football, and God. Other than being with his family, it was Paup's idea of a perfect evening.

Linebacker Bryce Paup helps a teammate make a tackle in 1992. Paup was the Packers' 1994 co-defensive player of the year, along with Reggie White.

By day, he was no less committed. Seeing a need to help others in the Green Bay metropolitan area, he started a charity called Good Samaritan. Paup and a partner ask people to donate used cars that still have some life and value on the auction block. Good Samaritan, with the help of participating auto dealers, cleans the vehicles, sells them, and sends the money to food pantries and Freedom House, a Green Bay homeless shelter.

Paup did leave the NFL with one wish unfulfilled. "I would have liked to have a ring with the Packers," he said in 2005, as he sat at the International House of Pancakes about a mile from Lambeau Field, where the Packers were conducting a minicamp at their indoor practice facility.

In 2002, Paup signed one more NFL contract—with the Packers. It was one of those one-day courtesy arrangements that let players like Paup officially retire with the team closest to their hearts. Having returned to Green Bay to live, Paup thought of the city as his home and certainly the place where his career took off.

When Paup left the Packers, he was fourth in team history with 32$\frac{1}{2}$ sacks, although Reggie White soon would pass him up. Green Bay defensive statistics only go back to 1975, so other well-known Packers players, such as defensive end Willie Davis and linebacker Ray Nitschke from the 1960s, would not appear in the record book.

Still trim, Paup sat across from me in a booth at the IHOP, drinking a glass of water and explained his life before, during, and after football, revealing his quiet, courteous personality. It's something you might expect from an Iowa farm boy—a young man who played in an NFL game, preseason, before he ever saw one—but not necessarily from an NFL defensive player of the year.

As he did when he was playing, Paup still feels a responsibility to take advantage of his opportunities in life. His faith in God, something that grew as he attended church every Sunday as a kid, is the foundation of his life: "I now have a platform to influence people. We're given responsibilities and positions to make a difference in people, and someday we'll be held accountable with what we've been given."

Although he says he's maintained a low profile in Green Bay, he has made himself available as a speaker around the Upper Midwest. "I still have that responsibility to be a good person. Your image speaks volumes about who you are as a person," he said, mentioning at least seven speaking engagements in the previous three months, including a father–son banquet and at a Catholic high school in Iowa.

His message often reflects how he played football: Set goals, work hard, don't quit when you lose. "If it's worth having, it's worth working for," Paup said. "There's no class on success. It's the little things that make a difference."

Paup applies his football philosophy to his daily life. He has dabbled in coaching, helping with his son's youth team. He also has worked as an assistant coach at East DePere High School near Green Bay and as an interim defensive coach one spring at Northern Iowa. However, he won't commit to coaching because he believes his next biggest job is spending time with his four children and helping families via Good Samaritan. "I've had coaching offers, but my kids already have paid the price once to chase my dream. There are only so many years to instill your values in your children," Paup said.

One of those values is helping others. Paup and his family have all but adopted a young boy whose single mother needed more than just a car or a handout. The boy has become a regular at the Paup house, where Bryce has become a father figure to him. Working with kids may lead him into another career; he would like to build a for-profit facility that not only would train young people physically but provide a safe, positive, after-school atmosphere. Long-range, Paup would like to build a different nonprofit facility to mentor young people.

For now, however, Good Samaritan fills his need to reach out and help others.

Paup knows how it feels to need help, too. One spring when he was growing up, 110-mph winds knocked down most of the corn in the region where his family lived. His father did custom farm work for other farmers. Without corn, his father didn't have much work. It was a difficult year financially for the Paups. "If people don't have the basics in life, they're hurting. Good Samaritan is a chance for me to give back to the people and the community. There are people that really need help," he said.

Paup said his parents relied on their Christian faith to get them through tough times on the farm. Even though it appears Paup has lived the American dream, he has had to rely on prayer and divine guidance to lead him through difficult periods in his life.

He wouldn't go into detail, but he said that he suffered a traumatic childhood event that made him a driven person as an adult and as an NFL player. "There are things that happened to me that shouldn't have happened," he said, saying only that the events were not family-related. "Eighty to ninety percent of NFL players—there has to be something in their past driving them, something traumatic in their upbringing. No normal person would do what we do," Paup said.

Paup has relied on God to help him escape his past and try to build a future away from the NFL. Leaving behind the outlet for his aggression also has been difficult for Paup. For the first couple of years after he retired, he couldn't bring himself to watch an NFL game or even highlights on television sports shows.

"Leaving the NFL is kind of like a depression. You're losing your profession. There's nothing like competition. It's you and the other guy battling and you defeat him. It's hard to give that up. Everybody knows it has to happen eventually, but you're never prepared for it. When it's taken away, it's a shock," he said.

Paup found fame and fortune in the NFL, but he believes without divine guidance he could have been the person on the side of the road hoping for a good Samaritan to come by and give him a hand. "If I didn't have God in my life, I'd probably be broke or divorced. There's a security that God is there and loves you for who you are and not what you did," he said.

As he sat unrecognized in the Green Bay restaurant, he was well aware that his very good—and almost great—pro football career slowly had faded away.

He was on a new mission, however, a mission to help get people on their feet. And Bryce Paup is just as determined and focused as ever.

UP NORTH
Ron Hallstrom (65)

College: Iowa
Position: Guard, 1982–92
Highlight: Played in 162 games as a Packer, 10th most in team history.
After football: Owner of Ron Hallstrom Sport and Marine,
    Woodruff, Wisconsin.

It was the summer of 1977. Ron Hallstrom was 18, and he had to make a decision. He had just graduated from high school in Moline, Illinois, and he wasn't sure what to do next.

At more than 6-foot-4 and 270 pounds, he knew that he could play football somewhere if he wanted, but the problem was he didn't really want to. He wasn't crazy about football. His two years playing high school ball didn't endear the sport to him; Hallstrom didn't like his coach or his school, for that matter, and wasn't really into the violence of football.

As a result of his take-it-or-leave-it attitude toward football, Hallstrom didn't have college coaches parked on his doorstep or flooding his family's mailbox with scholarship offers. He had pretty much made up his mind that summer that he would join the Navy when, unexpectedly, Coach Paul Shupe from Iowa Central Community College in Fort Dodge gave him a call.

Shupe always was looking for good athletes and he heard through the grapevine about this big, athletic kid over in Moline who no one seriously was recruiting. He invited Hallstrom to take a look at the school.

Hallstrom put his Navy plans on hold and made the drive from Moline on the Mississippi River more than halfway across the state to Fort Dodge, a northwest Iowa town with 40,000 people and one 19th-century military fort. "The kid came to visit. We didn't really have any money to offer him other than we could cover his tuition. He liked what he saw," Shupe said.

Hallstrom had made up his mind. Maybe college football would be more fun than high school ball. He wouldn't go into the Navy—at least not that summer. He would go to Iowa Central, a two-year school, and play football.

He returned to Moline, where his dad worked in a farm tractor factory, International Harvester, after the family moved to the Midwest from Massachusetts in the mid-1960s. Hallstrom was the sixth of seven children from a lower-middle-class family. One of his older brothers was a basketball star, a 6-foot-6 all-American sharpshooter who received a scholarship at Iowa but eventually transferred to Evansville in Indiana. His brother's success gave young Ron a role model, something he needed.

Hallstrom took out a loan for the rest of the money he'd need to make it in

Fort Dodge and headed northwest, past the state's ubiquitous hog farms and fields of corn and soybeans.

Maybe he still wasn't crazy about football, but at least he had one thing going for him. Since his senior season at Moline, he had grown close to two inches and put on another 20 to 30 pounds, all without lifting weights, which he wasn't crazy about either. When he arrived in Fort Dodge that fall, he was nearly 6-foot-6 and 300 pounds. And he could run, too.

That fall, Hallstrom began to like football at Iowa Central. Shupe put him at defensive tackle, where his impressive size kept him from getting pushed around and where his speed allowed him to chase down ball carriers and quarterbacks, even when the play didn't come his direction. Hallstrom's natural talent carried him until he learned how to play the game.

He liked the way Shupe ran the team. Through Shupe, he was getting discipline, structure, and focus, the same things he sought in the Navy. He wasn't the only one. Before he retired as coach in 1994, Shupe would see eight of his former players go on to play in the NFL, including Pro Football Hall of Fame inductee John Matuszak, and take the Triton to 10 junior college bowl games. Shupe eventually would be inducted into the National Junior College Football Hall of Fame. He was the right football coach at the right time in Hallstrom's life. "We made Ron work hard. We worked the hell out of him. We stressed discipline," Shupe said.

Hallstrom, however, still had one problem as a football player. "He was a nice guy, a super kid. He was just not tough," Shupe said. "He wasn't mean."

Somewhere along the line, Ron Hallstrom found his ability to play mean. Maybe, as a football player, it was a do-or-die situation: either be mean or get hauled off the field on a stretcher.

Maybe it had happened in 1978, when Hallstrom helped Iowa Central go undefeated and win the national junior college championship. After that season, University of Iowa Coach Hayden Fry offered Hallstrom a full scholarship for his final two seasons of college eligibility. Iowa needed defensive tackles, Shupe said. Hallstrom wouldn't need another loan to go to school at Iowa, although there still was some question about his ability. "I told him, 'Ron, I'm not sure if you can play at that level,'" Shupe recalled, "but he said he wanted to give it a try."

After he played one season at Iowa, Hallstrom was redshirted in 1980 and then switched to the offensive line in 1981. Apparently, Fry saw what Shupe had seen— Hallstrom wasn't naturally aggressive enough or didn't have the killer instinct to play defense.

At guard, Hallstrom blossomed in 1981 and helped lead the Hawkeyes to the Rose Bowl with most of their running plays to his side. He was all-Big Ten and picked to play in several college all-star bowl games. ·

The kid from Moline, who five years earlier didn't like football, was headed to the NFL. "He may be the pick [of the NFL draft] as far as I'm concerned," Fry told reporters. "He has everything you look for except experience. He has tremendously quick feet, he's intelligent, and he's highly motivated."

The Packers agreed. In the spring of 1982, Coach Bart Starr made Hallstrom the Packers' first-round draft pick.

Hallstrom was the third guard chosen in the draft and the 22nd overall selection. The first player chosen in the draft that year was Kenneth Sims, a defensive end from Texas, picked by New England.

Some people questioned the decision because Hallstrom only had one good season at Iowa. Just like in Moline, Fort Dodge, and the University of Iowa, Hallstrom had his detractors. But he was big, could run, and had a history of proving people wrong.

Starr and his coaching staff were impressed with Hallstrom's size—the move to massive 300-pound-plus lineman was under way in the NFL—and his tight-end type speed (5.25 seconds in the 40). They knew he could be a dominating run blocker and figured he would become a good pass blocker in time. "That's what got me drafted. Green Bay didn't have anybody like that," Hallstrom said of his rare combination of size and speed.

Guard Ron Hallstrom (65) and Tackle Tony Mandarich wait for the snap as Quarterback Don Majkowski gets ready to pass from the shotgun formation during the 1991 season.

Dick Corrick, the Packers player personnel director at the time, liked everything about Hallstrom, including his attitude, which was far different than when he left high school. "The main things about him are that he's got a mean streak and he's tough. He's competitive, and he has the size to dominate," Corrick said on draft day. Corrick's scouting reports were right. In his first training camp, Hallstrom got into a fight with teammate Kurt Allerman and wound up with a broken nose.

Hallstrom was ready to fight for the Packers, but it took him a couple of years to see action full time. He didn't see significant playing time until 1984, during Forrest Gregg's first season as head coach, and even then he thought he might be headed back to Moline based on the feedback he was getting from offensive line coach Jerry Wampfler. "[Wampfler] had the biggest ego of any offensive line coach in the NFL at that time. He told me if I wasn't starting by the end of training camp, I'd be cut," said Hallstrom, who believed when he was called into Wampfler's office at the end of camp that his career was over. "I thought, 'Well, that's my career. Two years'. It's one more than I thought."

However, lineman Greg Koch had been injured and the Packers needed Hallstrom. He didn't start immediately, but when the team began to struggle—losing seven of their first eight games—the starting job suddenly was his. "I remember, it was a Tuesday night. Gregg and Wampfler said they pulled out tape from Iowa and watched me play. They said, 'That's the player we want.' They said the position was mine to lose," Hallstrom said.

He never gave the job back. For the next nine seasons, Hallstrom was an anchor on the Packers' line through the Gregg and Lindy Infante coaching eras. By 1987, his teammates were effusive in their praise of his inspired play on the line. "He's just been mashing people," teammate Alan Veingrad said at the time of Hallstrom. Hallstrom was leading the team in the number of times he had knocked defensive linemen on their backsides, an obscure statistic to be sure but one that is a source of pride in the fraternity of linemen. It's a statistic that says, in essence, how tough you are, how you dominate battle lines of the game. "This year, he's been a lot more nasty," teammate Rich Moran said in 1987.

By the time he left the Packers in 1992—at his own request—he was one of the most consistent offensive linemen in team history, playing 11 seasons and 162 games. At a position that has few telling statistics, longevity may be the best measure of an offensive lineman's success. Players in recent decades tend to benefit from longer seasons, bigger contracts that commit them to being full-time players, and better conditioning and medical care, which prolong careers. Still, out of the more than 1,500 men who have put on a Packers uniform over the course of more than 85 seasons, only nine players, led by Brett Favre, have played in more games as a Packer than Hallstrom going into the 2005 season.

Based on his long and successful career, I expected to find Hallstrom succeeding somewhere else after football. I didn't expect to find him at Ron Hallstrom Sports and Marine, Highway 47 East in Woodruff, about 150 miles northwest of Green Bay. Most retired Packers tend to head south, away from the cold.

I arrived in Woodruff about an hour before I was scheduled to meet Hallstrom at his business, which is just outside Minocqua but has a Woodruff address. The side-by-side cities, along with Arbor Vitae, are on the edge of the vast Northern Highland-American Legion State Forest in Vilas County and next to the Lac du Flambeau Indian Reservation.

It's a civilized neck of the backwoods, but it's still the backwoods. The Minocqua–Woodruff area, including St. Germain and Eagle River to the east, is about as far as many tourists from southern Wisconsin and northern Illinois travel in the summertime when they take a trip "up north."

With dozens of picturesque lakes, deep-green forests, hidden golf courses, and lakeside restaurants, it's an easy place to fall in love with. Restaurant names include the Loose Moose and Paul Bunyan's Cook Shanty. Logging trucks rumble through town, dropping pieces of bark on the streets. A statue outside a taxidermy shop, like the Egyptian god Anubis, is half man, half animal (white-tailed deer in this case). One of the events at an annual summer festival is a woodtick race.

Green Bay, at about 100,000 people, is by far the smallest city in the NFL, but it looks like New York City compared with the settlements in sparsely populated Vilas County. Far northeastern Wisconsin is a good place to be if you want to get away from it all—count old gangster Al Capone among the converted—especially for the nine months of the year when the tourists are gone. You can head into town for necessities once a week and then disappear down a winding road the rest of the time.

When he was playing for the Packers, Hallstrom did some promotional work for Bombardier, a maker of outdoor recreational vehicles, including all-terrain vehicles. When he retired after the 1993 NFL season, he considered going into some type of business and then heard about a Bombardier dealership north of Green Bay that was for sale.

Within four months, Ron Hallstrom Sports and Marine was a reality. By the spring of 1995, he was living in a hotel in the Minocqua–Woodruff area and running a business for the first time in his life. Hallstrom didn't know much about ATVs, boats, motors, snowmobiles, and jet skis, although he liked riding snowmobiles. He didn't send for his family for a while, just to make sure he liked where he was, what he was doing, and that he wasn't in over his head.

If he ever felt unduly challenged by his new role, he handled that challenge as he did when he played his first game for the University of Iowa and got manhandled by a Nebraska lineman: He figured out pretty quickly how to survive and then move up the ladder. With a busy parts man behind the front counter and three large metal storage buildings for boats behind the showroom and office, his business looked to be doing well. A chain-link fence next to the office surrounded dozens of boats, ATVs, and jet skis.

As I hung out in the Ron Hallstrom Sports and Marine showroom, waiting for the boss to show up, I realized that he had been retired from pro football as long as he had been in it, but that in some ways his surroundings hadn't changed all that much. This was a place where, for the most part, men came to validate their manhood in some way. "Follow No One," read the slogan on a Bombardier product. "Leave Everything Behind," read another for a Sea Doo. "Your Engine is a Workhorse. Feed It Right," said still another slogan, which was next to a "Musclecraft" jet ski, a three-passenger, 215-horsepower, intercooled, supercharged, four-stroke engine. Change the setting and you could be talking about most any NFL coach giving a pregame talk to his players.

But this was Woodruff, a few county lines and several rural electrical cooperatives north of Green Bay, and when Hallstrom arrived for work he didn't come through a tunnel at Lambeau Field loaded for bear. Still a lumberjack of a man, he simply stepped out of his extended cab pickup, opened the glass front door to no fanfare, and headed for his office.

That's exactly the way Hallstrom wants it these days. After 12 seasons in the NFL, he's had enough public scrutiny to last the rest of his life; it's one of the reasons he's in Woodruff. Many of his customers are from Illinois, and they've never heard of Ron Hallstrom and don't care much for the Packers. "They think I'm just some big guy who runs a business," Hallstrom said from his 8-foot-by-8-foot office, which barely was big enough to hold him. Even an antique dealer down the road from Hallstrom's business didn't know who Hallstrom used to be, and the dealer was wearing a Packers sweatshirt.

Hallstrom, dressed casually, was 46 years old. His hair was beginning to turn gray, and he had just found out that he has high blood pressure. It was 54 degrees outside, but he cracked open a window behind his desk and talked about how happy he has been up north. "We've made a business of it. It's a tough business to be in, but we've done OK. It's been an interesting ride," he said. In addition to his business, Hallstrom said he had been dabbling in investment property, a hot venture up north, where the value of lakeshore property and other prime parcels of land have shot up as fast as professional athletes' contracts.

He likes the laid-back life. He's busy for about six months a year—three during the summer and three in the winter—and has time to enjoy other pursuits, like hunting, fishing, golfing, and snowmobiling. Hallstrom gets out snowmobiling a couple of times a week in the winter, then in March heads west with friends to do some extreme snowmobile riding in the mountains. He and his ex-wife, Mary Pat—they divorced in the early 1990s, reconciled, and are living together again—and their two daughters live next to a golf course. The oldest girl sometimes drives her snowmobile to school, like many of her classmates. The snowmobile is part of the culture in Vilas County (it was invented there in the 1920s), where the snow usually piles several feet high and an annual snowmobile race in Eagle River draws thousands of spectators.

Hallstrom's Packers connections are few. He has season tickets and his own sky-box at Lambeau Field, but he slips in and out of town with some friends and without any fanfare, seldom taking part in any event or promotion related to the Packers. His office decorations include two mounted fish. Other than a Lambeau Field seating chart, there is no indication that he ever played for the Packers.

After Hallstrom retired, he physically and mentally moved away from the crowd. "I have no desire to go south of Highway 29 anymore," he said, referring to the east–west Wisconsin road that goes through Green Bay and acts as an unoffi-cial border for the mostly undeveloped northern third of the state. "I know too many guys who need the [ego] boost, and I don't need it. My life has changed, and I've moved on. Football creates a different type of person than you really are. It builds your ego. I've never forgotten where I came from. I'm glad and proud of what I did in the NFL, but I don't need to be reminded," he said.

One of Hallstrom's friends in Minocqua and Woodruff is Dean Olson, who owns several automobile repair shops. Olson met Hallstrom when he ordered a snowmobile from him back in 1995. They since have gone on snowmobile touring trips to Montana, Wyoming, and Idaho; gone boating; worked on classic cars; traveled on their motorcycles to the Sturgis, South Dakota, cycle rally; and sat at Packers games in Hallstrom's Lambeau Field skybox. Olson and his friends have ribbed Hallstrom about using his name to get them a table quicker at Wisconsin restaurants because they know that's exactly what Hallstrom doesn't want. "He doesn't want to relive the glory days. Those days are done," Olson said. "He has some of his trading cards in his desk, but I don't think he really plays on the past too much."

Hallstrom's Green Bay career ended with a contract dispute. It shouldn't have been any surprise. He didn't see eye-to-eye with the Packers very often when it came to salary.

In 1986, he didn't attend minicamp because of a contract battle, but he proved his worth in 1987 by having the best year of any offensive lineman on the team, allow-ing just a half-sack for the season.

In 1988, he was a free agent well into training camp before signing.

In 1990, Hallstrom and fellow offensive linemen Rich Moran, Ken Ruettgers, and Alan Veingrad didn't report to camp after they saw what Tony Mandarich received the year before. Mandarich, the second pick overall in the draft, signed for $4.4 million over four years, the biggest contract in Packers history and the most ever paid to an NFL lineman. The other linemen figured they deserved more money, especially with the NFL signing a big new TV contract that would funnel more money to the teams.

Hallstrom eventually ended his 32-day holdout and signed just before the season began. He received $1.3 million over two years, nearly doubling his previous salary. He had been asking for almost $1.63 million. Hallstrom, Moran, and Ruettgers all signed within a week in late August.

Hallstrom hoped to get back in the starting lineup immediately, but Infante apparently took the holdouts personally. Although he was making three times as much money as Keith Uecker, Hallstrom didn't win back his starting job from Uecker until December, when the Packers were well on their way to a 6-10 season in 1990. Moran and Ruettgers also had to work their way back into the lineup.

Their holdouts, while big news for the offensive line, took a back seat to the holdout of Pro Bowl quarterback Don Majkowski. "I honestly think this was Lindy's demise. He felt it was more the system [that was responsible for the 10-6 season in 1989] than the players, that you could put anybody in there and be successful," Hallstrom said. Without the offensive line starters for so much of 1990, the Packers gave up a record number of sacks.

PHOTO COURTESY EAU CLAIRE LEADER-TELEGRAM.

Guard Ron Hallstrom (65) protects quarterback Don Majkowski in 1991. Hallstrom played in 162 games as a Packer from 1982 to 1992.

In 1992, Hallstrom signed a one-year contract under new Coach Mike Holm-gren and General Manager Ron Wolf. He was told he'd be a backup that season behind Mandarich but ended up starting and helping the Packers go 9-7, one of the surprise teams of the NFL. "I've been written off before," he said at the time, bristling. "People think I'm getting old, but I haven't missed a game since I've been here." At the time, Hallstrom also was going through his divorce, the death of a brother, and dealing with his mother's struggles with cancer.

He expected the Packers would want him back in 1993, when he was a free agent again, but contract negotiations fell apart. He was offered $1 million a year to play for the Los Angeles Rams but turned the deal down because he wanted to finish his career in Green Bay. But Wolf didn't want to pay him more than $800,000, even in incentives, so Hallstrom asked to be released. He was the last player from the Bart Starr coaching era, which had ended in 1983. Among his 162 games as a Packer, Hallstrom started 124 times.

In the fall of 1993, Hallstrom was signed by the Philadelphia Eagles, where he played just one season. He was cut by the Eagles—along with former Packers team-mate James Lofton—in June of 1994 and decided to retire at age 35. He didn't want to return to Philadelphia anyway. "I didn't like Philly. The grass isn't always greener on the other side, and out there it's concrete. If I would have just signed with Green Bay, I probably would have played two or three more years, and maybe I would have made it to 1996 [and the Super Bowl team]."

His retirement in 1994 may have been premature; even at age 35 Hallstrom was physically sound, having escaped major injuries. In some aspects of his game, he was improving because he finally began lifting weights seriously around 1989. He also had figured out how to balance the mental and physical aspects of the game. "There's a fine line between genius and insanity, between beating your head on a Coke machine and being a rah-rah guy. I knew what I had to do to be success-ful. Things came to me easier than some guys as far as handling pressure. If I screw up, I put it in my pocket and go on. I don't go into a shell. That's an intangible item called football ability," he said.

If Hallstrom has a fault as a businessman, his friend Dean Olson says, it's his frankness. Some things never change. Hallstrom always was considered one of the more loquacious Packers when it came to interviews and seldom lacked an opin-ion. Although he spends little time thinking about his past, he still has a few strong feelings—when asked—about the people in his old profession. He'll never forget the advice he received as a rookie from veteran Larry McCarren, the Packers' cen-ter from 1973 to 1984. "He was a great mentor. I had some growing up to do. He took me under his wing and saw some potential there. In my second year, he said,

'I've seen better guys than you get cut.' He impacted my career more than any other person," Hallstrom said.

He enjoyed seeing the rise of Don Majkowski, the rookie quarterback in 1987 who briefly became a star during the Packers' 10-6 season in 1989. Majkowski was one of Hallstrom's roommates on the road. "I was a mentor to some of the younger players around 1989 and 1990. I had some of them over to my house for Christmas, and I remember Majik saying he was just happy to make the team." Hallstrom still talks with Majkowski on occasion, but when the latter calls and says, "This is Majik," Hallstrom tells him, "Don, you're not Majik anymore."

He feels a little sorry for Tony Mandarich, the Packers' much-hyped top draft pick in 1989 who never lived up to expectations as an offensive lineman. Mandarich was moved briefly to Hallstrom's position when he had trouble fitting in, but he couldn't match Hallstrom's talent and only lasted three years in Green Bay. "I felt bad for him. He was just a made guy . . . just a made guy," Hallstrom said. Mandarich's college highlight video, which had NFL scouts agape as he flattened defender after defender, was a joke, purely a marketing tool, Hallstrom said. "I told him, 'Tony, I did the same thing at Iowa. There are plenty of pictures of me running over guys at Iowa.'"

Hallstrom even came to respect Forrest Gregg, the much-maligned coach from 1984 to 1987 who was a Pro Football Hall of Fame player at tackle for the Packers. "If he could make an example of you once in front of the whole team, then he respected you for the rest of your career. It was just to let you know you were going to be his guy. He blamed an entire [Bears] loss on me once. After that, everything changed. He never said anything again about my talent. I came to understand him."

Yet Hallstrom had his most fun as a Packer when Mike Holmgren arrived. Hallstrom enjoyed watching the emergence of Holmgren and his West Coast offense and Favre in 1992. He paid the staff the ultimate compliment in November of 1992—when the team was beginning to emerge as a playoff contender—when he said, "I think every year I've been here I've had to prove myself. I think this is the first year I felt appreciated by the coaches. They've treated me like a human being and let me go out and play as I can."

On the subject of his pro football career, Hallstrom was clear that he appreciated every year he wore a Packers uniform, win or lose. It was more than he had dreamed of. "If somebody had told me in 1977 that I'd play 12 years in the NFL ...."

He didn't finish the sentence, but he didn't have to. Clearly, the best decision Hallstrom ever made in his life was to take a look at Iowa Central Community College in Fort Dodge in the summer of 1977 before he almost joined the Navy. Coach Paul Shupe changed Hallstrom's life that day when he gave the unrecruited lineman a phone call.

The middle-class teenager from Moline has been separating himself from the crowd and heading north ever since.

RUNNING WITH DARRELL
Darrell Thompson (39, 26)
College: Minnesota
Position: Running back, 1990–94
Highlight: Rushed for 654 yards in 1993 to lead the Packers.
After football: Executive director of Bolder Options, a youth mentoring
   program in Minneapolis.

The situation seemed a little surreal. I was doing the running and Darrell
Thompson, the Green Bay Packers' former number-one draft pick who probably
still could rip off a 40-yard dash faster than I could run 25, was doing the watching.

We were in downtown Minneapolis on an early fall day with a fluid sky, a fast-
moving current of clouds, showers, and wind.

With Thompson on the sidelines in street clothes and a jacket, I started fast,
doing my best tailback impression as I headed straight upfield, dodged a few imaginary tacklers and broke into the clear. I have to admit, it felt pretty good running
past people, seeing them drop by the wayside like so many weary linebackers and
late-arriving free safeties.

For a while, before I began to wheeze and slow down, I experienced what it
must have felt like to be Thompson: running free with a head of steam. Who can
catch me?

My fantasy was only partly rooted in reality. Thompson was there watching all
right, but not to see me carry a football in a big game. At best, he got a glimpse of
my middle-aged frame shuffling down a blacktop recreational path along the gray
Mississippi River at the Bolder Dash, a 10-kilometer and 2-mile recreational running event.

I needed the exercise, but Thompson was there for a far different reason—to
help kids. Ten years and three weeks after his pro football career ended, he was running a different kind of race as executive director of an organization called Bolder
Options in Minneapolis.

Bolder Options has the seemingly never-ending job of working with at-risk
youth in the Twin Cities area who have been in trouble with the law or are truants. In
2001, for example, more than 8,000 Minneapolis youth were arrested for committing
crimes. Bolder Options trains volunteer mentors to reach some of these kids, attempting to get them—and sometimes their families—on the right track in life.

Bolder Options is more than just a social program, however. It's also a physical challenge. As part of a year-long commitment that kids and their mentors make,
they must participate together in running and/or bicycling events such as the
Bolder Dash. Setting a goal and reaching it can be a tonic for kids who may never

have experienced success before or who have been surrounded by negative influences in their lives. So while I was running just to feel better about myself, mentors were out there essentially trying to improve kids' lives, one success, one kilometer at a time.

It's a perfect fit for Thompson, who knows a thing or two about testing one's body as a means of shaping one's mind. Kids, along with a continuing connection to football, have been Thompson's second life. When his NFL career ended in 1995, he went to work for fledgling Bolder Options, a program that took root in Minneapolis in 1995 after being founded in 1993 by two runners in Boulder, Colorado. Thompson was the program manager at first, talking with troubled kids and telling them they either could keep going to dull meetings with probation officers or try his new approach. In the late 1990s, Thompson could be seen driving through the neighborhood with a half-dozen teens in his car, trying to steer them to a meeting with a mentor and a better life. About 15 kids a year graduated from the program at the beginning; in 2005, that number had risen to about 120 a year and about 500 total.

The program works. Surveys have found that more than 80 percent of the kids in Bolder Options earn better grades and don't get back into trouble. Nine out of 10 in the program move up a grade—a major achievement, considering that most of them were on a drop-out track. Kids respond to having a mentor, usually a young urban professional, by their side, as well as a safe place to study—the attic at the Bolder Options building.

A large part of the program's success in Minneapolis can be attributed to Thompson, who is its first executive director. With his determination and a name that helps him open fundraising doors, he has put Bolder Options on the Twin Cities charity map. Bolder Options had an annual budget of $500,000 in 2005. Thompson helped secure a three-year, $500,000 Department of Education federal grant, which gave Bolder Options a major financial boost and a higher community profile.

His is the chiseled 6-foot, 220-pound figure kids see and the firm but understanding personality donors and mentors trust when they buy into the Bolder Options philosophy. It's hard to say no to the Bolder Options mission: "To teach youth to succeed in all of life's races."

On the day of the Bolder Dash, Thompson really was on the move. Dressed in shorts and a windbreaker, he spent part of the morning at the race, greeting kids, shaking hands with program mentors and friends, and making sure everything for the race was lined up. He had one eye over his shoulder, however. Once the race was under way, he headed for the nearby Metrodome, the cloudlike white top of which could be seen billowing above other buildings less than a mile away.

Thompson is a radio commentator for University of Minnesota Golden Gophers football games. On that day, the Gophers were playing Purdue in an 11 A.M. Big

Ten game, so Thompson had to be in the booth before another Bolder Dash became history.

Thompson wasn't there to see me finish. With people passing me at the end, I didn't mind. It turned out to be a win–win day: the Bolder Dash was a success—pizza and T-shirts to the several hundred finishers—and the Gophers defeated the Boilermakers in overtime.

On the radio, Thompson praised the Gophers' high-powered running attack; he has a little experience in that area. A native of Rochester, Minnesota, the mid-size city about an hour south of Minneapolis best known for the Mayo Clinic, Thompson attended the "U of M," as most Minnesotans call it. He rushed for 4,518 yards in four seasons, setting the school's all-time rushing record. He had three 1,000-yard seasons and would have had a fourth if not for an injury his junior year.

With 4.3 speed in the 40 and the ability to shed tacklers with his solid frame, Thompson was a lock as a first-round pick in the 1990 NFL draft. In the draft that year, Green Bay had back-to-back first-round picks. With the 18th pick of the draft, the Packers took linebacker Tony Bennett from Mississippi. With the 19th pick, they took Thompson.

After the draft, running backs coach Willie Peete praised Thompson's toughness and said, "I really think Darrell Thompson's going to be good because he has really good work habits, and he's a smart young guy. And he's a quality individual. From that standpoint, I don't think we could have drafted a better person."

At the time, Thompson was excited to go to the Lindy Infante-coached team that finished 10-6 in 1989 and had just missed the NFL playoffs. The Packers' running game needed help, 1987 first-round pick Brent Fullwood having proved to be a disappointment. Fullwood gained only 1,300 yards total in 1988 and 1989, and seemed to lack the toughness and desire mandatory for a leading runner.

Thompson was a bigger, tougher runner, a man the Packers couldn't pass up. One scouting report used by NFL teams ranked Thompson the second-best back in the draft, behind Blair Thomas of Penn State. On a nine-point scale, Thomas received a score of 8.99.

Still, the Packers may not have taken Thompson if it weren't for the Dallas Cowboys. The Cowboys had the 21st pick that year but were worried that the running back they wanted—Emmitt Smith—might not be available that long. So the Cowboys gave up a third-round draft pick to Pittsburgh to move up four places and pick Smith at number 17. It was a genius move, as it turned out. Smith helped lead Dallas to three Super Bowl titles in the 1990s and contributed to many a Packer loss in the process. He played 15 seasons and retired as the NFL's all-time leading rusher with more than 18,000 yards.

Thompson's career fell well short of Smith's, especially for a man picked just two places behind him in the draft. Playing five seasons for the Packers, he totaled just 1,641 yards and seven touchdowns. Thompson always seemed to be on the verge of succeeding just as he or the Packers system broke down.

Making $1 million his rookie year, Thompson rushed for just 264 yards and one touchdown as a backup to Michael Haddix. It wasn't a good year in Packerland all around; the team was just 6-10 and had begun the slide that would result in Infante's firing by new GM Ron Wolf after the 1991 season. Thompson had a 37-yard touchdown run and a 76-yard kickoff return for a touchdown, but he gained just 18 yards rushing in the first six games as he worked on his blocking, something he didn't do much of at Minnesota. Still, Peete thought Thompson was as good as advertised. "Before you know it, he's going to be a guy everybody is talking about," Peete said early in the 1990 season.

When he did break loose for a 12-yard TD run against his home-state Minnesota Vikings on October 28, 1990, at County Stadium in Milwaukee, Packers Executive Vice President Tom Braatz was impressed. "He showed a burst of speed," Braatz said. On a second-and-one play 4:23 before halftime, Thompson started right, saw the hole filled and cut left, a block by tight end Jackie Harris opening a lane to the end zone. "He just did a nice job of running with his eyes," Infante said. "That's what you pay backs to do." The TD gave the Packers the lead, and they went on to win, 24-10. He may have been off to a slow start, but Thompson appeared to be on his way to a fine NFL career.

After beating out Haddix as the starting fullback in 1991, Thompson started 13 games. Despite a knee injury that sidelined him in October, he finished strong with 471 yards in November and December, including a 40-yard touchdown run against Atlanta.

Thompson had a chance to start over in 1992 under Holmgren. Although he had 10 running backs in minicamp in May, Holmgren immediately tabbed Thompson as a starter either at halfback or fullback. Thompson eventually settled in at fullback, but he missed the preseason when he suffered a torn quadriceps on August 2. He wasn't activated until mid-October. By that time, Vince Workman, Thompson's best friend on the team, was on pace for a 1,000-yard season.

However, Thompson got his chance on November 15 in Milwaukee. Workman started against Philadelphia and reeled off a 44-yard run before going out with a separated shoulder. With his quadriceps healed, Thompson took over and played well. He rushed for 72 yards on 15 carries, including a 33-yard run and a three-yard TD catch in a 27-24 win over Philadelphia.

It was the first of six straight wins, a streak that would keep Holmgren's surprising Packers in the 1992 playoff picture. Only a final-game loss to Minnesota knocked the Packers, 9-7, out of the playoffs.

But just when it appeared Thompson was back and had the ability to be a featured player, he was gone again. He sprained an ankle against the Eagles, and Edgar

Bennett got the start the next week against the Chicago Bears. The rookie Bennett, a fourth-round draft pick, responded with 107 yards in 29 carries in his first NFL start. Holmgren was impressed. "We all know that he has great ability," the coach said.

By 1993, with Bennett making progress at fullback, it was clear the Packers didn't have faith in Thompson. Wolf sent a draft pick to New England to get John Stephens heading into the 1993 season, and said Stephens most likely would be the team's featured halfback, ahead of Thompson. Stephens was a five-year veteran and had gone to the 1988 Pro Bowl when he gained 1,100 yards as a rookie.

Regarding Thompson, running backs coach Gil Haskell said, "There's part of me that says [Thompson] is a hell of a football player. You watch and say, 'My God, that's a big, strong, fast guy.' But we've got to see it," Haskell said in May of 1993.

In late October, not satisfied with Stephens or Thompson, Wolf traded again. This time he sent Stephens—averaging only 3.6 yards a carry—to Atlanta for retired NFL star Eric Dickerson. In the trade, the Packers also got cornerback Bruce Pickens for a draft pick. However, when Dickerson didn't pass a physical because of an injured neck—after falsely claiming to be 100 percent healthy—the Packers ended up getting just Pickens for Stephens. The whole Stephens–Dickerson–Pickens deal turned into a Wolf flop when Pickens did not return to the Packers in 1994.

So by mid-1993, after being touted and then demoted, Thompson was promoted to starting halfback. The door was open for him. "If he can stay healthy, he can be a very good back in this league. I mean really an outstanding player. I have a lot of confidence in Darrell," Holmgren said, even though he and Wolf had said otherwise with their actions when they put Stephens ahead of Thompson and tried to get an over-the-hill Dickerson.

Holmgren, true to his word, did show confidence in Thompson late in 1993. He did something for Thompson that he was planning to do if he had gotten Dickerson: change the offense to the I-formation to fit his halfback's skills. In the last two months of 1993, Thompson ran out of a modified I-formation, where the halfback lined up directly behind the quarterback. Holmgren typically used split backfields and not the I, but Thompson had run out of the I in college and was most comfortable with that approach. Backs who are in the I line up seven yards behind the line as opposed to five yards in a split backfield. Holmgren called Thompson a "north-and-south" runner who liked to ram through a hole rather than cut or slash through it.

The I-formation worked. The week after the Dickerson trade fell through, Thompson rushed for 105 yards against Tampa Bay, then followed up the next week with 68 against Chicago. Even Bennett, who became Thompson's blocker at that point, saw the merits. "Darrell is comfortable running out of the I. I think it helps him," Bennett said. With a revived running game, the Packers won six of seven games from mid-October to late November and got back in the playoff picture.

Their only loss in that stretch, 23-16 in Kansas City on Monday night, was at least partly Thompson's fault. Trailing, 20-16, with 5:57 to play in the fourth quarter, the Packers were on the Chiefs' 3-yard-line when Thompson got the ball. Running behind right tackle Tootie Robbins and right guard Harry Galbreath, Thompson was looking for the end zone. Three-hundred-pound Chiefs tackle Dan Saleaumua knocked lineman Rich Moran to the ground, then slammed into Thompson as the Packers' runner tried to cut toward the goal line. The ball flew into the air and wound up in the end zone, where the Chiefs recovered.

Despite the fumble, Thompson had another productive night with 12 rushes for 51 yards. The real culprit in the loss was Favre, who threw three interceptions and lost a fumble.

Thompson continued to play well late in 1993. Against the Lions on November 21 in Milwaukee, he rushed 18 times for 73 yards; Bennett had 66 and a pair of touchdowns. Thompson had just two fewer yards in the game than one of his idols, Detroit's Barry Sanders.

The day after Christmas, the Packers secured a playoff spot with a 28-0 win over the Los Angeles Raiders in Green Bay, thanks in part to Thompson. In what was the longest run of his pro career, Thompson scored from 60 yards out when he burst up the middle, broke two tackles, and outran a defender to make it 28-0. He finished with 101 yards on 21 carries while Bennett had 38 yards on 15 carries.

PHOTO COURTESY EAU CLAIRE LEADER-TELEGRAM.

Running back Darrell Thompson is all smiles on the sidelines during the 1993 season, when he led the Packers with 654 yards rushing.

Thompson led the Packers in the two playoff games, a 28-24 win in Detroit and a 27-17 loss in Dallas. He totaled 69 yards in 19 carries.

For the 1993 season, Thompson gained 654 yards—a career best—to lead the team for the second time in three years. "If I had played in the first couple of games, I could have gotten 1,000," Thompson said.

By 1994, however, Thompson was the odd man out in Wolf's continuing search for a lead back. Despite what Thompson did late in 1993, it wasn't enough for Wolf to change his opinion of the back he did not draft.

In 1994, the Packers drafted speedy halfback LeShon Johnson in the third round and fullback Dorsey Levens in the fifth round, and signed Tampa Bay star back Reggie Cobb, a free agent. "With Reggie Cobb, now we have the type of back we need to compete favorably within our division," Wolf said, calling Cobb the second-best runner in the division.

Wolf then made a phone call to Thompson, whose contract was up, and said he wouldn't be re-signed. "I'm sure it hurt him, but he took it well," Wolf said. Thompson was drafted 11 places ahead of Cobb in the 1990 draft, possibly because Cobb had failed a drug test at the University of Tennessee. Cobb, about the same size as Thompson, rushed for 1,171 yards in 1992 but was hampered by injuries in 1993.

Despite Wolf's lack of confidence in him, Thompson did return to the Packers in 1994. More than once. He took a pay cut—from $425,000 to $300,000—to sign on August 22 when the Packers cut Dexter McNabb. Thompson had gone from the starter to Cobb's backup but called the demotion "part of the game." He switched from jersey number 39 to 26.

It turned out to be a good season for the Packers, who went 9-7 and lost in the second round of the playoffs, again to Dallas. It was a trying year for Thompson. He was waived and re-signed by the Packers three times that season. Friends started calling him "Butcher Block."

He signed his last Green Bay contract on January 3, 1995, one month after the Packers had cut him for the third time. The team had just three healthy backs heading into the playoffs—Bennett, Levens, and Cobb after an injury to LeShon Johnson. Thompson, like he had been all season, was no more than an emergency fill-in for the Packers. He didn't stay long again, but this time it wasn't his fault. Five days after he signed, the Packers lost, 35-9, to Dallas.

With his contract up again, not to mention his patience with Green Bay, Thompson became a free agent in the spring of 1995. He wasn't the only one looking for greener pastures that year, as the Packers also lost Bryce Paup, Ed West, Cobb, and Don Davey to free agency.

Thompson signed a two-year contract with Chicago. He had made up his mind in Bears training camp in Platteville, Wisconsin, that if he didn't make the team he would look for another line of work. "Eventually you have to get on with life, and football takes a huge toll on you physically," he said that summer, when he was 27 years old. "To be honest, I'm starting to feel that toll." By running back standards, with four full seasons of being the featured back in college, he was physically older than some backs his age.

Thompson was one of eight running backs in the Bears' camp. Chicago was in the midst of a decade of losing, and the Bears that spring drafted Heisman Trophy-winner Rashaan Salaam, a back the same size as Thompson, in the first round. Thompson made it to the final roster cut with the Bears before he was released.

Four times in less than a year was enough. He retired.

Thompson went back to Minneapolis, where he started with Bolder Options. He was back on his home turf, a place where the name Darrell Thompson was associated with big things and where he could put his college studies in sociology to work. He and his wife built a home and started a family.

A few months after the Bolder Dash, I caught up with Thompson. This time, he was sitting in his spacious office on the second floor of the Bolder Options building on Stevens Avenue, a tree-lined street with older homes not far from where he starred as a collegian in the Metrodome.

He reflected on an NFL career that he's grateful for but that didn't live up to his expectations. He talked about getting "caught between coaches" with the Packers and fighting off injuries. "You've got to be in the right system, and I wasn't really in the right system. Edgar [Bennett] was tough and really fit their system. He played with a lot of confidence. I didn't realize until after one or two years that this is just not the right situation."

In addition to injuries, Thompson started slow in Green Bay because he had to change his running style. In college, he was taught to burst toward the hole, using his speed as soon as he touched the ball. In Green Bay, the coaches wanted him to "press" to the hole, waiting for it to develop before cutting loose. "I had to learn to be more patient."

Like the troubled and underprivileged children he tries to reach at Bolder Options, Thompson knows how circumstances can play a major role in peoples' lives. "I had an opportunity [in 1993], but it couldn't be enough. [The Packer coaches] figured my time was up. By the fourth or fifth year, if you're not a star they start drafting. There wasn't any room for me on the roster. I was just average, but they didn't draft me to be just average."

Still, he savors the second half of the 1993 season, when he was the go-to back. That experience left Thompson with a taste of what it was like to succeed in the NFL, to develop a rhythm and contribute to a team's playoff run. "I started to enjoy football a lot, and I was thinking I could have a real NFL career. I wish I could have had a whole career like that. My position coach [Gil Haskell] was happy for me because he knew what I went through," Thompson said.

Even though he never approached stardom, Thompson was glad he had a chance to emulate some of his childhood idols, running backs Dickerson, Sanders, and Walter Payton. "I enjoyed the whole experience," he said.

He fondly remembered scoring a touchdown in 1992 against the Bears. When he was spiking the ball in the end zone, Brett Favre, who had become the Packers' starting quarterback only a few weeks earlier, ran up from behind and tackled him. "I thought he was going to blow out my knee," Thompson said. He said Holmgren was so upset with Favre that he fined him $5,000 and told him never to do that again.

As we talked in the office, Thompson remembered that he was supposed to do a radio interview via telephone with a reporter from Wisconsin. The big Minnesota–Wisconsin college football game was the next day at the Metrodome, the annual battle for Paul Bunyan's Ax. As usual, Thompson spent about eight hours that week preparing for the game so when he interrupted our talk for a short conversation with the reporter, he sounded eloquent, rehearsed, and completely comfortable.

Watching him talk and seeing how he has acquitted himself so well at Bolder Options since retirement, it's hard to understand why Thompson didn't live up to expectations in the NFL. His personality is much like the way he ran—straight ahead, full speed, full commitment. Regarding Thompson's tenure as a Packer, no one ever said he should work harder, run harder, lift more. No one questioned his character. Where did he go wrong? Or was it the Packers, who were trying to find themselves as a team in the early 1990s, the ones who failed to live up to expectations?

If Thompson brought one life lesson out of the NFL to his work at Bolder Options, it's this: Life and its opportunities can be fleeting, so don't take them for granted or mess up when a gift lands in your lap. Thompson remembers Infante telling his players to enjoy every day in the NFL because one day—maybe sooner than they think—they will be on the outside looking in.

Thompson has one overriding goal in his new line of work. He believes disadvantaged kids should at least be given an opportunity to succeed. He wants them to have at least a piece of the gift he was given, the promise of a future while they're still young.

He talked about one boy, DeMont, who had been in trouble with the law but became involved in Bolder Options and blossomed. DeMont not only returned to high school but graduated early and joined the Marines. He eventually returned to Minneapolis, found a good job, and started a family. He didn't forget the man who helped pull him up by the shoestrings. When DeMont's daughter had her first birthday, Thompson was invited.

"What our kids typically need is someone to listen to them. They get ignored or slapped, or there's no one there for them. We try to give them a positive person to be involved in their life, and have them seek out healthy relationships. I'm blessed because our program works. It does benefit kids, and that makes it all worthwhile," Thompson said.

When I left the Bolder Options office, I felt like running again. I wanted to be like Darrell Thompson, to know the feeling of being out front and carrying the conviction that I could make a difference in someone's life.

MAKING AN IMPACT
Chuck Cecil (26)

College: Arizona
Position: Safety, 1988–92
Highlight: Selected to play in Pro Bowl after 1992 season.
After football: Defensive backs coach for the Tennessee Titans.

It didn't take long for Chuck Cecil to make an impact as a Green Bay Packer. In the sixth game of his rookie season, on October 9, 1988, Cecil was playing free safety late in the third quarter against the New England Patriots at County Stadium in Milwaukee. Patriots quarterback Doug Flutie threw downfield, over the middle of the Packers defense, as he tried to connect with wide receiver Stanley Morgan. The pass was overthrown and then intercepted by Ron Pitts. As Morgan reached for it, however, he was stopped in midair. Cecil had zeroed in on him and leveled him with a vicious hit, just below the chinstrap. Morgan fell to the turf, face down, and lay motionless as medical personnel rushed to his side.

Morgan, 33, a four-time Pro Bowl player, was unconscious for about five minutes. The stadium grew quiet, but no one felt the impact of the moment more than a man on the sidelines in a wheelchair. That man, Darryl Stingley, former Patriots receiver and now director of player personnel, thought back to the day in 1978 when a similar hit by Oakland defensive back Jack Tatum left Stingley in the same situation. Stingley never stood again—he was paralyzed for life. On this day, a decade later, Stingley lowered his head as Morgan was carried from the field on a stretcher.

The Packers were comfortably ahead in the game and went on to win, 45-3, but it wasn't until afterward that Cecil heard the news: Morgan was moving his limbs. He was in a hospital but would be OK. He wouldn't be paralyzed like Stingley. Cecil was relieved—he said he'd even thought of leaving the game because he was so upset—but he didn't offer any apologies. He would have done it again if he had the chance.

Hitting hard was simply the way he played football. "It was a clean shot. It was pure. No question about that. He went down like a domino," Cecil told reporters that day. "The big hit is part of the game. I enjoy it, and the fans enjoy it." Coach Lindy Infante, after looking at tapes of the play, agreed that Cecil had done nothing wrong.

Packers fans had to be relieved, too, when Morgan was released from the hospital the next day with just a concussion, but they also had to be wondering, "Who was this Chuck Cecil guy?"

Knocking out Stanley Morgan was just Cecil's opening act. Over the next few years, Green Bay fans would see Cecil play the game of football exactly the way they liked it—as hard and unforgiving as the ground in Wisconsin on a December day. Hit after hit, impact after impact, Cecil would become known as one of the hardest-hitting players ever to wear a Packers uniform. He knocked the wind out of opponents, knocked himself out in the process, and brought the air out of many a Packers fan as they cheered at the sight of his small, missile-like body slamming another body backward. Chuck Cecil played football with the mindset of a boxer: He went for the knockout punch. He wanted to make an impact.

The hard hit gave rise to Cecil's career, but it also became his downfall. By 1995, his aggressive style of tackling was curtailed by the NFL brass, his career was over after eight seasons.

More than a decade later, he hasn't changed the way he approaches life. He was at the Tennessee Titans offices when we talked by phone in 2005, his fifth season as a defensive backs coach. He discussed why he still loves being on the football field, still making an impact although he no longer is doing the hitting.

"The biggest thing in coaching is getting them to play better. When that happens, it's nice. I try to help them be better and help them capitalize on their abilities faster," Cecil said. "If I can impart my passion for the game and teach them to play it the way it's supposed to be played, then I'll have succeeded as a coach."

Beyond football, Cecil has another goal. In 2005, he and his wife, Carrie Gerlach Cecil, formed a committee to raise money for the trauma center at the University of Arizona Medical Center. The trauma center, the lone high-level center in southern Arizona, needed money to expand its services. The Cecils are UA alumni. With Chuck's work in pro football and his wife's connections to media and the sports world via her public relations firm, Anachel Communications, they knew they could make an impact on health care in the region. The Cecils live in Tennessee with their daughter, Charli, who was 1 year old in 2006.

Cecil's wife also has been a success story. Her first novel, *Emily's Reasons Why Not,* was published by HarperCollins and was turned into a television series by the same name, which debuted in 2006 on ABC.

Helping a trauma center seemed a natural thing for Chuck Cecil to do. As a football player, he has been around trauma and the threat of it most of his life.

When he was a skinny kid growing up in the San Diego area in the 1970s, he learned that hitting as hard as he possibly could was the only way he'd be able to follow his dream of playing football beyond high school.

He was a star quarterback, receiver, and defensive back in high school, but because he weighed only about 140 pounds as a senior, few major colleges were interested in him. Arizona did offer him a scholarship briefly, then reneged. He decided to go there anyway as a walk-on player and hoped to earn a scholarship.

The first year, he was "like 27th on the depth chart out of 27 defensive backs," Cecil said. "I didn't look like I belonged, but when I put the pads on, things changed. When you show you're not afraid of contact, it's a way to fit in, even though you may not fit in. Hitting people is something players respect."

Cecil knew, early on in college, that if he wanted to make the team he would have to hit hard to make the coaches notice him. That he did. He was redshirted, meaning he could practice but not play with the team. Although he impressed the coaches, Cecil apparently wasn't going to get the scholarship he coveted. He decided to quit football and go to work on a small dairy farm that his mother owned.

When the Wildcats coaches realized he was serious about farming, they changed their minds. Cecil finally was on a scholarship at a Pacific 10 Conference school, the thing he had aimed for since high school.

There was no chance that he'd squander his long-awaited opportunity. Before he was done at Arizona, Cecil set the Pac-10 record with 21 career interceptions. In his senior year, he was a first-team all-American and Pac-10 defensive player of the year. He had nine interceptions, tying for the best in the country.

He no longer was thinking about going home to work on a dairy farm. He wanted to work on Sunday in the NFL. He had put on nearly 40 pounds since high school, weighing about 180. NFL scouts ranked him the third-best safety in the draft. He was one of the leading contenders for the Jim Thorpe Award, an annual honor that is given to the best defensive back in college football. It went to Deion Sanders of Florida State. Still, NFL scouts loved Cecil's aggressiveness.

New Packers Coach Lindy Infante took Cecil in the fourth round of the 1988 draft. In practice, Cecil would get to cover the Packers' number-one draft pick, receiver Sterling Sharpe. As a rookie, he played in every game, started two, and finished with four interceptions.

His presence was felt almost immediately: In his third game in 1988, a Packers loss in Miami, Cecil intercepted a pass by Dolphins quarterback Dan Marino, ending his streak of 74 consecutive passes thrown without an interception. The Packers coaching staff liked Cecil, who wasn't as fast as preferred at the position but played all-out. "Chuck really does have a nose for the football. He has outstanding instincts for the game," said Dick Jauron, Cecil's position coach.

Then, a few weeks later came the hit on Morgan, but everyone agreed that it was a clean hit and that the Packers had a keeper from the 1988 draft class.

In 1989, Cecil's play in the secondary was one of the reasons the Packers finished 10-6 and nearly made the playoffs. In a big win that November over defending Super Bowl champion San Francisco, Cecil intercepted a Joe Montana pass and set up a key Packers touchdown. Montana, one of the league's smartest passers, had thrown 149 straight passes without an interception before Cecil picked him off. Cecil was proving not only that he could hit and tackle but outsmart receivers and quarterbacks.

After injuries limited him to nine games both in 1989 and 1990, Cecil made a name for himself in 1991 and 1992. Packers fans loved his hard-hitting style. Cecil often could be seen on the sidelines with blood coming from the bridge of his nose; so his biggest fans started coming to Lambeau Field with ketchup on their noses. Cecil loved the attention. "You try to put your nose through the ball carrier's body. I've always prided myself in playing good, clean football. Playing dirty is not necessary," he said.

He started every game in 1991, had 110 tackles, and made TV announcer John Madden's All-Madden Team, which usually is a compilation of players who best represent old-style, smash-mouth football. By 1992, Cecil was known as such a ferocious hitter that receivers became intimidated when they ventured into his territory. "I've

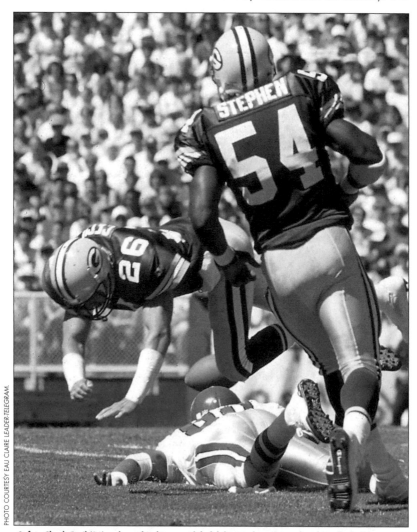

Safety Chuck Cecil (26) makes a big hit on a Philadelphia Eagles receiver, knocking the ball loose during a 1991 game at Lambeau Field. Closing in on the play is linebacker Scott Stephen (54).

been on the field quite a bit where guys short-arm balls they'd normally catch when they see Chuck coming," Packers linebacker Johnny Holland said in 1992.

Cecil again started every game in 1992, topped 100 tackles again, and capped his season by being named a starter in the Pro Bowl, along with teammates Sharpe and Brett Favre. Cecil played so well in 1991 and 1992 that when his contract was up, the Packers considered labeling him their "franchise" player—in other words, the one guy they didn't want to lose to another team through a free-agent contract.

Cecil, who thought back to the day when he quit the game at Arizona, couldn't believe he had become one of the NFL's best. Late in the year, especially, he came on strong. For example, on November 29, 1992, in Milwaukee, he had nine tackles, an interception, and broke up a pass in a 19-14 win over Tampa Bay. His Pro Bowl chances were helped when the Packers finished 9-7 and nearly made the playoffs.

First-year Coach Mike Holmgren said Cecil played with "ongoing rage" but was more than just the poster boy for big hits. "He's a total football player," Holmgren said.

Cecil, who started at safety alongside LeRoy Butler, led the 1992 team with four interceptions. When he wasn't making memorable hits, he was reading the receivers' routes, playing the angles, and either picking off or knocking down passes.

While the Packers were dangling big money in front of free agent Reggie White early in 1993, they couldn't spend much to sign Cecil. After his Pro Bowl season, Cecil's market value was up and several teams were interested.

He almost hurt his chances at a big contract with an embarrassing incident in 1992. The night after the team's—and Holmgren's—first win of the season when Favre threw his now-famous strike to Kitrick Taylor to defeat Cincinnati in the final seconds, Cecil went out and had a few drinks. He got into an argument over paying his bill, scuffled with the bar owner, got punched in the nose, and wound up being arrested for disorderly conduct. At the police station, he was charged with disorderly conduct a second time when he refused to let officers take his mug shot and get fingerprints. "Let's just say it was a misunderstanding," he said.

The 6-foot Cecil, who by 1992 was up to 190 pounds, loved nothing better than playing in Green Bay, but when the Phoenix Cardinals offered him a $2.25 million contract and the Packers said they couldn't come close to that, even Packers secondary coach Dick Jauron told Cecil it was a deal he couldn't refuse.

Cecil liked Jauron and Holmgren and could see that the team was headed places with Favre as its quarterback. "For all those reasons, I wanted to stay. I loved playing in Green Bay. It was a fairy-tale situation for me. My biggest regret is, people thought I was trying to get out of there. I hope the fans understand I really had no choice," Cecil said on the telephone from Nashville, as he took a break from his coaching duties.

Phoenix owner Bill Bidwell had opened his pocketbook and signed several free agents in the spring of 1993, including quarterback Steve Beuerlein for $2.5 million; defensive back John Booty for $3.3 million; and linebacker Tyrone Stowe for $2.7 million. The Cardinals had lost Pro Bowl safety Tim McDonald. By May, Cecil had signed and was going back to Arizona, where he played college ball, to help the struggling Cardinals head in the same direction as the Packers.

Cecil's stay in Arizona went south in a hurry, however. On September 12 that season, he made two of his trademark hits on Washington Redskins back Ricky Ervins and tight end Ron Middleton. He was not penalized for the hits, but the NFL had been keeping an eye on Cecil. In his final game as a Packer, he had been cited for two questionable hits in a game against Minnesota. He was fined $7,500 for another questionable hit during the preseason with Phoenix.

After taking his past into account, the league fined Cecil a record $30,000 for the hits against the Redskins. He was accused of using the crown of his helmet to make the hits, which is against NFL rules. He also was accused of hitting a receiver while the man was "defenseless."

Cecil appealed the fine. "I'm playing the same way I did 12, 13, 14 years ago in high school, and now all of a sudden it's illegal," he said at the time. NFL Commissioner Paul Tagliabue denied Cecil's appeal, leaving him "speechless."

Suddenly, football was a different game for Cecil. He was like a pro baseball pitcher who just had his favorite pitch taken away. Cecil had a nagging shoulder injury, adding to his woes in 1993. He didn't change his style of play because of the ruling but he said he was less effective and it "definitely changed things for me. No doubt, it had an effect on my career."

In 1994, he also didn't see eye-to-eye with Cardinals Coach Buddy Ryan. After being cut early that season and then re-signed, he was let go again and didn't play that year. Apparently, with his track record of illegal hits, teams weren't interested. "I guess nobody wanted me. Apparently there were some repercussions," Cecil said.

In 1995, he tried to return. He was signed by Cleveland and cut. "There was more politics going on," he said.

Then, he was picked up by Houston and played as a reserve. After experiencing more shoulder problems from 95 career NFL games, after 400 tackles and 16 career interceptions, he retired after the 1995 season.

Cecil, born on November 8, 1964, wasn't sure what to do with himself for awhile after his football career ended. He was a television analyst for University of Arizona games in 1999 and 2000. Then he realized he wanted to get into coaching and found a job with the Titans beginning in 2001.

A 4-handicap golfer, he also played on the Celebrity Golf Tour in 2000 and

2001. His best finish was second place in Lake Geneva, Wisconsin, when he shot even par for 27 holes, 3 shots behind Shane Rawley, a former pro baseball pitcher.

As a coach, the hours are long. The pay is much less than what he received as a player. He doesn't get to hit people anymore. But Cecil couldn't think of anything he enjoyed more than being back in football.

"Football is what I love," he said. "It's a perfect fit for me. I love coming to work every day. I love being around the players and coaches. The hours during the season are off the charts. It's high stress, but it's good work because it's football. The biggest thing is coaching and talking to the players, getting them to play better. When you work with a player and he says, 'Hey, thanks. That works,' that's the most rewarding thing. You just try to be one step ahead of them. I never get to step inside the white lines anymore, but it's still a rush on Sunday. It's almost an explosive feeling you get before a game."

I asked Cecil about his health. He had no ill effects from his NFL career, he said, but added that he likely will have neck problems as he ages because of the many head-first hits he made.

Then we talked about concussions. I asked him how many he suffered as a player, and he said, "Only a few." However, he only was counting the serious concussions. "Back then, you had to really be messed up to have a concussion," he said.

By today's standards, anytime a player is knocked unconscious, even momentarily, it's considered a concussion, he said. I asked him how many concussions he would have had by today's standards. "It happened with regularity. Seventy, eighty, ninety times," he said.

A couple of times, I asked Cecil about issues from his career that I figured he was sure to remember, and he didn't. "That was a few hits ago," he said with a chuckle. "I've never been the sharpest tool in the shed." Maybe he had forgotten, too, that he was pretty sharp when he was in school. Cecil had a 3.95 grade point average in high school and was an academic all-American in college.

What he hadn't forgotten was what turned out to be his last game at Lambeau Field. In the second-to-last game of the 1992 season, the Packers' final home game, Cecil played like a Pro Bowl star. His hard hits knocked three Los Angeles Rams players out of the game. Cecil had an interception, seven tackles, and broke up four passes, in addition to sending three players to the sidelines. After the last player had to be carried from the field, the fans began chanting Cecil's name. Standing in the huddle on the field, linebacker Brian Noble finally told Cecil to take a bow. "I still get goosebumps to this day thinking about it," Cecil said.

In 2000, he returned to Lambeau Field for the first time since 1992. Packers fans hadn't forgotten "the Hit Man." Some of them again began chanting "Cecil, Cecil, Cecil."

He remembered one more thing about the fans in Green Bay. In 1988, the

Packers were 2-12 under first-year Coach Lindy Infante and returned home to play the Minnesota Vikings. The Packers had scored just 36 points in their last six games and clearly were one of the worst teams in the league. Yet Lambeau Field was full. "It was five or six degrees and the wind was howling so much that the wind-chill factor was probably 30 below. I remember going out for the pregame warmups and there wasn't an empty seat in the stands. I thought to myself, 'What type of place is this?' Green Bay was a special place."

PART THREE:
A DIFFERENT ROAD

GOING PUBLIC
Esera Tuaolo (98)

College: Oregon State
Position: Nose tackle/defensive end, 1991–92
Highlight: As a rookie in 1991, had 3½ sacks and started all 16 games
for the Packers.
After football: Gay rights advocate, speaker, singer, author.

Trying to find a former Green Bay Packer who hasn't worn a "G" on his head for a decade or more can be frustrating or surprisingly easy. It's a lot like trying to catch a bouncing football—either it lands in your lap or bounces away from you each time you move in.

I once found Ray Nitschke and Tony Canadeo, members of the Pro Football Hall of Fame, simply by thumbing through the Green Bay white pages and giving them a call. Others were tougher to locate. For months, I tried to track down Herb Adderley, the defensive star whose image I remembered from my 1960s bottle-cap collection. He used to be right there—a dime-size face next to Zeke Bratkowski and Carroll Dale on my cardboard lineup. Now he always seemed out of my grasp, even though he kept appearing at Packers functions. Likewise, my attempts at finding Desmond Howard, the Super Bowl XXXI MVP, proved futile. Recent teammates had no idea how to get in touch with him. The closest I came to finding Howard was watching him on ESPN *College GameDay*, where he's a commentator. Apparently, he's just as elusive as he was while returning kicks for the Packers in 1996.

When most NFL players walk up the tunnel at Lambeau or some other arena for the last time, they slip quietly into a second life. Most realize their shot at glory has passed. They head back to their hometown or home state. They figure out pretty quickly that fame can be like an air squadron flyby on opening day as they lose touch with their teammates and eventually with the NFL. Reality, in the form of being a regular guy, sets in.

Esera Tuaolo is the exception. Few ex-pro athletes can say they are more famous after their careers end, but Tuaolo can. Since 2002, when he retired from the NFL, Tuaolo has been a rising star in American culture. Some might say counterculture. His lineup is impressive. Since he quit football, he has been a guest speaker at NFL headquarters in New York, addressed thousands of college students at campuses across the country, written about his life for *ESPN Magazine*, written a book about his life, been a guest on numerous television talk shows, and become friends with some of America's best-known celebrities. His fans can write to him on his Web site, *www.eseratuaolo.com*, where he weighs in with his latest activities, advice, and how you can join the Esera fan club.

The secret to his post-NFL career success is simple: He no longer has a secret. In 2002, on HBO's Real Sports with Bryant Gumble, Tuaolo said publicly for the first time three words that caught America by surprise and changed his life forever: "I am gay."

With that proclamation, Tuaolo became only the third former NFL player ever to announce that he was a homosexual. The first was running back Dave Kopay, who also played for the Packers in 1972; he came out in 1975 after he retired. Offensive lineman Roy Simmons, who played with the New York Giants and Washington Redskins from 1979 to 1984, was the second. He announced it on the "Phil Donahue Show" eight years after retiring. No active player ever has admitted to being gay. While Kopay said he knew of other gays in the NFL in the 1960s and 1970s, Tuaolo has said he did not know of any others in the 1990s.

When Tuaolo bared his soul, he figured he would be able to live in peace, one of the things he sought most; just the opposite happened. His story went across the country and the world, eliciting hundreds of news stories and becoming talk-show and news fodder for weeks. Almost overnight, he became a spokesman for gay rights and a role model for gay people everywhere. After all, he had played in the NFL, one of the most elite, all-male institutions in the country.

Tuaolo became so well known that for people like me trying to find him, he was the easiest of targets. Because he now makes a living off his name and new-found fame, giving interviews is part of his job. If Herb Adderley was the needle in the haystack, Tuaolo was the haystack.

He was easy to find but a hard person to find time to talk with. For much of 2005, I found him indisposed or dodging me. It probably was a little of both. Looking at just a few of the things he did, it was easy to see why. That May, he spoke to 200 students at the University of Hawaii in his home state in a speech called "Tackling Homophobia with Esera Tuaolo." Despite years of the gay movement, gays still live in fear in the United States, he said that day. Fear is why he didn't divulge his secret while playing in the NFL; some day that will change, he promised them.

That June, he gave motivational speeches aboard the cruise ship Norwegian Dawn, which was filled with gay travelers and entertainers. The charter group R Family Vacations, owned in part by gay activist Rosie O'Donnell and her lesbian partner, Kelli, was on its second annual cruise, sailing the East Coast. It was a reunion of sorts for Tuaolo, who called O'Donnell, the talk show host and actress, a "great role model for me."

In August, Tuaolo, an aspiring singer and actor, took the stage for the first time at the Illusion Theater in Minneapolis during the avant-garde Fringe Festival. He put on a one-man play about his life. The cabaret-style play received mixed reviews, but one critic compared his voice to that of Luther Vandross, the R&B crooner. Tuaolo already had produced two adult contemporary albums and one Christmas CD, which he unveiled the previous year at the Mall of America in Bloomington, Minnesota.

In September, Tuaolo was named ambassador for the 2006 Gay Games in Chicago. The Gay Games, founded by Tom Waddell, a former Olympic decathlete, grew from 1,350 athletes in 1982 to 11,000 in 2002. In an interview with the Gay Games staff, he said: "People ask me whether playing in the NFL was my dream. My answer is no. I am living my dream, being an out and proud athlete, having a committed relationship, two children, two dogs, and the house with the white picket fence."

Soon he was off to California to guest host a gay talk show, "Queer Edge," on a gay cable channel called "Q." Then he was in Memphis in early October to make appearances at another gay athletic event, where he answered his cell phone one night in a crowded place that sounded like a bar and said he'd be back in Minneapolis soon.

First, however, there was dinner in New York with NFL Commissioner Paul Tagliabue. Tuaolo, singer Cyndi Lauper of "True Colors" fame, "Queer Eye" star Kyan Douglas, and other leading gay activists were on hand as Tagliabue and his wife received an award from a gay and lesbian group, thanking them for their support. Tagliabue's son, Drew, is gay. The NFL has taken a stand on the issue: It offers same-sex domestic-partner benefits to its administration employees, although the NFL Players Association does not. The league also has a non-discrimination policy that includes sexual orientation.

A few days after being in New York, Tuaolo spoke at the University of Nevada-Las Vegas and he told students about his first NFL sack, when he pulled down Philadelphia Eagles quarterback Randall Cunningham in the 1991 season opener at Lambeau Field. "I sacked him, and I heard my name echo through the whole stadium, and I started shaking," he said at UNLV. Tuaolo lived in fear, he said, that someone would hear his name, divulge his secret, and seriously complicate his life.

So he covered up, going to strip clubs with players, dating women, and making sure teammates saw him kissing them. He had no choice but to hide his sexual orientation, he said, especially when one teammate called the other a "faggot" and a fight broke out. How would they react if they knew the truth about him?

Eight months of attempting to track Tuaolo down finally paid off after he got back from Las Vegas, New York, and Memphis. It was just a one-hour interview at his house in Eden Prairie, Minnesota, and I didn't hear anything that he hadn't already told people all over the country, but it was worth the wait. I walked through his front door, past the Hawaiian pineapple statuary on either side of his stoop, shook his hand, heard him talk about being gay, saw the family photo of him, his husband, Mitchell Wherley, and their two adopted children, I was able to make sense of everything that I had been hearing and reading about Esera: He has nothing to hide anymore. He's out with his secret, out with his feelings, and out to change attitudes toward gays in America.

It says something about a person's self-confidence when he opens his front door to you. When Tuaolo announced he was gay, he let the whole world into his living room. Why did he do it? Esera Tuaolo didn't want to be a prisoner of society any longer. To lead a normal life, he believed he had to open the door. Far from the radical that conservatives might depict him as, Tuaolo is a pleasant, thoughtful, friendly man who played arguably the toughest position in the NFL.

Even for a heterosexual, life in the NFL isn't the norm. Athletes receive undue public attention, make salaries about 30 times higher than the average American, have little job security, work odd hours, and must deal with persistent temptations, which include forward women, illegal drugs, and alcohol aplenty.

Those are just the peripheral issues. They work in a world of controlled violence, a world that celebrates male toughness. Every play in the NFL, when one man's skills are matched against another's, is a test of physical superiority. Muscle vs. muscle. Grit. Determination. Raw power. The men who play in the NFL are America's tough guys, strong and unflinching. They work in mud, spit, and sweat. To paraphrase actor Tom Hanks in the baseball movie, *A League of Their Own*, there's no crying in the NFL. It's an image that conflicts with the traditional stereotype of a gay male.

Many NFL players struggle psychologically when their careers are over. They wish they could keep playing, hesitant to leave what they feel are the best years of their lives. Not Tuaolo. Many bad things—anxiety attacks, suicidal thoughts, fear for his own sanity—happened to him while he was in the NFL. When he quit, he didn't shed a tear.

He looked like a happy man the day we met. He and Mitchell and their adopted twins, a boy and a girl, live in a spacious, modern house in Eden Prairie, not far from the headquarters of the Minnesota Vikings—one of the teams Tuaolo played for in his nine-year career. As he sat at his kitchen table, fumbling with a mini-football and checking his e-mail on a laptop computer, he made it clear that he's never had second thoughts about his decision to come out. It changed his life for the better.

"For 35 years of my life, I had been in the closet. This is an opportunity to just enjoy our lives, a chance to walk down the street and know we're a family," Tuaolo said, with the two-husband family portrait in a tan wood frame behind him on a coffee table.

Tuaolo was alone at home on this Friday morning; Mitchell was at work and the twins were at preschool. He and Mitchell met in the Minneapolis area and became partners in the mid-1990s, when Esera still was playing in the NFL. They privately adopted the twins from Samoa in 2000 when they were a week old. Tuaolo is mostly Samoan by descent and grew up in Hawaii. The twins' picture is on a Christmas CD, "First Christmas," that he produced in 2004.

He discussed his new role as a gay advocate, which he has happily accepted, even if it has delayed his singing career. "I'm trying to make a difference in this world. I'm trying to help people understand that [gays] are not like what people saw on TV in the seventies and eighties. I've sat down with Christians and non-Christians. I'm not trying to change their mind but give them a different perspective of what a gay man is," he said. Tuaolo is a Christian, although he has had to endure many a Christian message condemning his sexual orientation, he said.

As someone who is used to being scrutinized by the media, Tuaolo is comfortable as a role model. Moreover, he's passionate about speaking for gay rights because he suffered so many indignities as a closeted gay man. "I have a duty now to help people," he said, referring to other gays. Gay rights issues such as marriage and same-sex adoptions are close to his heart. "They want to take away my marriage and my children," he said of anti-gay activists. "We all can change the world in our own way."

With the NFL more popular than ever, Tuaolo knows he has a rare opportunity to reach people. He hopes to make a difference in how people perceive gay men, the gay movement, and in the lives of other still-closeted gay people. "We have good gays and bad gays. People think we're all the same, but we're not," Tuaolo said, as he discussed harmful gay stereotypes.

The job has been easier than he expected. He didn't receive as much criticism as he expected when he came out. He has taken his son to Vikings games and been accepted by the fans. He has been to bars in mostly rural northern Wisconsin, and Packers fans still recognize him and buy him drinks. Gay or not, "Once a Packer, always a Packer," Tuaolo said with a smile.

NFL reaction to his announcement was mixed. Former Vikings teammate Todd Steussie said Tuaolo's secret wasn't a big deal. Former Packers teammate LeRoy Butler said he was proud of Tuaolo for coming out but also said that he would be uncomfortable showering in the locker room with a man who he knew to be gay. Packers defensive back Darren Sharper had a similar concern, and San Francisco running back Garrison Hearst said, "Hell no! . . . I don't want any faggots in this locker room."

Tuaolo, nicknamed "Mr. Aloha" and the "Singing Samoan" while in the NFL, had more than 50 teammates with the Packers in 1991. He heard from only a few after his 2002 announcement. His former defensive line coach, Greg Blache, called to apologize if he ever said anything anti-gay that might have offended Tuaolo.

Former center James Campen offered Tuaolo his support. He didn't hear from his old drinking buddy, Favre, but heard Favre and Butler support him in interviews. "That's basically it," Tuaolo said. "It doesn't surprise me at all, but I didn't do this to look for approval from anyone."

One of the first people who called was Don Davey. In 1991, Davey was a rookie defensive end on the line with Tuaolo, and they quickly became friends. So when Tuaolo announced he was gay, it only seemed natural for Davey to call and support him. "The hard part was hearing how miserable he was. I wish he would have told me at the time," Davey said, "but I understand why he didn't. He was petrified for his career and for his safety on the field." Davey, who in 1998 started a financial portfolio management company in Neptune, Florida, said Tuaolo made friends wherever he went, even though there were signs that he might have been gay. Davey and the woman that he eventually married often went out with Tuaolo, but he never had a date. It didn't matter to Davey, who grew up in Manitowoc, Wisconsin, and was an academic all-American all four years—the first in NCAA history—when he played for the University of Wisconsin. "We were friends almost instantly, and we've been friends ever since," Davey said.

Since Tuaolo's announcement, he has been accepted wherever he has gone, supported by the gay community, and respected by non-gays for his decision to tell the truth, he said. "It's not about being gay; it's about who I am. My story has inspired a lot of people in the GLBT [gay–lesbian–bisexual–transgender] community as well as people in the straight community. I get thousands of e-mails a month. I've helped kids."

First, however, he had to help himself. He felt so trapped while he played in the NFL that he considered suicide. "I'm a survivor. Yeah, I feel I should be dead," he said.

The fact he made it through his childhood is a testament to his toughness. Tuaolo was born on July 11, 1968, to a Samoan mother and Samoan-German-French father. The last of nine children, Esera's philandering father died when he was 10.

Losing his father was just one of his traumatic experiences while growing up. He witnessed an aunt being shot to death. One of his older brothers was gay and died of AIDS. One of his uncles was a drug dealer. Worst of all, another uncle sexually abused Esera. That uncle eventually was murdered.

Esera helped on the family's 15-acre banana plantation while he was growing up, skipping freshman football to lug fruit. He often piled 50-pound or heavier bundles on his shoulders and carried them down the hillsides.

When he was 14, his mother thought he needed a role model and male influence in his life, so he left Honolulu as a sophomore in high school to live with another uncle, a pastor, in Chino, California. Tuaolo started playing football. After being named defensive player of the year in his high school conference, he picked Oregon State out of a pile of scholarship offers.

He started three years at OSU, moving to nose tackle his junior year. When he began blowing past centers and guards to make 13 tackles for losses that season, NFL scouts paid attention. Along the way, his ability to sing also put him in the spotlight, starting as a child in the Pentecostal church. By the time he was in college, he was singing the national anthem at a Portland Trailblazers pro basketball game, Oregon State basketball games, the Senior Bowl, and other places. And he was named the best defensive lineman in the Pac-10 Conference.

Despite a knee injury that kept him sidelined for part of his senior season, Tuaolo was destined for the NFL. For a kid who didn't come from much, it was everything he had hoped for, although secretly he knew better. He would have to live life on the run, so to speak, if he were to survive in the macho world of the NFL. His first gay relationships in college were short-lived, and he would have to live the same way in the NFL—pretend he was a straight male so that his teammates wouldn't suspect anything, and only let his guard down a little when he went home to Hawaii in the off-season. He wanted the financial security that the NFL offered, but he feared the notoriety that went with it.

As a rookie, Tuaolo started every game at nose tackle in 1991 for the 4-12 Packers. He was the team's second-round draft pick, behind cornerback Vinnie Clark, and was the 35th player picked in the draft. He proved he could play one of the most physically demanding positions in the game, earning the starting position over veteran Bob Nelson. Tuaolo had 48 tackles to rank 10th on the team, $3\frac{1}{2}$ sacks, an interception and a forced fumble. Jay Hilgenberg, all-pro center for the Chicago Bears, said Tuaolo would be "a great nose guard for the Packers for years and years." His position coach, Greg Blache, praised Tuaolo's explosiveness off the ball, his work habits, and intelligence. "He's as intense on the field as he is personable off it," Blache said. But even as Tuaolo was succeeding in the NFL, he was battling his emotions more than his opponents.

At 6-foot-2, 284 pounds, Tuaolo was average size by nose tackle standards but was agile—and he could sing. A natural talent as a tenor, Tuaolo shocked his teammates in training camp when, as was the custom, he was asked to sing a song. His melodic version of "Mary Had a Little Lamb" had the dining hall hooting and hollering for more. Then, in October of 1991, in a nationally televised Thursday night game against Chicago at Lambeau Field, Tuaolo became the first Packer—and possibly the first NFL player ever—to sing the national anthem. He sang it in his full uniform, wearing number 98.

Life in the NFL may have looked like fun for Tuaolo, but it wasn't. "When I was there, I didn't trust anyone. So a lot of times I didn't get too close to players. How close can you get when you can't share your life?" Tuaolo asked.

In a tell-all story in *ESPN Magazine*, Tuaolo described his low points, such as anxiety attacks and thoughts of committing suicide. "I would get a sack, force a fumble, stuff a play on the goal line. And hours later, in the middle of the night, I'd wake up sweating, clutching my chest, and gasping for breath . . . . By Monday night, the hurt and the panic would change to numb depression. That's when I'd start to drink. The one thing I could never do was talk about it, because the NFL is a super-macho culture. It's a place for gladiators. And gladiators aren't supposed to be gay."

This gladiator was. Tuaolo played so well his first year in Green Bay that he made two of the NFL's all-rookie teams. "I usually kicked butt," he said. However, it was his only full season in Green Bay. In 1992, Coach Lindy Infante was replaced by Mike Holmgren, who started over. Tuaolo played four games as a reserve—with six tackles and one sack—in 1992 before Holmgren released him. Second-year nose tackle John Jurkovic won the starting job in training camp, when Tuaolo fell behind, his internal struggles intensified by the recent loss of his brother.

Officially, Tuaolo was waived to make room on the roster for the signing of free agent defensive end Keith Millard, a former Minnesota Viking. Tuaolo then was picked up by the Vikings. (Interestingly, while the defensively talented Vikings saw promise in Tuaolo at nose tackle, they let go of rookie nose tackle Gilbert Brown in 1993. Brown became one of the keys to a Packers' defense when they won the 1997 Super Bowl.)

Tuaolo was productive as a Viking from November of 1992 through 1996. His best season in Minnesota was 1995, when he had a career-best 59 tackles and three sacks, including one against the Packers, while starting all 16 games. He led all Vikings defenders in 1995 with six tackles for losses and two fumble recoveries. He had the best game of his career that season, recording eight tackles Oct. 8, 1995, against Houston.

Scheduled to make $1.1 million in 1997, the Vikings released him that spring. Tuaolo then bounced from Jacksonville in 1997 to Atlanta in 1998 to Carolina in 1999, before retiring. Considered a solid defender against the run, he finished with 12 career sacks and one interception in 99 NFL games. His best year for sacks was his first, $3\frac{1}{2}$ with the Packers in 1991.

With Atlanta, Tuaolo played in 13 games and all the playoff games as the Falcons made it to the 1999 Super Bowl, where they lost to Denver, 34-19. During the game in Pro Player Stadium in Miami, Tuaolo's old fears returned. When he made a tackle and heard his name announced, he realized that more people were watching him and hearing his name on worldwide television than ever before. Would someone he knew divulge his secret? He had his first gay relationships at Oregon State. Would someone tell?

He had kept his secret for eight years from NFL teammates, coaches, and fans. He knew there had been rumors back in Minnesota because the family of his partner,

Mitchell Wherley, owned a spa frequented by some wives of Vikings players. When would it all end?

"If somebody would have found out, it all would have been taken away. If opponents knew, they would have tried to hurt me. 'Get the gay guy.' If the so-called sissy dominated you, you'd be all embarrassed. It wasn't a safe environment to come out," Tuaolo said.

Tuaolo won't soon forget some good things about the NFL—like his friendship with Brett Favre. "I was good friends with Brett," Tuaolo said about a friendship that grew when they discovered they both enjoyed a night out on the town. They hit it off as friends in training camp in 1992, Favre's first year, when Tuaolo saw Favre rifle a pass. Amazed by the velocity on the ball, Tuaolo told Favre he had a bright future in Green Bay. Their shared love of partying got out of hand one night in Mississippi in 1992. Tuaolo, Favre, and Favre's younger brother, Jeffrey, were arrested after a fight in a nightclub. Favre faced three charges—public drunkenness, using profanity and disorderly conduct—while Tuaolo was charged with disorderly conduct.

Then there was the time Tuaolo bought his teary-eyed mother a ring when she came to visit him in Green Bay. Growing up poor in Hawaii, the ring was something his mother never could have afforded. As much as he hated his situation at times, the NFL also was a drug that he couldn't resist.

Tuaolo, who has a quick smile and an easy-going manner, has done all right for himself, if his house can be used as a measuring stick of financial success. At his two-story house on a winding, hillside street, the lawn was perfect on an early fall day, as were the lawns of all his neighbors, their homes neatly spaced, white concrete driveways breaking up the expanse of green.

There was no white picket fence, but there may as well have been. Everything about the house fit the traditional American dream, except for the two-husband picture on the coffee table. No matter how hard he tries to convince them, Tuaolo knows that some people never will be able to get past that part of his life. It's one reason he wrote his book, *Alone in the Trenches: My Life as a Gay Man in the NFL*, which came out in March of 2006. When he was suicidal, he read a book, *The David Kopay Story*, written by Kopay, the first ex-NFL player to admit he is gay. Tuaolo said Kopay's book helped save his life because he knew for the first time he wasn't alone.

Tuaolo played for the Packers one full season, but the lower portion of the dust cover of his book has just one NFL picture—a color shot of number 98 in a Packers uniform. He seems to take pride in the fact that he played for one of the most storied teams in NFL history. All of Tuaolo's pro and college uniforms hang in giant frames on a wall in his living room, and a Packers helmet is among his prizes sitting atop a kitchen cupboard.

Eden Prairie, Minnesota, named Eden in the 1850s for its lovely prairie, is on the trendy southwestern edge of the Twin Cities metro area, not far from the Mall of America, the international airport, and the multimillion-dollar new headquarters for Best Buy corporation along busy Interstate 494. The Tuaolo and Wherley home is close to parks and lakes, a perfect location to raise their children in an area that epitomizes "Minnesota nice."

After more than a decade of searching for it, Esera Tuaolo found his Eden and is tackling what he believes is his responsibility to make sure it isn't taken away.

BRAVE GAY
Dave Kopay (40)
College: Washington
Position: Running back, 1972
Highlight: Special-teams standout on the Packers' 1972 Central Division
  championship team.
After football: Manager of Linoleum City, Hollywood, California.

In 1975, David Kopay read a series of stories in the *Washington Star* about gay men in the National Football League. As an ex-NFL player who had just retired, he was upset about the stories, but not because the *Star* had dared to discuss an issue that was taboo in the all-male, he-man world of pro football. Kopay thought the stories, while revealing, didn't go far enough. None of the players in the stories who talked about homosexuality in the NFL dared to identify themselves, which Kopay considered duplicitous. The series ultimately left people asking questions: Who were these gay players in the NFL?

Kopay didn't just get upset. He did something about it. Kopay called the *Star* and told the lead reporter in the series that he knew the name of a gay NFL player and that they could publish it: his.

When a subsequent *Star* story about Kopay hit the presses and then was picked up by wire services, newspapers, magazines, radio and television stations across the country, Kopay had made U.S. history: He was the first man to admit he loved other men while playing in the NFL. And the men he loved and had relationships with included other NFL players.

Kopay wasn't acting on impulse when he decided to go public about his private life. Fed up with living a double life and having to hide his sexual preference, he almost came out three years earlier while he was a Green Bay Packer. All it would have taken was for another man, a Packers teammate, to stand up to him and ask him point-blank.

In 1972, Kopay was a backup running back and special-teams player for the Packers, who were coached by Dan Devine and who had Bart Starr on the coaching staff. Kopay had been in the NFL since 1964. The Packers were his fifth team, and at age 30 he not only had grown up but come to fully realize who he was: He could not be completely happy in a traditional heterosexual relationship.

Born in Chicago, Kopay was the son of a Croatian man, a former Marine who was forced to drop out of school after sixth grade. Growing up in a strict Catholic home, Kopay received a football scholarship and played one season at Marquette University in Milwaukee before the school dropped its program. His family had moved west by then to North Hollywood, California, and he transferred to the

University of Washington. In Seattle, Kopay's life became more complicated as he fought homosexual urges. He tried the straight life. Kopay dated girls and women in high school and college, including the Rose Bowl queen in 1964 when he was co-captain of the 1964 Washington Huskies. As an adult, Kopay fell in love with a woman and got married. And yet he had a sexual relationship with a college football teammate and then throughout his nine seasons in the NFL, again sometimes with teammates.

By the time he reached Green Bay, Kopay knew he would live the rest of his life as a gay man and that his marriage wouldn't last much longer. He was aware that other people in the NFL knew or suspected that he was gay, and he didn't care. "I was in a challenging mood," he said.

One day in Green Bay, his secret almost came out. One of his Packers teammates—he wouldn't say which one—began making comments about Kopay, suggesting that he might be gay. "I was ready. I was getting so angry," Kopay said, and he challenged the teammate to simply ask him if he was gay. Kopay planned to tell the truth, if asked.

However, the man backed off, and it would be another three years before Kopay, prompted by the newspaper stories, would make his announcement. "That would have been really something. God knows what would have happened in the middle of the '72 season," Kopay said in 2006, thinking back to the team that went 10-4 and won the Central Division title.

Green Bay offered him little in terms of a gay-friendly environment, but Kopay was happy he had the chance to play in the NFL's smallest city and slow down his life a little. He called Green Bay a pleasant escape from life in the big cities, although he still sometimes drove to Milwaukee to find a gay bar and have a drink. He played in San Francisco, center of the gay pride movement, from 1964 to 1967; Detroit in 1968; Washington in 1969 and 1970 (where he fell in love with teammate Jerry Smith); New Orleans, where he lived in the sexually liberal French Quarter in 1971; and then part of the 1973 season with Oakland.

Kopay's best season was as a rookie in 1964 with the 49ers. He had 271 yards rushing to lead the team and 135 yards receiving. That team, which finished 4-10, was coached by Jack Christiansen and led by quarterback John Brodie. Two years later, Kopay rushed for 204 yards with a career-best 4.3-yard average per carry, including a 32-yard touchdown run. In nine NFL seasons, he totaled 876 yards rushing, 593 yards receiving, and scored seven touchdowns.

In Green Bay, he wasn't completely careful about his secret and wasn't worried because he was married. It was his cover-up, although he never intended it to be. However, with his wife living out east and only coming to Green Bay for an occasional visit, he was free to pursue his search for other relationships.

His teammates suspected something was up with the blonde, tanned, 6-foot-1, 205-pound back who turned ladies' heads and once was asked to pose in *Playgirl* magazine. "They knew, but they didn't know," Kopay said. John Brockington, the team's starting fullback in 1972, said teammates thought Kopay was a little different but didn't think much about it because he was from California.

Kopay remembered that once he was in the shower at Lambeau Field and teammate Carroll Dale commented on Kopay's lack of tan lines. Kopay used to visit nude beaches in California to run and catch some sun. "Carroll, you're not supposed to notice things like that," Kopay said half in jest to Dale, the veteran wide receiver who had played on three of Green Bay's championship teams of the 1960s. Dale was married, a devout Christian, and one of the Packers whom Kopay admired because of his straightforward, honest manner. "Carroll just laughed," Kopay said.

Kopay said he secretly was attracted to his Packers roommate, wide receiver Paul Gibson, whom he said was the fastest man on the team, faster even than dart-quick defensive backs Willie Buchanon and Ken Ellis. "[Gibson] wasn't gay, but I wish he was," Kopay said. "He probably knew I was gay. We joked about it," said Kopay, who didn't know of any other gay players in Green Bay that season. He knew of other gay players in the NFL, he said, including Smith, the all-pro Redskins tight end who set NFL records and was nicknamed "Mr. Touchdown."

His 1972 season with the Packers turned out to be Kopay's last full one in the NFL. He rushed 10 times for 39 yards, caught three passes for 19 yards and did not score, but he also played special teams for the Packers. Kopay took part in 14 games and was there when the Packers lost to his old team, the Redskins, in the first round of the playoffs.

Kopay returned to Green Bay in 1973, determined to make the team again, but he was cut—along with Dale—when training camp ended. Although Dale went on to have a fine season with Minnesota in 1973 and help the Vikings reach the Super Bowl, Kopay spent the season on the practice squad in Oakland. He played briefly with a World Football League team in California in 1974 before retiring.

In his best-selling 1977 book, *The David Kopay Story*, he recalled the day he was cut by Packers Coach Dan Devine, who had four rocky seasons in Green Bay, suffering from a lack of respect by players and questionable personnel decisions. "After the usual deadline for cuts, Coach Dan Devine sent one of his assistants with the message for me to turn in my playbook. I was too disgusted to try to find out why. I went to my locker and got my stuff. Several of the other players were in a huddle, talking about it. They were also feeling how easily it could have been one of them. Gale Gillingham, the all-pro captain of the team, put his arm around me and said, 'Dave, he doesn't have any idea what he's doing. You definitely deserve to be here.'"

Kopay's life wasn't the same after his 1975 announcement. He instantly became a household name in the gay community and opened himself up for praise and criticism. Some of the latter came from his shocked parents. He would have no trouble speaking out about his feelings but would have plenty when he looked for a job or sought approval from his former employer, the NFL. "Companies were afraid to hire me or they'd be identified as a gay company," Kopay said. "The NFL has hardly recognized I exist. It's been shameful."

Much of Kopay's life after football has been spent in Hollywood, where he works for his uncle, the owner of a retail business called Linoleum City. Kopay has made a good living buying and selling carpets and other floor coverings. His good taste has made Linoleum City a favored supplier for set designers on television shows and in movies, he said.

Kopay owns a fine house, travels, and still is a sought-after speaker on gay-rights issues. When women's pro basketball player Sheryl Swoopes announced she was a lesbian, Kopay and former Packer Esera Tuaolo appeared on a talk show together to discuss her announcement.

Much like when he was a Packer, Kopay works out regularly, despite total shoulder-, hip-, and knee-replacement surgeries. He had four knee operations before the knee replacement. "When you play special teams for 10 years, that's what happens," he said.

Kopay lives in a city where his gay lifestyle isn't questioned, but he is disappointed that the NFL's attitudes toward gays haven't changed in the last 30 years. Just four NFL players have been known to be gay: Kopay, Tuaolo, Roy Simmons (another former Redskin), and Smith. "We're not the only four in the NFL. I can assure you of that," he said. "There are a number of great ballplayers who aren't out."

He believes gay players in 2006 and beyond face an even more hostile, homophobic environment than he did in the 1960s and 1970s, partially because the NFL refuses to be upfront with players about the issue. "They treat us like lepers," he said. Yet, even if the NFL welcomed gay players, Kopay wouldn't expect a flood of them to admit they are gay for fear of being ostracized.

It's not easy being a gay gladiator. Tuaolo fought depression and was suicidal. Smith only tacitly acknowledged his homosexuality before his death from AIDS in 1987. Several of Kopay's gay and bisexual NFL friends said they couldn't do what he did and risk ruining their lives.

One of the highlights of Kopay's NFL career was his chance to play for Vince Lombardi when he coached the Redskins in 1969. The year before, he played in Detroit and was beginning to realize who he was. At Detroit, "Alex Karras and Bill Munson had befriended me and, although I was never really able to help them or the team [because of injuries], they remained very close. In fact, Alex practically threw me out of the closet. Yet he never embarrassed me when a number of the players would get on me for not chasing the ladies. In private, he let me know that he simply didn't care. The next year, when Lombardi and the Redskins would pick me up off waivers, I remembered [Karras'] support, and that empowered me to be more myself and creep out of the closet a little more," Kopay said in his book.

After Lombardi led the Packers to five titles in the 1960s, he came out of retirement to coach the Redskins for one season before dying of cancer in 1970. He was no stranger to the issue of gay men. His brother, Harold Lombardi, years earlier had divulged to his family that he was gay and still was accepted by the strict Catholic family. In the Lombardi biography, *When Pride Mattered*, David Maraniss wrote: "Here was an area where the coach showed an open mind, according to friends and family. He ignored Catholic teaching against homosexuality and instead considered gays another group deserving of respect, like blacks and American Indians and Italians. In later years, he would have players who were gay, and quietly root for them at training camp, hoping they could show they were good enough to make his team."

Lombardi's philosophical approach to football and life made the soul-searching Kopay more introspective. After beginning a gay relationship with the Redskins tight end, Smith, and other men in Washington, Kopay took an even harder look at his sexual orientation. He took pride in being one of Lombardi's chosen men. After years of wondering who he was, his gay pride finally began to take root in the nation's capital. "By the end of the 1969 Redskin season, I had finally admitted to myself that I was homosexual," Kopay wrote.

By 1972, he was ready to divulge his secret—something that in 2005 no active NFL player had yet done—if only his suspicious Packers teammate had been brave enough to ask.

PART FOUR:
REMEMBERING THE 1980s

PENALIZED FOR LIFE
Charles Martin (94)

College: Livingston
Position: Nose tackle/defensive end, 1984–87
Highlight: Played in 48 games as a Packer.
After football: Died of kidney disease on January 23, 2005, in Houston at age 46.

Mention the name Charles Martin to Green Bay Packers or Chicago Bears football fans and they most likely will furrow their brows and say, "Wasn't he the guy who…?"

Yes, he was the Packer who unnecessarily hurled Jim McMahon to the Soldier Field turf in 1986, damaged the quarterback's shoulder, and essentially killed the Bears' chance of a second straight Super Bowl title. It has become one of the more infamous plays in the history of pro football's oldest rivalry, one that Packers fans, despite their decades-old dislike for the Bears, aren't proud of.

Hard hits and tacit violence are part of what draws fans to football, but no one likes a bully. On November 23, 1986, Martin let his temperament get the best of him. In the second quarter, McMahon threw a pass that was intercepted by Green Bay's Mark Lee. After the throw, as McMahon was beginning to walk off the field, the 280-pound Martin rushed toward McMahon, lifted him in the air, and slammed him, shoulder first, into the turf. Unlike many dirty plays in the NFL that go unnoticed because they occur in the middle of the line or the bottom of a tackling pile, this one was plain to see and involved one of the Bears' stars. The play drew howls of protest from Bears fans and the media, as it was replayed time and again on television.

The repercussions were many. The pro-wrestling-style body-throw further injured McMahon's bad throwing shoulder, and he missed the rest of the season. Martin was penalized, escorted off the field, and ejected from the game. Later, he was suspended for two games without pay by the league and fined $15,000. His ejection was believed to be the first in NFL history for something other than a fight.

Critics of the Packers, including some of their fans, said the play was symbolic of the team's losing ways and lack of discipline under Coach Forrest Gregg. Making matters worse, Martin, some teammates, and at least one Packers assistant coach didn't apologize. Martin and teammates allegedly wore towels on their uniforms with hit lists; McMahon's number was at the top of Martin's towel, which could be seen dangling from his waist as he knelt over the injured McMahon.

The play so disgusted the NFL that a caveat was added to the rules of the game: A player could be ejected for "stuffing" a quarterback. It was the word used by veteran referee Jerry Markbreit when he announced to the crowd at the game why Martin had been ejected.

The McMahon play followed Martin to his grave. When he died at age 46 on January 23, 2005, in Houston of kidney disease, news stories about his death focused on the one thing that everyone seemed to remember about Charles Martin—one late hit in 1986.

Martin's friends and former coaches—Danny Cronic, Jack Street, Joe D'Alessandris—and a teammate wished that people knew a few more things about the man they said was much more than one bad play. As much as they don't condone what he did to McMahon, they always admired the carefree big man who made them smile and made something of himself when the odds in life were stacked against him.

Officially, Martin played five NFL seasons as nose tackle for the Packers, Houston Oilers, and Atlanta Falcons. He had 11 sacks in 76 NFL games. Before that, he played for the Birmingham Stallions of the USFL. Facts about Martin's pro career, however, don't begin to explain why he might have slipped up that day in Chicago and hurt McMahon.

Martin grew up in Canton, Georgia, a city of about 7,700 in the northwestern corner of the state, just north of Atlanta. Canton used to be the home of a large cotton mill but then became a major chicken producer, billing itself the "Chicken Capital of the World." It was a blue-collar town, and even there Martin started at bottom.

Martin didn't have much of a life as a child, said Danny Cronic, his high school football coach. Martin came from a broken home of seven children with no father, had few clothes or material goods, and once said his mother was a bootlegger. One day, Cronic gave a ride home to another Canton player and saw Martin sitting under a porch, wearing filthy clothes. Martin was 14 and had dropped out of school. He expressed an interested in playing for the Cherokee High School football team in Canton. Cronic didn't know what to think of him. "I said, 'Son, you can't play football. You've got to be in school.' The next day, he was in school," Cronic said.

Although Martin was behind academically at first, he pushed himself to succeed at school and football, Cronic remembers. Martin needed to put on weight to play football so he began eating at all three school lunch periods—until school officials found out. He would go out the door of the lunch room then turn around and go right back in. To get stronger, Martin would carry a washing machine on his back through his neighborhood. He gradually grew into his size-14 shoes, caught up in school so that he could be eligible to play football, and became one of the Canton starters.

In what might have been a sign of things to come, Cronic said Martin was naturally aggressive on the football field. He never quite knew when to quit. "He didn't like the sidelines. People would run out of bounds, and he'd still hit them," Cronic said, remembering the time Martin and the ball carrier he was pursuing disappeared down an embankment beyond the sidelines. "Charles didn't like the whistle because he was going to be in on the tackle. It was a boy's innocence in a way. We had a few penalties. One time, I put him at defensive end, and the other team was running plays away from him. I looked up, and we had two defensive ends on one side. He said, 'Coach, I couldn't tackle them over there,'" Cronic said with a laugh.

Martin's nickname was "Too Mean." Harvey Martin of the Dallas Cowboys had that nickname, but Cronic said, "we nicknamed him because this was the real 'Too Mean' here. He wanted to get there and to hit the guy. There was no defeat in him. He just wanted to play. He loved the game. He was a special guy. He had a big heart. I have his picture up on my wall."

Jack Street was an assistant coach at Canton. Street's son, Robert, also was on the team and was one of Martin's friends. "One day Robert came home and said, 'Daddy, I know you don't have much money, but if you have an extra dollar or two, send it to Charles because he don't have anything.' I went to visit his house once, and it was bare," Street said. "Part of the reason I could relate to Charles was that his life was tough like mine. My dad worked in the textile mills and was killed in a car wreck when I was 5. But my life wasn't as tough as Charles.'"

After high school, Martin went to Western Carolina to play football in 1978. There, he met Coach Joe D'Alessandris. The coach and his wife helped Martin manage his money in college and supplied him with used clothes. When D'Alessandris left to be an assistant coach for Livingston, Martin transferred and become one of D'Alessandris' first key players. Martin, by then 6-foot-4 and 235 pounds, struggled academically his first year, went back to Canton, and worked in construction. He returned in 1980 and made a name for himself at Livingston. "We had him on the kickoff teams. He was a leg buster. He would scatter bodies all over the place. Boy, could he run. He was athletic as all-get-out," said D'Alessandris, who in 2005 was an assistant coach at Georgia Tech. Martin once ran a mile in training camp in less than six minutes, D'Alessandris said.

Martin had about 10 quarterback sacks as a senior and earned several honors, including Division II all-American in 1982. "You talk about strong. I've never seen a man as strong as Charles. He was all work on the field. Whether it was practice time or game time, that guy across from him was going to take a whuppin'. That's just the way he played. He was hungry. He knew his ticket out in life was the NFL. He was on a mission with football," D'Alessandris said.

By the time Martin was a senior, he had matured and was ready for bigger things. He was close to getting his degree from Livingston when he began playing in the USFL for the Birmingham Stallions. "His people skills improved tremendously, his character and work habits. He was very polite, respectful, and hardworking. I'd take a ton of Charles Martins," D'Alessandris said.

Martin didn't go directly to the NFL, but after being rejected twice in lower leagues, he made it nonetheless.

After playing one year in the USFL, Martin was cut by Birmingham after the 1983 season. He went to the Canadian Football League and was cut by Edmonton early in the 1984 season. Then Coach Forrest Gregg and the Packers signed him to a two-year contract, $60,000 for the first year and $70,000 the second. By 1986, as he showed promise at nose tackle, the Packers boosted his pay to $115,000.

Martin impressed one player, veteran Pittsburgh center Mike Webster. One week before the fateful game against the Bears, Webster said Martin was "already one of the better guys in the league." Webster was watching film one day of future opponents and saw Martin demolish an opposing center and explode into the opponent's backfield. Webster sat upright in his chair, impressed with Martin's speed and power, and knew he'd better be ready to play against Martin.

As a Packer, Martin was childlike at times in his approach to life, easy-going and unpolished. A friend said Martin never opened a bank account in Green Bay, left piles of cash sitting out, and ate mostly fast food.

On the field, he worked ferociously. "He worked very hard on the practice field and in the weight room, extremely hard. He didn't take a break. He would push very hard," said Karl Swanke, an offensive lineman for the Packers in the mid-1980s.

Safety Ken Stills saw Martin for the first time in a hallway in the Packers offices. Martin was with defensive tackle Robert Brown. Martin and Brown were wearing workout shorts and T-shirts, with the arms cut off to the shoulders. "Robert and Charlie were all muscle and all neck. Charlie looked like the 'Incredible Hulk' when I first saw him. He was just rippin' out of his shorts. I was glad they were on our team," Stills said.

Stills, for one, thinks Martin deserves better than to be remembered as a Green Bay thug. First, Stills said that Martin did not intend to take McMahon out of the game, despite McMahon's name being listed at the top of Martin's uniform towel. The supposed "hit list" of Bears players simply was a guideline of key players the Packers needed to focus on, Stills said. "It wasn't a hit list to hurt anybody. There was no plan to hurt Jim McMahon. That wasn't in Charles' mind—no way," Stills said.

Second, Packers defensive coaches at the time preached old-school aggressiveness, Stills said. They preached hard the week of games against the Bears. The history of the bitter Bears–Packers rivalry goes back to the 1920s. Forrest Gregg, the Packers' head coach in 1986, played in close to 30 games versus Chicago in his 14-year Packers career from 1956 to 1970. "He hated the Bears," Stills said. One of the Bears' team colors is orange; Green Bay players wore orange wristbands the week before the McMahon incident.

Packers assistant coaches picked up on Gregg's animosity. "Take out the best player and make them play with a backup. If you got close to the quarterback, you dove at his legs," Stills said, referring to what defensive coordinator/defensive line coach Dick Modzelewski and linebackers coach Dale Lindsey taught Packers defenders. And when a quarterback throws an interception, the coaches said, knock him down because he is one of the last people who could make a tackle on a return, according to Stills.

Nose tackle Charles Martin (94) of the Packers puts pressure on New York Giants quarterback Phil Simms in September of 1985 at Lambeau Field.

When McMahon threw the interception, Martin simply was doing what he was told—he went for McMahon. Martin, however, got carried away, possibly as a result of all the buildup to the Bears game or his tendency, going back to high school, to ignore the whistle. "Charlie was really impressionable. I really believe he just snapped. Jim McMahon was our friend. We played golf and basketball with him in the off-season. After the play, Charles was like, 'Wow, I can't believe that happened.' I could see in his face that wasn't in his plan. I knew he was hurt about it. He felt sorry," Stills said.

Stills remembers the fun-loving Charles Martin who was his pal around Green Bay, the guy who could go into a nightclub, uproot the disc jockey, and start playing the music he wanted. They, and other teammates, had Christmas and Halloween parties together. They would tell stories and get to laughing so hard that tears would stream from Charles' face. "As big as he was, he was as soft as a baby's butt," Stills said.

Sometimes, Martin would have too much to drink. In 1986, he was suspended for two games by the team for a sexual incident at a bar.

If anyone can sympathize with the "thug" label pinned for life on Martin, it's Stills. As a rookie in 1985, Stills suffered through his own incident with the Bears when he was penalized for a late hit on running back Matt Suhey when Suhey was walking toward the sidelines. "He stood by me," Stills said, remembering Martin's support.

Although Stills' mistake wasn't nearly as well known as Martin's, Stills says people often remember him for that one ill-advised hit even though he played seven years in the NFL, including 65 games with the Packers from 1985 through 1989.

An eighth-round draft choice of the Packers in 1985 from the University of Wisconsin, Stills had something else in common with Martin. He came from a single-parent family, raised mostly by his father, a military man, and his sister. Stills, one of nine children, left home at age 17 but eventually made it into a junior college and then the University of Wisconsin. Martin, Stills, and other Packers who were single and had difficult childhoods gravitated toward each other and bonded. "There were no silver-spooners in that group. We all came from hard backgrounds. I loved Charles to death," Stills said.

Trouble seemed to follow Martin around after the McMahon incident. Two months later, in January of 1987, he spent a month in an alcohol abuse center, saying his drinking problem went back to high school days.

In the fall of 1987, Martin's name was linked to a Green Bay bar fight, although he denied being involved. Gregg, who was under pressure to clean up the Packers' image, waived Martin anyway on September 22, two days after the reported incident. Around the same time, Martin was arrested and charged with disorderly conduct for throwing an egg at the car of a replacement player during the NFL players strike.

When the Houston Oilers picked him up in 1987, Martin was hoping to start over. "People think I'm a big thug, but I really am a nice guy. I can play good, clean football," he told reporters. When asked about the McMahon play, he said, "I just got caught up in the moment. I grabbed him without thinking about it. If I could take it back, I would. I'm trying to live it down."

Martin played his final year in the NFL in 1988 with the Atlanta Falcons. He made $165,000 that season before he was waived in the summer of 1989.

After his football career, Martin struggled even more. He developed chronic high blood pressure and was unemployed and living off his NFL pension for about a decade before he died. His kidneys began to fail and he was on dialysis. Doctors said he died when his spleen ruptured and his kidneys failed.

Stills lost touch with Martin after they no longer were teammates. He had heard Martin was ill but didn't know the seriousness of it until Martin passed away. He heard rumors that Martin may have used steroids and that the muscle-enhancing drugs eventually may have contributed to his fatal health problems. However, Stills said, "I never saw him take a pill or inject himself."

Martin left behind two ex-wives, a 19-year-old son, Charles, and many friends, who filled First Baptist Church in Canton for his funeral. The people who knew him best admired his grit and determination.

Charles Martin was much more than one late hit. Coaches like Cronic and D'Alessandris often used Martin's rise from nothing to the NFL—on pure persistence—as an example to inspire other football players and students. Martin crawled his way out from under a porch at age 14 and made it to the NFL a decade later.

"He came from a tough background. He was so dedicated and single-minded, how he pulled himself up and made himself a better way, a kind of *Man of La Mancha* story," Cronic said. In the Cervantes novel, the endearing Don Quixote wears armor and fights imaginary foes as he strives to become a hero, if only in his own mind. Martin forever will be one of the most endearing players Cronic ever coached. "Charles was a special guy," Cronic said. "We loved him."

NOWHERE TO RUN
Eddie Lee Ivery (40)

College: Georgia Tech
Position: Running back, 1979–86
Highlight: Retired with seventh-most yards in Packers history.
After football: Georgia Tech strength and conditioning coach.

Eddie Lee Ivery was in the mood to celebrate. Finally, things seemed to be going his way. After four years of pain and struggle as a Green Bay Packer, it looked like he finally had made it. The Packers and Coach Bart Starr seemed to think so. Heading into the 1983 football season, they had just given Ivery a new contract. For the first time in his life, Ivery had the things he craved most—financial security and a future carrying the football.

The trip had been a long one, when he looked back at it. The years growing up without a dad in the poor part of Thomson, Georgia. Becoming a Georgia Tech football star and getting drafted in the first round in 1979 by the Packers. Then ripping up his knee in his first pro game. Would he ever be the same after rehabilitation? Then injuring the same knee in 1981. Would he even play again—and would the Packers want him back? He had proved all the doubters, including himself at times, wrong. "A lot of people said I couldn't come back," Ivery said. "I was sure they had no more plans for Eddie Lee Ivery. I thought about retiring."

Instead, he hit the weight room and rigorously followed doctors' orders to get his knee back in condition to play football again. "I rededicated myself," he said.

In 1982, he not only returned but, amazingly, played like the Ivery of old. He helped the Packers reach the playoffs for the first time in a decade. In the strike-shortened year, he rushed for nearly 500 yards in nine games and scored nine touchdowns rushing and one passing. "I proved the critics wrong," Ivery said. The Packers were impressed. They boosted his salary from $70,000 to $200,000 and looked forward to 1983. Finally, the pieces of Bart Starr's team seemed to be falling in place.

Indeed, it was time to celebrate. After signing the contract with the Packers, Ivery went to a party in Atlanta with several Packers teammates . . . . Someone there offered him cocaine. It wasn't the first time he had seen it. One of his Packers teammates, kicker Chester Marcol, became addicted after using it at a party in 1980 in Green Bay. "It was in about every city where I played. There was always some form of party going on. When you go to Green Bay and see other players doing it . . . . I thought it was the thing to do," Ivery said.

He was in the mood. He knelt down and snorted it. "It was one of the most unwise decisions in my entire life," he said.

By the time he returned to Green Bay for training camp in the summer of 1983, he was hooked, a crack cocaine addict. The highly addictive street drug appealed to him because the high helped chase away, at least for a while, some of the demons from his difficult past, including worries that his knees might again give out and end his career. He craved the feeling. Cocaine was the only thing that made him feel as good as football.

Ivery had priorities, however. He made a promise to himself: He wouldn't use cocaine during training camp or the football season. He loved football too much.

As strong and elusive as he was, more than 200 pounds and able to shed blockers with smooth, fluid moves, he wasn't strong enough to avoid the lure of cocaine. He found a street supplier and began using cocaine again as the Packers kicked off the 1983 season.

After the eighth game, Ivery heard that Coach Starr wanted to talk to him. Ivery felt he had come into camp in the best condition of his life. Yet he hadn't met expectations. He had just 340 yards rushing and two touchdowns. After a team meeting, all the players went to lunch except Ivery, who went to Starr's office, closed the door, and sat down. Then Starr asked Ivery, "Do you have a drug problem?" Starr had received an anonymous letter from someone who claimed to have been supplying Ivery with cocaine.

Thoughts began to race through Ivery's head. Who would say such a thing about him? Who would want to hurt him? "You can't do things in Green Bay without somebody knowing your business. I didn't think the news about me would leak out. I didn't do anybody harm. I didn't think nobody would do that to Eddie Lee Ivery," he said.

So at first he told Starr that he did not have a drug problem. The NFL was just starting random drug testing of players. He could lie his way through it, he thought. "I was in big-time denial."

Then he got up to leave. "When I left the office, I had tears in my eyes. I got to the door and began turning the doorknob. Then I turned around and told him that I had a problem," Ivery said.

Still crying, the 26-year-old Ivery stood there while Starr got up from his chair and gave him a hug.

Ivery soon realized what he had done. The team had just lost an overtime game to Minnesota, falling to 4-4, well below preseason expectations. He loved Green Bay, the Packers, his football career. He respected and admired Starr as the coach and mentor who had drafted him and given him the chance to come back from knee injuries twice, and then rewarded him with the big new contract. He had a wife and young daughter. He had done worse than just become an addict. He had let his teammates and Packers fans down. He let all of them down.

Starr called a news conference to announce that Ivery had been placed on a non-football-related illness reserve list without divulging the nature of his problem. For sure, it was one of the saddest days of Ivery's young life. The worst, how-ever, was yet to come.

When Ivery turned around and sat back down in Starr's office, he and Starr came up with a plan. The coach made arrangements eventually to send Ivery to the respected Hazelden Foundation in Center City, Minnesota, to begin a 28-day out-patient drug treatment program. If Ivery made it through the program and stopped using cocaine, Starr would give him a chance to play again in 1984. It was all Ivery could hope for.

One of Ivery's closest friends on the team, fullback Gerry Ellis, had no idea that he needed help. "He never acted like he had a problem. I sat next to him most of the time at team meetings. It didn't hurt his performance from what I could see," Ellis said. "It was hard for me to see him leave the team, because I thought we made a pretty good tandem."

For Ivery, it was the beginning of a 15-year roller-coaster ride, one that would take him lower than he ever thought he could go, lower even than the life he had as a child. And one that would end with one more Eddie Lee Ivery comeback.

Born in 1957, Ivery grew up in the Cherokee neighborhood of Thomson, a city of about 6,500 in northeastern Georgia, not far from the South Carolina border. Thomson is 36 miles from Augusta, home of the annual Masters golf tournament, but Ivery never thought about playing golf at a rich man's club like Augusta National. That was the other side of the tracks to him.

Cherokee was the poor part of Thomson, a corn- and cotton-growing area. Most residents of segregated Cherokee were black and on welfare. "I thought that was normal," he said. His mother paid $27 a month for their tiny, wood-heated home, where his sister and grandmother also lived. Neither his mother nor his grandmother worked. His mother hadn't gone to school beyond first grade. Ivery's father left home when he was a baby. He saw his dad one time while growing up—at his funeral.

Ivery's mother wanted a different kind of life for Eddie Lee, however, so every-day when he got up each morning she had his school clothes laid out. She told him, no matter what, he had to go to school. It was his only way out of poverty. Eddie Lee did have one dream. Whenever his uncle, Jimmy Lee, would come to visit, he'd bring along the football uniform he used to wear in high school. Eddie Lee loved to try it on and dream a little.

Ivery didn't think anything was wrong with his life until he went to high school. For the first time, he was going to school with white kids, and he realized that he was from a different world. He had to take a bus to Thomson High. When he got there, most of the other kids were being dropped off by parents in cars or driving their own cars. Ivery's mother never owned a vehicle of any kind. Most kids wore different clothes each day, but Ivery owned one pair of jeans. "I was ashamed to let anybody even know where I lived," he said.

Soon, however, everyone knew about Eddie Lee Ivery. In his sophomore season on the Thomson High football team, Ivery scored four touchdowns in one game for the junior varsity. He quickly was promoted to varsity and blossomed. In his senior year, he rushed for 1,710 yards for the Thomson Bulldogs, averaging a first down—more than 10 yards—every time he touched the ball. He was all-state and prep all-American. Scholarship offers poured in from 90 colleges across the country. Ivery chose Georgia Tech and ran wild. In four years for the Yellow Jackets, he gained more than 3,500 yards, set seven school records, and was a college all-American.

In his senior year, 1978, he had one of the greatest games in college football history. Against the Air Force Academy in Colorado Springs, Colorado, he rushed for 356 yards on just 26 carries. It was a national collegiate record, made even more remarkable by the fact that Ivery started the game with an upset stomach, and the contest was played in a storm that dropped three inches of snow on the field, ruining the footing for most players. The wind-chill factor was zero, but Ivery didn't seem to notice. He reeled off touchdown runs of 80, 73, and 57 yards. Georgia Tech Coach Pepper Rodgers called Ivery the best player he had ever seen. Coaches, players, and fans marveled at his ability to run, catch passes, return kicks, and elude tacklers with a rare blend of speed, power, and total body control.

In the 1978 Heisman Trophy voting, an award that goes to the best college football player, Ivery finished just eighth, well behind the winner—junior running back Billy Sims of Oklahoma. Sims rushed for 1,762 yards and Ivery for a school-record 1,562 yards. Despite Ivery's spectacular running, Georgia Tech's mediocre 7-5 record in 1978 didn't help his run for the Heisman. Oklahoma was 11-1, won the Orange Bowl, and finished third in the final college rankings.

Ivery was labeled as a can't-miss NFL prospect. He was too good to pass up when it came the Packers' turn to pick 15th in the first round, even though they already had Terdell Middleton. In 1978, Middleton rushed for more than 1,000 yards.

Immediately, Ivery impressed his coaches and teammates. During a preseason game, Ivery caught a short pass out of the backfield and headed upfield. He slipped the first couple of tacklers, hurdled another, and sped past the rest of the defense—virtually untouched—for a long touchdown, quarterback Lynn Dickey remembers. "We looked at each other and thought, 'Wow, we ain't never seen anything like that before.' Ivery was the real deal," Dickey said.

He was, until his first official game as a Packer in 1979. He had carried three times for 24 yards at Soldier Field in Chicago when he got the ball again. He saw a hole in the defense and cut back. It looked like he was on the way to a 67-yard touchdown run. "I had broken the play downfield and had one defensive back to beat. I tried to make the cut against the grain," he said. And he fell over, writhing in pain.

He hadn't been touched by a defender, but a ligament in his left knee tore when he planted his leg on the Astroturf surface. He couldn't believe it. Some of the first artificial turfs, such as Astroturf, were infamous for the number of players who limped off with knee injuries. Yet Ivery had made it through his entire college career at Georgia Tech on artificial turf without injury. "It was very disappointing. I had a good preseason," he said.

He came back, however. Football was his life, the only thing he was passionate about. He wasn't ready to try another career because he was at least a year away from a college degree. He had a solid year in 1980, rushing for 831 yards and three touchdowns as the Packers finished 8-8. He averaged a respectable 4.1 yards per carry and also caught 50 passes. In one of his best games that year, Ivery rushed for 145 yards on 24 carries as the Packers defeated Minnesota, 25-13. Ivery put the game away with a 38-yard scoring run in the final minute.

With the Metrodome under construction in downtown Minneapolis, it was the final Packers–Vikings game at old Metropolitan Stadium in Bloomington. What made it more special is that Ivery's backfield partner, Gerry Ellis, also rushed for more than 100 yards—115 in 15 attempts. In the team's 60-year history, the feat had been accomplished just once before, by John Brockington and MacArthur Lane against Chicago in 1973.

Eddie Lee Ivery (40) looks for running room in October of 1986 against the Detroit Lions at Lambeau Field.

PHOTO COURTESY EAU CLAIRE LEADER-TELEGRAM.

Ellis, a rookie that year, thought Ivery was a special player even after the knee injury. "He was so quick. He had deceptive speed. He could take a five-yard pass and take it all the way to the house. He was a gifted athlete," said Ellis, who still lives in the Green Bay area and works as a commercial lender.

After the 1979 knee injury, Ivery figured he might be a little slower than he had been coming out of college with 4.49 speed in the 40, but not much. After a solid 1980, he was poised to become one of the premier backs in the NFL. "I know I'm completely recovered," he said at the time.

Then it happened again. In the opening game of the 1981 season, the Packers returned to Chicago and Soldier Field. Ivery had rushed 14 times for 72 yards in the game when he got the ball in the third quarter. Bears safety Lenny Walterscheid dove to tackle him, hitting his helmet on Ivery's left knee, damaging other ligaments in the seemingly snakebit joint and ending Ivery's season. "He's an outstanding running back, so it's a big loss," Starr said that day.

The second left knee injury meant another long year of rehabilitation. When he came back with another solid season in 1982, defying numerous people who thought his career was over, Ivery couldn't have been happier. Neither could the Packers. Even at less than full speed, Ivery still was pretty good, the Packers realized.

The third rehab program of Ivery's career, at Hazelden, was his own doing. With two knee injuries and a drug problem, he didn't give himself much of a chance at making the Green Bay roster in 1984. The Packers had fired Starr and replaced him with Forrest Gregg; however, they didn't draft any running backs in 1984. Ivery was back, along with Ellis and Jessie Clark, a 1983 draft pick.

· From the time he left the team in 1983 to the start of the 1984 season, Ivery struggled with his personal failure. "I was living with a lot of remorse, shame and guilt, but somewhere along the line I had to put that behind me," he said.

Gregg gave Ivery a chance. One more time, he responded and revived his career. He struggled to regain his form in training camp and the first half of the season. Ivery did not carry the ball until the ninth game and still gained 552 yards—a 1,000-yard season pace—and scored six touchdowns.

Still, all wasn't well. Although he stopped using cocaine, he couldn't resist his other demon, alcohol. Ivery had his first drink when he was 12. He drank socially in college at fraternity parties and then drank plenty with his Packers teammates. After away games, the Packers had beer ready for players when they got on the plane. One of the most popular and easy-going guys on the team, Ivery enjoyed a party, especially if the beer was free.

Ivery's drinking problem grew worse after he gave up cocaine. "I thought I was just a social user, but it was progressing. I started drinking throughout the week and after practice. After being in Wisconsin for a few years, that seemed to be the thing to do." On Mondays, typically a day off for players, Ivery and teammates would head to their favorite bar, where he usually got drunk. "I would never leave without having a little too much. I wasn't smart enough to get someone to drive me home. I was just grateful I didn't harm myself or anybody else," he said.

Also, Ivery made headlines in the mid-1980s when he and wide receiver James Lofton were accused of sexual assault but not charged.

Ivery was patching up the problems in his life but not fixing them. Slowly, he was heading in the wrong direction again. But he managed to hold his football career together. Ivery gained more than 600 yards, averaging a very good 4.8 yards per carry, and caught 28 passes in 1985.

Then, in 1986, he developed back problems. He played in 12 games but ran with the ball just four times for 25 yards. He was used mostly as a receiver, catching 31 passes. He had back surgery for the second time after the 1986 season. In 1987, he decided to retire, and Gregg didn't argue.

Without football, Ivery's life came unhinged. "Football was my life, my whole life. It was like an earthly god to me. When I was not playing I felt like something was wrong in my life," he said. "Once that was taken away from me, I didn't have anything else I wanted to do."

With a giant void in his life and no longer faced with random drug tests by the Packers, Ivery began using cocaine again. His life slowly spiraled out of control. He and his wife, Anna, also had a son, Eddie Lee Jr., and the four of them moved to Tampa after he retired. By 1990, his bad habits ruined his marriage, and he and Anna separated and divorced; Anna took the children.

Ivery sobered up, if only briefly. He went back to Georgia Tech in 1992 and earned his degree in industrial management, fulfilling the promise he had made to his mother. He returned at the urging of a former Tech assistant football coach, Dick Bestwick. Ivery stopped drinking and using cocaine, spent nearly a year in school and received the National Student-Athlete Day Giant Steps award at a dinner in Boston. The award, sponsored by the National Consortium of Academics, honors students who have excelled in the classroom, and athletically and made a significant contribution to their community. The NCA had paid Ivery's expenses when he returned to school.

His life was looking up. In 1993, he took a sales job with Russell Athletics in Alabama. Then he started drinking again, was arrested for drunken driving, and lost his job. "I thought I had turned my life around," he said, "only to run into some of my old playmates in the old neighborhood. I had so-called friends, but they were buying me drugs and bringing me alcohol. I'd say I wouldn't use again, but then, damn, here comes somebody with a six-pack, and all it took was one drink. I feel there were people who were glad to see Eddie Lee Ivery down. I was running from myself, but wherever I ended up, there I was," he said.

One more time, he sobered up. He was given a job at a day care owned by his cousin and regained custody of his children. That lasted for three years, until 1998, when he relapsed again and hit the lowest point of his life.

He spent thousands of dollars—most of what he had made in pro football— to support his cocaine habit. By 1998, he not only had lost his wife and children, but his house and his car; he couldn't afford to make the payments. Essentially, he had reverted to what he had come from, a kid from the poor part of Thomson who needed the charity of others to help him survive.

Ivery was all but homeless until an aunt took him in. "I had hit rock bottom. I lost material things and my family, and lost respect for who I was. I used cocaine every time it was available. When I got paid, I'd cash my check and the first thing I'd do is get a drink and look for some drugs. When you go to the liquor store before you pay the bills, you're not in control of yourself," Ivery said.

Then, on October 28, 1998, he was in his aunt's bathroom when he saw himself in the mirror, through the smoke of his marijuana cigarette. Holding onto a 12-pack of beer, he didn't recognize the haggard-looking man in the mirror, and the sight startled him. "I didn't know who that person was. I really didn't. I was possessed by drugs and alcohol," he said. With his heavy, bloodshot eyes, unshaven face, and untrimmed hair, he didn't look like the Eddie Lee Ivery he remembered.

Ivery realized what he had become. He walked outside, fell on his knees, and asked God for help. The next day, he called the NFL Players Association and asked whether they had some way to help him. They told him they didn't. "I was very angry because I figured I was paying my union dues, and they weren't trying to help me. Something told me to call back," Ivery said.

He did, and the NFLPA eventually put Ivery in contact with a man who directed him to the Oakhurst Recovery Center in Atlanta. For the next 16 months, he dried out at Oakhurst and tried to understand how to heal the wounds in his life for good.

He started doing little things he never had done in his life, like making his bed every morning, balancing his checkbook, and paying his bills. He began every day with meditation. Counselors helped him understand "unresolved" issues in his life, like not growing up with a father and being ashamed of his childhood home. "I didn't know drugs and alcohol weren't the only problems. God laid down the red carpet in my life and started to straighten things out," he said.

He had come full circle. Atlanta was where his downfall began at that party in 1983, and it was where he put his life on the right track at Oakhurst. When he was released, he stayed sober and straight, and began to repair the relationship with his wife and children. In 2000, he took a job at his alma mater, Georgia Tech, as an athletic department weight-room strength and conditioning coach.

In 2006, Monday through Friday, he was working with a variety of athletes, including football players, the swimming and diving team, and the cheerleaders. He not only is a mentor—"I'm a good motivator" —but talks to them about not heading down the wrong road in life.

One of the young men he supervised was his son, Eddie Lee Jr. Born in 1984 when his dad still was a Packer, Ivery's son rushed for 1,430 yards his senior year in high school and accepted a scholarship at Georgia Tech. At 5-foot-10 and 165 pounds, not as big as his 210-pound dad, he played wide receiver at Georgia Tech. Then, like his father, he suffered season-ending injuries to the same knee twice. The injuries cut short his college career.

In 2004, Eddie Lee Ivery Sr. remarried. When he worked at Russell Athletics in Alabama, a young woman, Antoinette Young, who modeled on the cover of the Russell catalog, caught his eye. They went on a few dates. A decade later, now living in Decatur, Georgia, near Atlanta, Ivery recognized the woman in a Wal-Mart checkout line. They were living five miles apart. They began dating again and were married six months later.

As part of what he feels is his new mission in life, Ivery takes time to speak at high schools, Boys and Girls Clubs, churches, and other places about the dangers of drugs and alcohol. He also is a peer counselor at Oakhurst. His advice is simple: "When you put your mind to it and believe there is a God, you can do anything. God will always put the right people in your life."

He still lives by the three Ds—discipline, determination, and desire—the same intangibles that helped him survive two knee surgeries as a Packer and helped him come back to lead the team in rushing.

Much has been repaired in his life, including his relationship with the people in Thomson, who helped him get started. In August of 2004, the town and its high school held a ceremony to retire his number, 44, which he wore as one of the Thomson Bulldogs. Only one other Thomson player has had his number retired, NFL punting legend Ray Guy. A reception was held at a restaurant owned by Ivery's cousin. The mayor of Thomson proclaimed it Eddie Lee Ivery Day. After a heartfelt speech thanking the people of his hometown, and some tears, Ivery received a framed jersey from the booster club and posed for pictures in his running back stance one more time.

Ivery knows that, as an addict, he never can consider himself cured. His goal simply is to live drug and alcohol free one day at a time. "I haven't felt the need to drink for years. To have that serenity is more than I ever could get from playing football. I love who I am. I'm a happy-go-lucky person, and I enjoy life," he said.

Despite his personal and physical problems, he also can live each day knowing that he had a successful NFL career. He played for seven seasons, totaling 2,933 rushing yards, 1,612 receiving yards, and 30 touchdowns for the Packers. He led the team in rushing three times. Going into the 2005 season, he still was 11th all time on the team rushing list. He was seventh when he retired.

Even after football, when he had nowhere to run, resilient Eddie Lee Ivery found a way to survive. Now, he's making the most of his latest chance in life. "I learned a very, very costly lesson. For some reason, I was meant to suffer through my addiction," he said. "Today, I'm living out that purpose by sharing with young people the destruction of life and dreams by alcohol and drugs. Like my momma always told me, you live and learn and grow. You can't be living in your past."

PAST THE PAIN

Lynn Dickey (10, 12)

College: Kansas State

Position: Quarterback, 1976–77, 1979–85

Highlight: Set several Packers passing records, including 4,458 yards passing in 1983.

After football: District manager for Mechanical Breakdown Protection Inc., which provides training and programs for auto dealers.

In the NFL, where some of the biggest, fastest, strongest men in the world crash into each other at full speed week after week, body parts take a beating. During a 16-week NFL regular season, bones from head to toe get broken, cracked, dislocated, and separated from their connecting joints; muscles, tendons, and ligaments are snapped, bruised, and torn; cartilage wears away; teeth get knocked out, noses flattened, eyes jabbed, necks jammed, appendages twisted, skin and flesh scraped, cut, gouged, and punctured; blood is left on the green grass every Sunday. An ambulance always is in the stadium, a team doctor and a cadre of trainers and medical supplies always on the sideline.

If you want to have a long career in the NFL, you'd better be ready to suffer. Pain is part of the game. Training camp can be grueling enough, with its twice-a-day drills in the August heat and its wind sprints that leave players gasping for air—but it's only a warm-up until the pads go on and the full contact begins.

Injuries are what players fear most—not because they are afraid of the pain but because an injury can cost them a game, a season, or even the career they've dreamed of since they were children. Packers running back Eddie Lee Ivery suffered season-ending knee injuries two of his first three years in the NFL while playing on artificial turf. From then on, whenever the Packers had a game on turf, Ivery would tense up and could be seen rubbing his knees before going on the field, according to Gerry Ellis, another back at the time.

Playing with and recovering from injuries isn't a badge of honor in the NFL because everyone in the league experiences it sooner or later. It's just part of the game that players accept or are forced to accept. If they don't, they can start looking for other work.

When players suffer an injury, their first instinct is to keep playing. When Packers quarterback Bart Starr took a hit to the face and suffered a split upper lip, he gritted his teeth and got back in the huddle. When center Larry McCarren, a man of the trenches, broke a finger, looked down and saw it pointing sideways, he got back in his stance and hiked the ball again. Ellis once dislocated three toes when he was tackled, asked for a shot from the trainer to numb the pain, and returned to the field.

Then, he sprained his ankle on the other foot, asked for another shot, and returned to finish the game.

If players suffer a serious injury, they nearly always will try to resume their careers. Ray Nitschke hurt his knee as a young player. As a result, one of his legs was shorter than the other and not nearly as muscular. He became one of the best linebackers in NFL history on one good leg. Jerry Kramer played part of his career with a piece of wood the size of a small harmonica in his groin. The wood, embedded as a result of a childhood accident, made him deathly ill in the early 1960s. He lost weight, and teammates thought he was dying. The wood eventually was discovered, Kramer underwent an operation and played the next season. Packers star defensive back Bobby Dillon, who had vision in just one eye (also as a result of a childhood accident), tore ligaments in both knees on a Thanksgiving Day game in 1953; he returned to make all-pro or the Pro Bowl every year after that for the rest of his career, which lasted until 1959. Not even his prosthetic eye, which once popped out on the field, slowed him down.

Pro football has plenty of such stories, but few are more compelling than the tribulations of Lynn Dickey. The Packers' quarterback from 1976 to 1985 knew how to play with pain and how to come back from it. He didn't look like the type. Hardly a grizzled warrior, Dickey was a pleasant, baby-faced, curly-haired man from a tiny town in Kansas, but he was as tough as anyone in Green Bay history, including Dick "The Bruiser" Afflis, a gun-toting, fist-fighting 1950s guard with a 52-inch chest who went on to become a pro wrestler.

Dickey was more than a survivor. Despite a badly broken and dislocated hip in 1972 in his rookie season with Houston, a separated shoulder in 1976, a severely broken leg in 1977, and other physical problems, Dickey became one of the Packers' best quarterbacks ever. He had one of the best seasons of any Packers quarterback and had such a solid career that when it was finished, one could only wonder: What if he hadn't gotten hurt and lost several seasons? What if he hadn't taken such a battering and had even a modicum of mobility? What if the Packers had had a defense to go with Dickey in 1983?

Indeed, one could only wonder what Dickey still was doing in the game late in the fourth quarter on November 13, 1977. The Packers were losing, 24-6, to the Los Angeles Rams at Milwaukee County Stadium. With only a few minutes to play, Coach Bart Starr told Dickey to go back on the field and just run out the clock. Dickey called a short pass play and transferred his weight to his front foot as he dumped the ball over the middle of the defense to running back Eric Torkelson.

As Dickey threw, Rams defender Larry Brooks closed in and tried to sack him, cracking his helmet on Dickey's shin. Dickey remembers going down and then looking up and seeing his left foot flopping in the air at an odd angle. When he hit the ground, Rams defenders Fred Dryer and Jack Youngblood began screaming for medical attention. When Packers trainer Dominic Gentile reached the field, he took one look at Dickey on the ground and said, "Well, this is a fine mess you've got yourself into."

That it was. The hit by Brooks broke both the tibia and fibula in Dickey's left leg below the knee. Dickey's season was over, not that it mattered much anyway to the Packers' hopes that year. They were 2-7 and on their way to a 4-10 record. The next week, on Monday night, rookie David Whitehurst was Green Bay's starting quarterback as Dickey watched with a cast on his leg.

When he reached a hospital in Milwaukee, doctors had two options: They either could set the bones and let them fuse on their own or, given the seriousness of the injury, do something more drastic. Team physician Doc Brusky chose the latter. Dickey flew to Green Bay the next day and had surgery. A steel plate was inserted into the leg, and the plate and bones were connected with six screws. Dickey spent the next four months in a long cast.

By spring, with the cast off, Dickey began running on the leg to prepare for the 1978 season. Five days a week, he would work out in the team weight room and then run laps around the concourse at Lambeau Field; however, it wasn't going well. He told Gentile, "This really hurts, bad, when I run."

PHOTO COURTESY EAU CLAIRE LEADER-TELEGRAM.

Quarterback Lynn Dickey warms up during the 1976 season, his first with the Packers after being acquired in a trade from Houston. Dickey, who set several Packer passing records in the early 1980s, later wore number 12.

189

When the pain continued and Gentile didn't have an answer, Dickey decided to go to the Mayo Clinic in Rochester, Minnesota, to see what was wrong. A doctor there took an X-ray of his leg, put it up on the viewing stand and immediately took it down.

"Your leg is still broken," he told Dickey.

"What?" Dickey said. "You've got to be kidding me."

"Your leg is still broken. It has not mended."

"I've been running on it five times a week," Dickey said.

"I bet that hurt," the doctor replied.

"You bet your ass it hurt," Dickey shot back.

Dickey wasn't even halfway into the ordeal, which would test his Job-like patience and prompt Starr to say, "Lynn, I regret that I ever put you back in that game."

Dickey had surgery again. This time, his leg was cut open and bent, and the patella tendon on the knee pushed aside. With his bone exposed, a steel rod was pushed down through the top of the tibia, through the bone marrow, connecting the two broken parts, to help stabilize them and bring them back together. Dickey had to wear a large brace on his leg. He spent six weeks on crutches. The patella tendon ached because of a reaction to the steel rod. Unable to put weight on the leg, he swam a mile five times a week to stay in shape.

More importantly to him and the Packers, he had to miss the entire 1978 season, when the Packers actually showed some promise with a rookie wide receiver named James Lofton and Whitehurst at quarterback. They finished 8-7-1.

Dickey wasn't able to play football again until October 28, 1979. He had been out of action for almost two years.

Dickey was talking, and I was listening. We were sitting at Bravo bar and restaurant in Brookfield, Wisconsin, on a rainy Thursday afternoon in August of 2005. The strange thing was that I had not physically been that near Dickey since the day the injury happened in old County Stadium, just a few miles down Interstate 94, later to be torn down to make way for the Milwaukee Brewers' new home, Miller Park.

I was there that day when Dickey went down in the fourth quarter. In fact, my friends and I were on our way out of the stadium—along with thousands of other Packers fans—because the game essentially was over. We were descending the concrete ramps in the stadium and keeping an eye on the game when we saw the commotion, and a crowd of players and other people in the Packers backfield. Someone said it was Dickey. Someone else said, "What was he still doing in the game?" We were on the same end of the stadium as him, and could look down and see him prone on the brown, muddy field.

Starr, a quarterback of no small repute himself, should have known better. He had staked part of his future as a coach and general manager on Dickey in the Packers' seemingly never-ending search for a quarterback in the 1970s. Since Starr retired from playing in 1971, the Packers had gone through too many quarterbacks to remember—Jack Concannon, Jim Del Gaizo, Carlos Brown, Scott Hunter, Jerry Tagge, Don Horn, Charlie Napper, Frank Patrick, Dean Carlson, and others.

As a result, Starr traded for Dickey on April 2, 1976. It was Starr's second season as coach. He gave up plenty to get Dickey: defensive back Ken Ellis, a third-round draft pick, a fourth-round draft pick, and the Packers' starting quarterback from the year before, John Hadl. An ill-advised trade for the aging Hadl in 1974 still didn't sit well in Packerland. That trade cost the team two first-round, two second-round, and one third-round draft pick, and all but cost Coach Dan Devine his job. But he left before the team could fire him, and the Pack was in disarray.

Needing a young leader to build around, Starr was taking a chance on Dickey. The 6-foot-4 Dickey played five years with the Houston Oilers but had little chance to prove himself behind starter Dan Pastorini. Besides, Dickey already had suffered one career-threatening injury.

More than three decades later, as he sipped an iced tea at the bar, the affable Dickey told me about his first brush with pain and disappointment, how he came back from all of it to become a Packers Hall of Fame inductee and one of the great long passers in the game.

Dressed in a polo shirt and slacks, his hair was above the collar and straight, unlike his curly-haired days as a Packer. He always was considered one of the best interviews among Green Bay players in the late 1970s and into the 1980s, and he maintained a pleasant demeanor even as he talked about his injuries, divorce, and the loss of most of his pro football money through business failures. Dickey is laid-back and unpretentious, just the kind of person you'd expect from a small town in Kansas. When his cell phone rang, Dickey joked to an assistant in his office that he was being interviewed by a man who wanted to do a book on broken down, old Packers. "I certainly qualify for that," he said.

Once, during his career, Dickey was asked why he kept playing pro football after suffering a broken leg, shattered hip, dislocated hip, severe tendonitis, and other maladies: "What's one more torpedo in a sinking ship?"

Dickey's struggles with injury began his second season in the NFL. A third-round draft pick from Kansas State, he was sacked during a preseason game in 1972. The force of the tackle broke his hip socket and dislocated the hip. "I sailed through high school and college without hardly any injuries," he said. "What a traumatic thing that was to my body, and to rehab and get back in shape.

"I was scrambling to get out of bounds and ran back into a defensive lineman. He put all his weight on me. It was on the third-base path in the [Houston] Astrodome, on a Thursday night, the fourth preseason game. They had to re-set the bone on the field. The next day, I flew to Boston by Lear jet and had surgery

Saturday morning. The tackle broke off a chunk of my pelvis, so they put a chunk back in with screws. I was immobilized and in traction for three weeks.

"After a week, the bar [on the traction device] was pinching my leg. I still remember lying in the Boston hospital crying, my leg hurt so bad. It was a Saturday night, and nobody was on duty. I called a nurse and told her I needed to see a doctor. She said no one would be in until the next day. I finally passed out from the pain and woke up at 6 A.M. When the doctor came in, he chewed the nurse's ass out."

The doctor proceeded to probe Dickey's leg with a long needle: Dickey couldn't feel it. The young quarterback suffered nerve damage in his leg and lost the reflex in his Achilles tendon, causing his foot to drop. Three weeks later, when Dickey finally recovered enough to take a short walk on crutches down the hospital hall, he stood on a scale. "I had been eating like a horse—lobsters, cheeseburgers (in the hospital). I weighed 170 pounds. I had lost 40 pounds in three weeks. All my muscles were atrophying. I was just shrinking away."

He was wondering if he'd ever play football again. Not only did Dickey have to contend with the bad hip and nerve damage to his foot, but he was totally out of shape. The pain was so bad in his foot that he needed nine shots a day in his spinal column with a six-inch needle. He spent much of the fall of 1972 in a wheelchair and didn't start working out until January of 1973. After an intense weightlifting program in Florida, Dickey showed up at the Oilers' camp in May. Players were tested in the 40-yard dash. Top speeds in the 40 for NFL players are around 4.3 seconds, with many quarterbacks around 5 seconds or slightly more. "I ran it in 6.8 seconds, and I was thrilled," Dickey said.

He might have been able to match that time in a wheelchair, but Dickey just was excited that he could run 40 yards. "I figured I had one chance to play," he said. "I'll give it everything I've got. So I kept working and working. If I had to play any other position, I couldn't have played. I was never a real mobile quarterback, but that injury took away any mobility that I had."

Slowly, he healed and proved he still could play. He had solid statistics as a backup in the next couple of seasons. That's when Starr saw Dickey's potential and made the trade. Then, in his first season with the Packers, Dickey suffered a separated shoulder in November 1976.

After he returned from the broken leg in 1979, Dickey had to wonder if he ever would get the chance to prove what he felt all along—that he was a bona fide starting quarterback in the NFL. "I never had any doubt I could perform," he said.

The statistics weren't on his side. Going into 1980, Dickey had missed 30 of his 60 games as a Packer and didn't exactly have glowing statistics—25 touchdowns and 60 interceptions. Not much to show for a 31-year-old quarterback.

Still, the Packers had faith in him. In the 1978, 1979, and 1980 drafts—when Dickey's return from the broken leg still was questionable—Starr drafted only two quarterbacks; both of them were low-round picks, Dennis Sproul and Keith Myers, in the eight and ninth rounds, respectively, in 1978. (Oddly enough, when Dickey did start to play well, Starr, ignoring the pleas of some staff members, drafted weak-armed quarterback Rich Campbell in the first round in 1981.) The job was Dickey's, if he could stay healthy.

Finally, in 1980, he began to look like the quarterback Starr traded for in 1976. He played in all 16 games, completed 58 percent of his passes for more than 3,500 yards, and had 15 touchdown passes. He also had 25 interceptions, however. On October 12 of that year, he set the team record with 418 yards passing against Tampa Bay (eight yards more than Don Horn's 1969 record). That season was the start of a six-year period in which Dickey would become one of the premier quarterbacks in the NFL.

His success was due partly to offensive weapons that went with his strong, accurate arm. During that time, James Lofton hit his prime as a future Hall of Fame receiver, the Packers traded for standout wide receiver John Jefferson, and had Pro Bowl tight end Paul Coffman, and Gerry Ellis and Eddie Lee Ivery providing a steady, if not spectacular, rushing attack. Ellis and Ivery also were sure-handed receivers out of the backfield. The offensive line was strong, too, with Karl Swanke, Greg Koch, and Larry McCarren.

Dickey also believed in offensive coordinator Bob Schnelker, a gruff, headstrong type who didn't have the support of everyone on the team. "All our guys had a great feel for what we were doing. Schnelker was as good of an offensive coordinator as we could possibly have. Schnelker was not there to make friends. If you didn't know your assignments, he'd chew your ass out right in front of the team. He told me when he came to Green Bay, 'I'll say things you're not going to like, but you've got to forget them and move on,'" Dickey said.

The Packers began to click on offense. In 1982, they made the playoffs for the first time in a decade. They scored 41 points in a first-round playoff game against St. Louis as Dickey threw four touchdown passes, including a 60-yarder to Jefferson. They put up 26 points the next week in Dallas but lost because the Cowboys scored one more. A Dickey interception that led to a Dallas score didn't help.

By 1983, the Packers led the NFL in offense, piling up 6,495 yards. Their defense, however, was the worst in the NFL. It gave up even more yards—6,674.

The season started with a memorable performance by Dickey in Houston. Finally injury-free and playing up to his ability, he was looking forward to going back to the city where he started his career. Dickey had back spasms that week and, as a result of the epidural shots needed to control the spasms, was suffering from migraine headaches that morning. He was dizzy and sick to his stomach, forcing him to lie down on the bus on the way to the game and on the training table at the stadium. He didn't even get dressed for the game.

"I thought, 'Here it is, opening day. This sucks. I went out and just tried to walk around the field a little bit. I asked Bart, 'Do you mind if I try to play?' He said, 'You look really bad, but it's OK with me if you want to try,'" Dickey recalled.

He proceeded to complete his first 18 passes, a Packers record, and he remembers that his 19th pass was on the money but dropped. "We really had a good game plan for Houston. Everything was clicking. I was getting time to pass. Guys were getting open," he said.

After four quarters, Dickey had completed 27 of 31 passes for 333 yards and one interception. He also tied a team record with five touchdown passes (a feat he would accomplish one more time in his career with the Packers). His quarterback rating of 152.1 also was a Packers record for 20 years, until Brett Favre topped it. With the score tied, 38-38, after four quarters, Dickey was so ill he had to be taken from the field in a cart. The Packers won, 41-38, in overtime on a Jan Stenerud field goal, but the story of the day was Dickey. "I'm glad it's over. I was wishing it was over in the first quarter," Dickey said after the game. "Lynn always looks woozy and sick in the huddle," joked Lofton, who caught a 74-yard bomb from Dickey.

That season provided Dickey with another lifelong memory. He always will remember the Monday night game on October 17, in which the Packers upset the defending Super Bowl champion Washington Redskins, 48-47. Dickey completed 22 of 30 passes for 387 yards and three touchdowns. What he remembers most is a news clipping on the Packers locker room bulletin board in which one of the Redskins was quoted as predicting the game would be a rout.

"On Wednesday, Bart put the clipping up on the screen at the team meeting. We had heard all that type of talk before so we didn't think much of it. We had a really good week of practice. Just before the game, Bart held up the clipping again and said, 'He said it's going to be a rout, but he didn't say which way. Now let's go out and kick their ass!' I had never heard something like that from Bart before. I looked at James Lofton and said, 'Wow. All right. Let's go!'" Dickey remembered.

The teams traded touchdowns the entire game, and when Washington kicker Mark Moseley missed a 39-yard field goal in the closing seconds, the Packers won. "I remember sitting on the sidelines and thinking, 'What a shame to score so many points and we're going to lose, 50-48.' I was the holder for Moseley at Houston before he got cut and went to Washington. That was an easy kick for him. It's like a guy missing a one-foot putt [in golf]," Dickey said.

In 1983, Dickey didn't miss much. He led the league and set a Packers season passing record with 4,458 yards. Heading into the 2006 season, that still was a team record, 45 yards more than Favre threw for in 1995 despite the fact that Dickey had nearly 90 fewer passes than Favre. Favre, however, had more touchdowns (38-32) and far fewer interceptions (13 to Dickey's team-record 29). Dickey, the most immobile player in the league, also was sacked 40 times that season.

Lack of mobility was the only thing that kept Dickey from being great, said Gerry Ellis, a Packers fullback from 1980 to 1986. Dickey threw a great ball and had a knack for figuring out defenses. "He'd throw the ball where you could catch it. He would put it in the right spot," Ellis said. "He was so smart, too. He would go up to the line and, if he saw something, he'd audible. One year against Seattle, on the first play of the game we had a running play called. Dickey saw press coverage on James Lofton and audibled to a streak route and, bang, touchdown."

A pocket-only passer, Dickey could throw every pass and had a great touch, especially on long throws. His average gain per pass in 1983 was 9.21 yards, one of only five NFL players since 1970 to top 9 yards per pass. Not even Favre or Starr managed to do that.

It was a big year for Dickey but not Starr, who was fired after the Packers finished 8-8 and missed the playoffs. Dickey was sad to see Starr go. He was the man who gave Dickey a chance when he traded for him in 1976, and again in 1979 when his leg finally mended. "Bart's one of the few guys who believed in me," he said.

For his career, Dickey threw more than 3,100 passes and completed 56 percent of them for 23,322 yards, 141 touchdowns, and 179 interceptions.

Dickey wasn't fond of Forrest Gregg, whom he said did not treat players with respect like Starr. Nevertheless, Dickey continued to play well under Gregg. He had another solid season in 1984, passing for nearly 3,200 yards. In an October 15, 1984, game on Monday night in Denver, future Hall of Famer John Elway took a back seat to Dickey. Although the Packers lost, 17-14, Dickey passed for 349 yards; Elway managed only 101 as the Packers outgained the Broncos by a margin of 423-193 yards in snowy conditions. The loss wasn't Dickey's fault; the Broncos returned two Jessie Clark fumbles for touchdowns.

Dickey also was reaping financial rewards for not giving up on football when he was hurt. He had a $600,000-a-year contract in 1983 and 1984, and signed for $850,000 in 1985, making him what was believed to be the second highest paid player in the NFL.

As the 1984 season came to a close, he was 35 and not even thinking about retirement. He was planning to play until at least age 38. "I was feeling good and throwing the ball as well as ever," he said.

He was feeling fine physically as well when the 1985 season wound down, although the team was struggling under Gregg. Dickey felt especially good after the December 1, 1985, win over Tampa Bay, 21-0, at Lambeau Field. In that game, Dickey completed 22 of 36 passes for 299 yards—despite 13 inches of snow that fell before and during the game, which Packers fans now simply refer to as the "Snow Bowl." A strong north wind made conditions even worse. The smallest crowd in Lambeau Field history, 19,856, watched Dickey carve up the frozen Buccaneers, who often were seen huddling by heaters when they weren't on the field.

Dickey figured he would have an advantage passing that day because defensive linemen wouldn't be able to get good footing to mount a pass rush. Tampa Bay quarterback Steve Young, who would go on to star with the San Francisco 49ers, apparently didn't enjoy the same advantage. The Packers gained 512 yards on offense, and the Buccaneers just 65. "The Tampa Bay guys had just left Florida the day before where it was 80 degrees. I think they just wanted to go home," Dickey said.

Packers offensive lineman Karl Swanke said the thing that sticks out in his mind about the game was how the ball disappeared in the snow when it was punted. Punt returners couldn't see the ball through the howling blizzard, so they waited for it to land, found it, then picked it up and ran.

That game turned out to be Dickey's last as a Packer. The next week, while lifting weights, he strained his neck, thanks to an old whiplash injury he suffered while being sacked in 1981. Dickey missed the rest of the 1985 season.

When he tried to come back in 1986, his neck again acted up in the preseason. Besides, Gregg had indicated he wanted to give Randy Wright the chance to start, and use Dickey as a backup. Gregg was cleaning house, dumping many of Starr's key players, including linebacker Mike Douglass and offensive lineman Greg Koch. Gregg wanted to cut Dickey's salary to the NFL minimum of about $200,000 a year. Dickey had pretty much decided to retire when Gregg called him into the office. "He said, 'Lynn, I'm really sorry. You've done a lot for this club.' I told him, 'It's OK. I can't do it anymore.'"

Dickey left Gregg's office. "I could see my career flash before my eyes," he said. "I thought, 'God, that was fun.' There are so many guys who were not quite good enough. I thought of all those guys."

Coffman and Dickey both had played at Kansas State, at different times, and were close friends. Coffman had a different memory of the day. "Lynn and I had both gotten cut, and I was riding with him over to his house to get his playbook. He was going too fast, and a cop pulled us over. Lynn told him he was having a bad day, that he had just been cut. The cop couldn't believe it. He went back to his squad car and started telling everyone. He forgot about the ticket," Coffman said.

As Dickey talked in the Brookfield, Wisconsin, restaurant in 2005, he reminisced about his own restaurants, the ones that cost him all his money. After he retired, he tried coaching briefly with the Lions but didn't like it. Then he opened restaurants/sports bars in 1989 in Kansas City, St. Louis, and Beaver Creek, Colorado.

For more than two years, the money poured in. Then the St. Louis site failed when crime increased and drove away customers. Dickey blames himself for the failures of the other restaurants. He was out of business and out of money by 1993.

"I trusted people too much. There were a lot of things I should have done," he said. "I lost about everything. I didn't have a penny. It was back to ground zero. I got divorced at the same time. I don't have a lot more than that now but enough to pay the bills," Dickey said. "When I was making $850,000 a year, someone told me, 'You can't blow that kind of money. You'll never have to work another day.'"

Dickey, a native of Osawatomie, Kansas (population 3,500), goes to work every day now for a company called Mechanical Breakdown Protection. He sells training programs, extended service programs, and various other products and services to business managers at auto dealerships. He travels between Kansas, Missouri, and Wisconsin. He has used his contacts in Packers country to pick up new business. Plus, when he's in Wisconsin he's able to attend various Packers functions, where he's still a sought-after autograph and household name. He was inducted into the Packers Hall of Fame in 1992.

Dickey had three daughters with his first wife, all of whom are grown. He also has a granddaughter. He remarried, and he and his new wife have a daughter who was eight in 2005.

He plays golf on the weekends, watches the Packers every chance he gets and thinks about how fortunate he was to play 13 seasons despite having 10 surgeries—four on his broken left leg, three on his wobbly left knee, two on his well-worn throwing shoulder, one on his screwed-together hip—along with migraine headaches, a weak neck, and a nerve-damaged left foot.

He pulled up the pant on his left leg and showed me the white scars that circumscribe his knee. His left calf, the one that had broken bones floating around inside it at County Stadium in 1977, looked normal and healthy. Dickey himself looked fit, healthy, and happy, like everything in life had gone his way. Then he got up and walked out. He didn't even limp.

ALL FIGURED OUT

Karl Swanke (67)

College: Boston College
Position: Tackle/center, 1980–86
Highlight: Played in 84 games as a Packer, starting in all 16 in 1983 when the team set numerous offensive records.
After football: Project engineering, operations for IBM.

The Green Bay Packers of the early 1980s were difficult teams to understand and to follow. It seemed as if every time the Packers did something worth cheering about, the players, coaches, or the organization then would do something that made people wonder whether they ever would get out of the rut they had been in since the late 1960s. One cleat forward, one back.

For a time, that decade of franchise history was referred to as the "Eight and Eight Eighties" when the Packers finished with 8-8 records in 1981, 1983, 1984, and 1985. And those were some of the good years; four other seasons in the 1980s, they failed to win more than five games.

For sure, there were good times: The early '80s saw bespectacled Chester Marcol returning his blocked field goal for a touchdown and a last-second win over the Chicago Bears in the 1980 opener; the feeling in 1982 and 1983 that Coach Bart Starr and the Packers were on the verge of becoming Super Bowl contenders; James Lofton streaking deep down the sideline, hauling in a perfectly thrown bomb from Lynn Dickey and then using his world-class sprinter's speed to break away for a touchdown; the trade with San Diego for John Jefferson, giving the Packers two of the best wide receivers in the NFL; the 1982 playoff win at Lambeau Field over the St. Louis Cardinals, 41-16, the Packers' first home playoff win since the Ice Bowl; the classic 48-47 Monday night win in 1983 over the Washington Redskins at Lambeau Field; hope for a "fresh start with Forrest," when the Packers dumped Bart Starr after the 1983 season and hired ex-Green Bay great Forrest Gregg; and the 21-0 "Snow Bowl" win on December 1, 1985, over the Tampa Bay Buccaneers played in 13 inches of snow and in front of fewer than 20,000 hardy fans.

But the good times in the early 1980s never seemed to last or always were tempered by some negative development. The early '80s in Green Bay also gave us top 1980 draft pick Bruce Clark deciding he'd rather play in Canada; Eddie Lee Ivery's knee problems; the Packers slowly realizing that top 1981 draft pick Rich Campbell would not be the quarterback of the future; Starr's frosty relationship with the media; the loss to Dallas in the second round of the 1982 playoffs, the closest the Packers would get to the Vince Lombardi Trophy for another 13 seasons; Starr crying in his office on December 19, 1983, after he was fired as the team's coach; Ivery's and Marcol's substance abuse problems; Ivery's, Lofton's, and Mossy Cade's run-ins with the law; Charles Martin body-slamming Chicago quarterback Jim McMahon; the death of wide receiver Ron Cassidy's infant son in a home accident; and the Packers slowly realizing that Gregg wasn't the answer either.

It was the first half of a decade that, compared with the proud history of the Green Bay Packers, didn't amount to a whole lot: One playoff victory, two winning seasons, two head coaches, and at least four team employees in court. Maybe the 1980s were a set-up that made the team's success in the 1990s seem that much sweeter.

Love or hate them, the schizophrenic Packers of the early 1980s were Karl Swanke's Packers. For seven seasons, from 1980 through 1986, Swanke saw all the excitement and disappointment unfold from his stance at left tackle and center. As a player and person, Swanke was the opposite of the early 1980s Packers teams: Steady, dependable, studious, a model citizen. He was a low-key starter who seldom made headlines but always made the Packers look good after they drafted him in the sixth round in 1980.

Two decades after playing his last snap as a Packer, Karl Swanke talked by phone from his home in Vermont. I asked question after question, for more than four hours, about what he had done with his life after retiring from football.

I knew where many of Swanke's teammates had ended up: Jefferson was at the University of Kansas as an assistant athletic director; Campbell and linebacker George Cumby went into the ministry, and Campbell then went into the newspaper business; Dickey went into restaurants and then selling automotive protection plans; linebacker Mike Douglass went into bodybuilding and personal training; running back Gerry Ellis went into commercial lending; tight end Paul Coffman went into farming and prison ministry; Ezra Johnson went into semi-retirement and the restaurant business; and Lofton went onto a longer NFL career, the Pro Football Hall of Fame, a job as a football TV analyst, and then worked as an assistant coach in the NFL. Charles Martin was dead.

What had Swanke done with his life? He has been called one of the smartest Packers ever. He feared for a time that he wouldn't even be drafted or given a fair chance at playing because teams thought, with his degree in physics from Boston College, that he might not be serious about pro football, where physical strength is stressed far more than brain power.

Swanke thoughtfully explained where he'd gone and how he remembers his career. It seemed clear enough: The Green Bay Packers may have been a tough team to figure out in the early 1980s, but Swanke never took on the personality of his former employer. He was ahead of the game that the Packers played back then.

Few ex-football players end up working at such high-tech companies as IBM. Swanke said he never wanted to be considered just a football player, and that's why when his career ended he pursued another line of work away from the game.

He works for "Big Blue" in Essex Junction, Vermont, where the company manufactures computer chips for video games, like Nintendo, and for high-end retail computers. He lives about three miles from work with his wife and family. It reminds him of Green Bay, where he lived only a mile from Lambeau Field. Now in his mid-40s, however, he no longer puts his body on the line every day: Now, his brain is tested.

"I've done almost everything for IBM—sales, marketing, project management, operations," Swanke said. His latest positions have been working in a department that helps refurbish parts for million-dollar production line tools and in product engineering. He works with the intricate computer chips that run PlayStation and Xbox video games, high-definition televisions, and phones.

He's had a successful second career, thanks in part to what his first career taught him. Swanke strives to look beyond the day-to-day work routine and set high goals for himself and the people around him. "If you don't have a goal or a vision, you just flounder. The challenge for me has been to go beyond the status quo," he said. "Football has burned in my psyche that you need to continue to persevere and strive to do what is important, not to be distracted by things that are around you. When you were playing in front of 60,000 or 70,000 people, you had to focus on the quarterback, the snap count, the defensive linemen. You can't let people distract you from what you want to accomplish."

He has challenged himself not just at work but in his personal life. Swanke has returned to the game of football as an official, and someday he even may return to Lambeau Field in that capacity. In recent years, he has been an official for Arena League games, NCAA Division III games, and an NFL Europe internship officiating program, one that could lead again to NFL stadiums.

He has been a ref in such games as Tufts versus Middlebury, attendance 846, and Bowdoin versus Wesleyan, attendance 550. He once umpired an Arena League game and recognized one of the coaches, former Packers teammate Brian Noble. Surprised, Noble got on his cell phone and called another ex-teammate, Rich Moran, now a sports agent, and "we had a little reunion right there on the field," Swanke said.

As an umpire, playing in the middle of the field, Swanke has taken hits, just like the old days, and gotten right back up. His take-home pay for an officiating job well done is often about $100 a game. He doesn't care about the money; he's just happy to walk in the gates of a football game for free and still be part of the action—even if his bad knee, the one that has no cartilage left after seven operations, aches days later.

His destiny as a football man and his connection to the Packers was at least partly determined before Swanke was born. His great-great-grandfather, Johan

Schwanke, emigrated from Germany to the United States. He and his wife settled and farmed in the Ripon area of east-central Wisconsin. His great-grandparents ran a lumber company in Tigerton, Wisconsin. His dad, Roy, grew up in Tigerton, not far from Green Bay. Karl was born in Elmhurst, Illinois, on December 29, 1957.

The Swankes were Packers fans even after they moved east, where Karl's father eventually became president of Waring Blenders in Connecticut. Roy Swanke was a football player and fan; he played at Purdue, where he was a teammate of future Kansas City Chiefs Coach Hank Stram. "We always rooted for Green Bay, even though we only got the New York Giants on TV," Swanke said. One summer, the family went back to Green Bay and saw the Packers in training. Young Karl got autographs from two men who someday would play a role in his future, Bart Starr and Forrest Gregg.

At age 14, Swanke's world changed. His father died, most likely because of heart problems. Karl was one of eight children—seven boys—in the family. "We all admired Dad and looked up to him," Swanke said.

After that, Swanke set a goal to play pro football. He threw himself into football, and track and field. He was the Connecticut state high school champion in the javelin and discus. He spurned scholarship offers from a number of big-time football schools, including his dad's alma mater, and picked Boston College for football.

He weighed just 225 pounds coming out of high school but had plenty of room to add weight on his big frame. He wound up on the offensive line, where he faced BC nose tackle Fred Smerlas, a future NFL star for the Buffalo Bills. While juggling classes such as thermodynamics, molecular physics, and quantum theory, Swanke battled the likes of the snarling Smerlas on the practice field.

PHOTO COURTESY EAU CLAIRE LEADER-TELEGRAM.

Offensive lineman Karl Swanke (67), right, listens to quarterback Lynn Dickey (12) call out the signals in September of 1984 against the Chicago Bears.

Swanke also remained active in track and in the weight room. One year in the Big East Conference track meet, Swanke took first or second in the javelin, discus, hammer throw, and shot put. Track and field, with its emphasis on correct body position and timing, helped keep Swanke on track as a football player.

It paid off. At age 22, on April 29, 1980, Swanke spent the whole day alone in his dorm watching the NFL draft. He had played well enough at BC—despite the team's 0-11 season in 1978—to draw serious interest from NFL teams. When the first day of the 12-round draft had nearly come and gone, he still was waiting for a phone call. Then, about 6 P.M., the phone rang and the caller was Starr, whom Swanke had admired since he was a boy. "We're happy to have you as a Packer," Starr told Swanke.

He was a sixth-round draft pick of the team he'd seen win the Ice Bowl out east when he was 10 years old. He couldn't have been happier to go to Green Bay, unlike top draft pick Bruce Clark, the defensive lineman who wanted no part of the Packers. Swanke still had relatives in the Midwest, including an aunt and uncle a short drive away from Green Bay in Shawano, Wisconsin.

After biding his time as a rookie—the Packers were 5-10-1—Swanke's career was on the right track in 1981. In an exhibition game that August, Swanke more than held his own against Dallas Cowboys star defensive tackle Randy White. In Swanke's first career start, albeit an exhibition game, he held White to one tackle and also showed some speed when he ran 15 yards to recover a fumble by receiver Aundra Thompson.

Swanke was playing regularly as a backup early in 1981 when he tore the anterior cruciate ligament in his left knee. Despite cartilage problems, he returned to start all eight games in the strike-shortened season of 1982 but missed the Packers' two playoff games when his knee gave out again, requiring arthroscopic surgery.

Swanke came back again, however, and started all 16 games in 1983 when the Packers were at the peak of their offensive power.

Swanke, 6-foot-6, came into the league at 250 pounds and wound up playing at close to 290, thanks to drinking two 500-calorie shakes a night along with plenty of McDonald's and hearty Wisconsin food. In 1984, Packers coaches told Swanke he had to get up to at least 270 pounds. When he married Maggie in 1983 and she started preparing veal parmigiana, spaghetti, pecan pies, and the like for Karl and his offensive line teammates at pregame get-togethers, he didn't have any trouble gaining weight.

He refused to take steroids. One of Swanke's teammates had a bottle of pills labeled "Anabolic Steroids." They were prescribed by a doctor, Swanke said. The teammate suggested that Swanke take some, but he didn't. He never saw the teammate use them, he said. "I read a *Sports Illustrated* article about signs of steroid use. I started to link it with some of the things I was seeing in [pro football]. I wasn't going to mess with something that could be so destructive to my body," he said.

Why mess with a well-made machine? Swanke wasn't just big; he was a sprinter on the high school track team and could run the 40-yard dash in 4.8 seconds, as fast as most linebackers. "God blessed me with athletic ability. My technique was good. I had quick feet. I could run fast. Anybody in the NFL is a little bit of a freak of nature."

He enjoyed the challenge of going one on one against an opponent for an entire game, but not necessarily the pressure put on by coaches and trainers to play when he was hurt. "The pressure was intense. The trainer would say, 'Do what you can do.' How much pain could you put up with? You didn't want to fail at what you were doing," Swanke said.

Fear of failure is why Swanke once straightened his own broken finger. He was going against Frank Warren, a 6-foot-5, 300-pound defensive end for New Orleans. "He was one of my worst nightmares," Swanke said. Warren would line up wide, get a head of steam, and come at Swanke like a train. After one encounter, Swanke was steamrolled and looked down to see a pinky finger facing sideways. Instead of going to the sidelines to get tape on the snapped appendage, Swanke—in a classic display of NFL toughness—gave it a yank and kept on playing.

Swanke was a key member of a powerful Green Bay offense. As left tackle, his job was to protect the blind side of quarterback Lynn Dickey, who, after numerous injuries, was one of the least mobile drop-back passers in the NFL. One measure of Swanke's success is that in 1983, his first full season as starting left tackle, Dickey was able to lead the team to numerous club passing records.

One of Swanke's greatest joys was to hold off a defensive lineman and look up to see long-legged James Lofton sprinting down the sidelines for one of his 50 Packers touchdowns. It was a sight that let Swanke know he'd earned his paycheck.

When it came to blocking, Swanke the physics whiz knew all about angles, leverage, and torque, things that helped him stay one step ahead of his opponents or to bring them down. His teammates called him Dr. Swanke or Professor Swanke. The physical challenge of football, for Swanke, was more trying than the mental demands. A visual and auditory learner, when coaches told him or showed him something in practice or at a meeting, he didn't forget.

Swanke said that in 1986, rookie lineman Alan Veingrad wanted to know about different roles of the offensive linemen. Swanke explained them all in detail. He knew not only his position but everyone's on the line and how they all interacted.

At the end of his Packers career, Swanke was playing center, which he found a lot more fun than the other offensive line positions because it was more mentally challenging. "It was a chess match. You could play mind games with the defense," he said.

How much faith did the Packers have in Swanke's ability to understand the offense? In one 1981 game, he played four offensive line positions and tight end. Lynn

Dickey even called an audible pass play to him once while Swanke lined up at tight end. "It was a Y sneak, where the tight end sneaks behind the defensive linemen," Swanke said, as he recalled turning back to see Dickey throwing the ball his way, good for a 2-yard touchdown pass. "It was like a slow-motion experience." Swanke still has the ball from his only NFL score in his basement, and the cherished memory.

In Green Bay, Swanke grew as a person, thanks in part to Starr and his wife, Cherry. Swanke still has a picture of Cherry bringing groceries to his apartment in 1981 when Swanke was isolated for three days with mononucleosis and recovering from knee surgery. "I was miserable," he said.

The Starrs were like parents to the young Swanke and many other Packers. "The compassion was there," he said, although Starr wasn't Mr. Compassion on the field. In fact, the veteran of the Lombardi system was the most physically demanding coach Swanke ever had.

Despite Starr's and Gregg's different styles, Swanke liked both coaches. To him, they were obvious products of Vince Lombardi's tough-love school of coaching. They pushed players to their physical and mental limits but tried to show compassion, as well. "The combination of the two men showed the essence of who Vince Lombardi was. Bart was first-class citizenship. His integrity was not something you could call into question. I really admired him for that."

Starr was known for grueling practices—like Lombardi—but always bought pizzas on Mondays for the team. Likewise, Gregg could be demeaning and demanding, but Swanke and his wife once had Christmas dinner with Gregg and his wife. "I can't say Gregg didn't show compassion. There's something more to him than a lot of people know about. Having a Hall of Fame lineman as a coach—he knew everything I was doing. To say I was frustrated with him at times is an understatement, but to say he didn't have a heart also is wrong. Both coaches at times were frustrating, and both at times you could appreciate," Swanke said. "Both showed a side of Vince."

Swanke can't forget the scenario that cost Starr his job. The Packers were 8-7 and needed to win their final game of the 1983 season to have a shot at the playoffs. Late in the game, as they watched other NFL scores come in, the Packers realized they simply had to beat Chicago to qualify. They drove close to 80 yards to score and take the lead. "But we left too much time on the clock," Swanke said.

With 3:08 left to play, the Bears came back and sliced through the porous Green Bay defense. Jim McMahon drove the Bears 58 yards in nine plays, and Bob Thomas kicked a 22-yard field goal with 10 seconds to play to give the Bears a 23-21 win in Chicago. "Gary Lewis, our tight end, was 6-foot-6. He already blocked a few kicks that year. It was one time I wished he could have jumped up and blocked it. If we had made the playoffs two years in a row, it would have been almost impossible to fire Bart. We thought Bart was becoming a better coach. He started to turn things around," Swanke said. In a news conference after the Bears game, Starr said it was "the most discouraging defeat I've ever experienced." About 16 hours after the 1983 season ended, Starr was fired.

The loss to the Bears typified the Packers' entire season: They couldn't stop anybody on defense. Five times in 1983 they gave up more than 30 points, twice more than 40 points. The 439 points allowed by the Green Bay defense was the most in team history. Based on yards gained and allowed, the Packers were in the bizarre position of having the best-ranked offense in the NFL in 1983—and the league's worst defense. Swanke traced the problems to the defensive line. The Packers didn't re-sign end Mike Butler and lost nose tackle Terry Jones to an injury. With a weak line, Swanke said, "the linebackers were getting decimated. We couldn't score enough points to overcome that."

PHOTO COURTESY EAU CLAIRE LEADER-TELEGRAM.

Lineman Karl Swanke, right, and fullback Jessie Clark (33), left, listen to quarterback Lynn Dickey (12) call a play in the huddle in September of 1984 against the Chicago Bears.

They tried. In 1983, the Packers beat New Orleans, 41-38, Tampa Bay, 55-14, Cleveland, 35-21, and Chicago, 31-28; they scored 41 points but lost to Atlanta by a touchdown. They scored 49 points in the first half against Tampa Bay before easing up on the hapless Bucs.

They also beat the defending Super Bowl champion Washington Redskins, 48-47, at Lambeau Field in the highest scoring game in "Monday Night Football" history. Redskins kicker Mark Moseley missed a 39-yard field goal as time expired. Swanke recalls several things about the memorable Redskins game. "There was no punter on the field the whole game. We had 48 points and called 53 plays. That game was the pinnacle of [offensive coordinator] Bob Schnelker's career. Every play he called worked."

During that game, Swanke's job was to pass block feared Redskins defensive end Dexter Manley, who, like many of the Redskins, had predicted it wouldn't be much of a game. Manley may have gotten one sack, but Swanke neutralized him so well that he was one of the Packers who received a game ball in the euphoric locker room. Quarterback Lynn Dickey remembers Swanke's performance. "Manley was a great pass rusher. Early on, he got in Karl's face and Karl stopped him in his tracks. He gouged Manley in the neck or something. Karl was not a mean guy, but that night he came ready for bear," Dickey said.

Starr's replacement as head coach, Gregg, continued the Packers' losing ways, despite having taken the Bengals to a Super Bowl in 1982. Speculating on Gregg's failure to win in Green Bay, Swanke observed that he had gotten away with having a gruff personality in Cincinnati because his offensive and defensive coordinators softened the effect. Lindy Infante, who would follow Gregg as coach of the Packers, was Gregg's offensive coordinator in Cincinnati.

Gregg wasn't able to hire the coordinators he wanted in Green Bay, instead winding up with two top assistants, Dick Modzelewski on defense and Jerry Wampfler on offense, who were more like him. "Something was needed to offset Forrest's personality. The dynamics in place in Green Bay didn't work," Swanke said.

Some of the negativity from the late Starr era carried over and actually grew worse under Gregg. By the end of Swanke's Green Bay career, he was supporting teammates on trial for sexual assault. "It was just a mess, a mess. It started snowballing," Swanke said. Lofton was tried and acquitted on second-degree sexual-assault charges involving a woman outside a Green Bay nightclub, the Top Shelf Lounge. Defensive back Mossy Cade was convicted of sexual assault of a relative and sent to prison. On another occasion, Lofton and Ivery were accused of assault but not charged.

In mid-May of 1987, Lofton and Cade were tried at the same time in the Brown County Courthouse. Despite Lofton's trade to the Raiders, he still had the support of the Packers in the courtroom, as many of them attended the trial. They included Bart and Cherry Starr, who sat in the front row at Lofton's trial. Gregg and his wife sat in the front row at Cade's trial. Among the spectators were Packers defensive end Ezra Johnson and Swanke. Lofton was accompanied by his wife, Beverly, who was pregnant.

Swanke still dislikes the memory of his teammates' legal problems. "The fact that was going on was very disconcerting to me and my wife. I still remember going from one courtroom to another to support my teammates. There was so much negative press. It was a bad perception and very unsettling to me as a player. This is not why I came to play football. They were affecting my life because people were assuming I was like the rest of the players [on trial], and that wasn't the case," Swanke said.

One of Swanke's teammates, Ron Hallstrom, said, "We were sending more people to prison than to the Pro Bowl."

The seeming lack of discipline and player character issues that plagued the Packers in the mid-1980s would have surprised Vince Lombardi. Gregg was one of the most disciplined players under Lombardi, who preached personal integrity to his 1960s championship teams.

Swanke wasn't like the Packers who sullied their images. He wasn't a big name by NFL standards, but he garnered respect for the way he conducted himself on and off the field. He was on the board for the Midwest Athletes Against Childhood Cancer Fund charity of Milwaukee, worked with the Special Olympics, conducted marriage seminars with his wife, and volunteered with her at the Green Bay Family Violence Center. He and Maggie taught religious classes at a Green Bay Catholic parish, formed a spiritual recreation club for high school children, and worked at a shelter for women.

Unlike many of his teammates, Swanke liked Green Bay. He was one of just four Packers at the time who lived in Green Bay year-round. His name was in the phone book. In 1985, he was the Packers' NFL Man of the Year and was given the team's Ed Block Courage Award, voted by teammates for "commitment to the principles of courage and sportsmanship."

Swanke had football figured out, but there was one thing he couldn't get a handle on—trying to find peace in his life. Because he lost his father as a teenager, Swanke looked to football to fill the void. "I thought I would feel the love somehow from him if I performed well," he said. "He never got to see me play organized football, which was very frustrating. I was always seeking that love from my father that I never got."

For years, during and after his football career, he struggled to find happiness, even though he had a good marriage and three children, who also have excelled in sports. He thought that his career at IBM might be enough. At times, he dealt with so much anxiety that "I couldn't even read a book to my daughter."

Finally, one day he remembered reading a story about an NFL player with the same problem; that player looked to God for help. Swanke knew he'd found his answer. Years after he retired, Swanke found peace and greater happiness than he'd ever known when he became a follower of Jesus Christ. "That experience far outshadows any other experience in my life," he said. "It has changed my life. It all stems from looking for the love of my dad and needing the love of my eternal father."

In 1994, Swanke was inducted into the Boston College Athletic Hall of Fame. A handful of other Packers have come from Boston College, including 1990s quarterback Matt Hasselbeck, who went on to star with the Seattle Seahawks, and tight end Mark Chmura.

Playing in small-town Green Bay, much like playing for the Packers teams of the early 1980s, had its ups and downs, as well. Fans might bend over backward to befriend players but also could make life difficult for them. During some of the losing seasons in Green Bay, Swanke had eggs thrown at his house, tires slashed on his vehicle, and answered prank phone calls. And he was one of the good guys. "In Boston College, people could care less if you played football. In Green Bay, people are saying, 'Hi, Karl.' One coach said, 'Take a ride around Green Bay and see how small it is. You're in a fishbowl. People know where you are and where you've been at any time of the day.'"

Yet Swanke acknowledges that Green Bay fans, in general, are the best around. Although he isn't a marquee name in Packers history, he returned to Lambeau Field for a recent Packers alumni game. When he walked into the stadium, nearly 20 years after he retired, a man turned to him and said, "You're Karl Swanke." Soon, Swanke was signing autographs. "It's unbelievable. I still get people sending me playing cards in the mail to autograph."

As much as he tried to do the right thing in Green Bay, the losing, the court cases, and his injuries piled up. Swanke played center in 1986 but only after another off-season knee injury. By 1987, his knee felt even worse, and he retired. He announced his decision on August 4, 1987, in Green Bay at training camp. He wasn't getting rich. He made $36,500 his first year and topped out at $186,500 his last year. He was far from the stereotypical million-dollar athlete, plus he was in the 50 percent tax bracket, he said.

He had second thoughts. Later in 1987, he tried out for the New York Giants. In 1988, it was the Chicago Bears. His knee failed team physicals both times.

Swanke could put two and two together. In 1989, he went to work for IBM. At age 31, once and for all, his pro football roller-coaster ride was over. The thrills were so memorable, however, that if Bart Starr called him again with that draft ticket to the NFL, Swanke would be on board.

LEARNING TO KICK

Jan Stenerud (10)

College: Montana State

Position: Kicker, 1980–83

Highlight: In 1981, made 22 of 24 field-goal attempts, then an NFL record for accuracy. In 1991, inducted into Pro Football Hall of Fame.

After football: Director of business development for HNTB, a sports stadium design firm in Kansas City.

How do you kick a football soccer-style? It's easy. Just follow the directions inside the package for Jan Stenerud's Kicking Tee. "Learn to kick like the pros in your own backyard. Kicking instructions written by the Hall of Famer included. Official tee of the NFL," the package says.

When I was a teenager, I thought for a time that I might like to become a kicker on a football team. I saw Don Chandler and then Chester Marcol kick footballs through the uprights on television for the Packers and had heard of other famous kickers, like Stenerud, Pete Gogolak, and Garo Yepremian. I had the size of a running back without the speed. Becoming a kicker was my only realistic chance at making the NFL

I had some success experimenting at the local middle school football field. My brother and I took turns being the gopher in the end zone, teeing up the ball at about the 10-yard line, and kicking. At first, we'd run 10 yards to get up a head of steam before pummeling the ball with our canvas, high-top basketball shoes, leaving a puff of dust as we planted. We thrust our young legs into the lower center of the leather ball and watched the brown zeppelin spin end over end toward the goal posts. Eventually, we realized that we only needed a half-dozen steps or so to get the leg properly loaded and the ball off the ground.

For weeks, yard by yard, we closed in on an NFL contract. A kick from the 10-yard line—which amounted to a 20-yard field goal because the goal posts were at the back of the 10-yard deep end zone—was no problem. Up and through, time and again. It was about the equivalent of an extra-point kick in the NFL. Then we connected on 25- and 30-yard field goals, and our heads began to fill with dreams.

After a few weeks of practicing, I stood at the doorstep of fame—the 30-yard line, ready to attempt a 40-yard kick. As my brother waited in the end zone, and with all the leg strength I could muster, I rushed toward the ball, let fly, and watched the awesome sight. The ball, in perfect rotation, flew high and straight, and cleared the crossbar by a few feet. A 40-yard kick; pros sometimes missed from that distance, I told myself. At age 14, it arguably was the greatest accomplishment of my life.

Then winter came, and the kicking tee and all the hope it brought became buried in the garage, to be replaced eventually by other dreams.

About 40 years later, I roamed the aisles of the local Wal-Mart store, and there it was, long-lost hope in a clear plastic package. It was Jan Stenerud's Kicking Tee, for $5, including a 14-page booklet on how to kick soccer-style. Stenerud himself had told me about it on the telephone.

If I only had this when I was 14, who knows where I could have gone, I thought. Still, I bought the tee, read the instructions, and then hauled my son, Matthew, 16, out to the blacktop street in front of our house to see what we could do.

For an old, conventional-style kicker like myself, getting the hang of soccer-style kicking wasn't as easy as Stenerud's instructions made it sound. Soccer-style involves hitting the football from an angle, with the side of the foot instead of the front of the toes. Today, all NFL kickers kick this way. Straight-on kickers went out in the 1970s after men like Stenerud, Gogolak, Yepremian, Chester Marcol, and others—all immigrants who had grown up playing soccer—proved that they could kick the ball farther and straighter with the new-fangled method.

So Matthew and I gave it a try. I struggled, often sending the ball low and with an ugly spin, 25 yards or less and into the trees along the boulevard. I eventually resorted to straight-on kicking again. Matthew, having grown up watching soccer-style NFL kickers and playing youth soccer, fared better. After a few tries—and without bothering to read Stenerud's instructions—he came at the ball from the side and sent it 40 yards down the middle of the street. I began to fill his head with dreams of the NFL.

Stenerud himself did not dream of the NFL while growing up in Fetsund, Norway. He didn't even know what it was. Stenerud spent much of his youth doing what most Norwegians do for recreation: skiing cross-country, skiing downhill, going off ski jumps, and playing hockey and soccer. He dreamed of Olympic ski-jumping fame. As a junior jumper, he was one of the top 10 prospects in Norway.

He had never seen a football or a football game until he came to the United States, bound for Montana State University on a ski-jumping scholarship. When he saw his first football game, with his sister, Berit, and her sportswriter boyfriend, he thought the game looked rather crazy; he didn't understand why all the players kept jumping on each other.

All that changed, as his often-told story goes, when he was running the steps one day at the Montana State football stadium, trying to get his legs in shape for ski jumping. He saw the football kickers practicing and thought he'd give it a try. When he began kicking balls more than 50 yards soccer-style, the football coach was alerted and Stenerud was encouraged to try out for the team.

He didn't have any trouble making the roster. As a junior at Montana State, he began kicking the ball almost unheard-of distances—60-, even 70-yard kickoffs.

He once kicked a ball through the end zone and over the stands out of the stadium. In his first year on the team, 1965, he made a 59-yard field goal, at that time the longest field goal ever made in college or the pros.

His life was about to change forever. When Stenerud was a senior in college, the Kansas City Chiefs of the American Football League played the Green Bay Packers of the NFL in the first Super Bowl on January 15, 1967, in Los Angeles. The Packers won, 35-10, and Kansas City Coach Hank Stram wasn't happy. He had the foundation of a championship team but needed a few more key players. When he went to see Stenerud kick in a game, the ski jumper's first kickoff sailed through the sky, the end zone, and seven rows deep into the stands.

Stram had seen enough; he signed Stenerud and gave him an $80,000 signing bonus. Stenerud already was doing better financially than he ever could have hoped to as a ski jumper. He bought a new Oldsmobile Toronado and moved to the heartland. At age 24, the fiords of Norway were his past and the football fields of America his future.

When he arrived in Kansas City, he still was working on his English but he had kicking pretty much figured out. His first field-goal attempt as a pro was from 54 yards; he made it. The Chiefs knew they had a powerful new weapon in the right leg of the 6-foot-2, 187-pound Norwegian. They began putting an "X" on the stadium beyond the end zone where Stenerud's unreturnable kicks banged off the wall.

By 1970, Stenerud was a household name in America. In Super Bowl IV on January 11, 1970, in Tulane Stadium in New Orleans, Stenerud led the Chiefs to a 23-7 upset victory over the Minnesota Vikings. He scored the first nine points of the game on three field goals, including a 48-yarder, which was a Super Bowl record at the time.

He wasn't invincible, however. On Christmas Day 1971, he missed, by a few inches, a 31-yard kick at the end of regulation that would have sent the Chiefs to the Super Bowl again. In what turned out to be the longest game in NFL history, Miami beat Kansas City, 27-24. Stenerud took the miss hard, saying it probably was the biggest miss in NFL history. Weeks after the miss, he told reporters, "I can't get over it. I was really disappointed in myself. It's going to be the most famous miss of all time until someone comes along and misses a bigger one." He was capable of worse: In 1977, he had a completely forgettable final regular-season game, missing an extra point and three field goals—including a 25-yarder as time expired—as the Chiefs lost by one point.

But despite occasional failings, Stenerud not only lived the good life of the NFL, he helped change the game. He made all-pro and Pro Bowl teams, and became one of the best-known players in the league. By the early 1970s, Stenerud and kickers like him, including Chester Marcol of the Packers, were so good that coaches became conservative on offense. They began to settle for the sure field goal rather than risk going for the touchdown. Between 1963 and 1973, the ratio of touchdowns to field goals rose from 5 to 2 to 5.5 to 4. Kickers were taking over the game, some feared.

So the NFL did something about it. Starting in 1974, the NFL moved the goal posts from the goal line 10 yards to the back of the end zone. The league also ruled that when a kicker missed a field goal, the opposing team would start at the spot of the kick, instead of the 20. The goal was to discourage field-goal kicking and encourage coaches to go for more touchdowns. In another attempt to neutralize the super-kickers, the NFL also moved kickoffs back from the 40- to the 35-yard line.

Stenerud said the soccer-style kickers were being made scapegoats. The real problem, Stenerud said, was improved defenses. Although people complained about kickers dominating the game, he seldom heard that argument come up when it was time to renegotiate his contract, he joked. But the rules changes had widespread support, including that of longtime NFL Coach George "Papa Bear" Halas of the Chicago Bears and even pro golfer Jimmy Demaret, who commented, "When a Norwegian soccer kicker beats you, that's not football."

But the Norwegian Stenerud, the Pole Marcol, the Hungarian Pete Gogolak (the first pro football soccer-style kicker), and other immigrants were in the NFL to stay. They were part of a long immigrant tradition in football, dating from before the days of Stenerud's countryman, Knute Rockne, the famous Notre Dame coach of the 1920s who helped revolutionize football with the forward pass. These new men were pure kickers, specialists who did not play other positions. Coming to the game at a time when coaches and even the kickers themselves had placed little emphasis on kicking, when all the games were played outdoors and always on grass, they were a major improvement over those who came before them, part-time kickers such as Packers guard Jerry Kramer in the early '60s.

They wrought a dramatic change in the game. For example, during the Packers' championship years in the 1960s, Don Chandler was dependable but never made more than 65 percent of his kicks in any one season. Stenerud hit almost 92 percent one season and averaged 67 percent for his career with far more long-distance attempts than Chandler. Stenerud's longest field goal in the pros was 55 yards.

By the late 1970s, American kickers, after a decade of training, caught up to the foreign-born kickers. After the 1979 season and 13 years of success for Stenerud, new Chiefs Coach Marv Levy picked Nick Lowery as the team's kicker over Stenerud as the 1980 season began. At first, Stenerud was stunned, thinking it meant the end of his career. It would turn out to be one of the best things that ever happened to him. It was good for Lowery, too, as he booted a 57-yard kick his first season and became one of the NFL's best.

Stenerud didn't know it, but Chester Marcol was having trouble in Green Bay at the start of the 1980 season. He had developed a drinking problem over the previous few seasons and had recently started using cocaine. One month into the season, it was obvious that he wasn't the same player he had been when he was drafted in 1972, went on to lead the NFL in scoring, and became all-pro.

Coach Bart Starr cut Marcol early in the 1980 season—unaware of his personal problems—and signed Tom Birney, who had challenged Marcol in camp that summer. When Birney, a straight-on kicker, didn't perform well either, Starr made one of his better moves as coach; he signed Stenerud for the remainder of the season. At age 38, maybe the Norwegian wonder still had something left in his right leg. No one else had signed Stenerud that season. Certainly, he could do better than Birney, who hit on just 6 of 12 kicks.

Stenerud made Starr look good. He made three of five kicks at the end of 1980 and then had an incredible season in 1981. That year, Stenerud made 22 of 24 kicks, including a 53-yarder. His success rate of 91.7 percent set an NFL record for a season. Stenerud's performance was all the more impressive, considering he had returned to a grass surface—Kansas City went to artificial turf in the 1970s—and had to deal with Green Bay's late-season inclement weather.

Maybe Stenerud felt at home in Wisconsin. Norwegians were one of the first immigrant groups to populate the state and had brought many lingering cultural connections to which he could relate. Wisconsin not only had snow, but residents in the Badger State liked it. Stenerud went to ski-jumping competitions in such places as Iola, Westby, and Eau Claire. The state also was home to the annual American Birkebeiner cross-country ski marathon, a race patterned after one of the most famous European sporting events, the Norwegian Birkebeiner. Stenerud attended the "Birkie" and once even completed it. Churches, towns, roads, and businesses carried Norwegian names, and he could find lefse and lutefisk in the supermarkets.

Green Bay also was Stenerud's kind of place because Starr and the Packers gave him a chance to revive his career. In three seasons plus a month, Stenerud kicked 59 field goals and missed only 14 in Green Bay. He proved he still had it.

Two decades later, he hasn't forgotten Green Bay. Now living in Colorado Springs, Stenerud said that the fans in Kansas City and Minnesota, where he finished his career in 1984 and 1985, were good but didn't compare with Green Bay's. "They treat the game like a religion. I was thrilled, and cherished the opportunity to go up there," he said, adding that playing in Green Bay made his career more complete and satisfying now as he looks back on it. "After I left Kansas City, I may have had my best years."

He made people forget about Marcol, the "Polish Prince," if not immediately. In December of 1980, the Packers needed to defeat Tampa Bay to stay in the playoff hunt. Stenerud made his first kick as a Packer, a 40-yarder, but missed badly on a 45-yarder in the final seconds in Milwaukee as the Bucs won, 20-17.

In fact, Stenerud didn't know whether he'd make the Packers roster in 1981. In competition with several kickers, Stenerud got his chance in a preseason game. Punter

Ray Stachowicz, a rookie third-round draft pick, was struggling and hearing boos. Rather than let Stachowicz punt again and risk more damage to his psyche, Starr let Stenerud try a 54-yard field goal. When he made it, Starr had no choice but to pick Stenerud as his kicker. The next day at practice, Stenerud's competition was gone.

Stenerud was almost the perfect choice as the 1981 Packers kicker. He missed only two of 24 attempts as he closed in on George Blanda's record of 335 career field goals. That November, he made four kicks, including his 300th, in a 26-24 win over the New York Giants in Milwaukee. Before the year was done, he tied Jim Turner for second on the all-time list with 304 field goals.

In 1983, his last season with Green Bay, Stenerud zeroed in on Blanda's mark. After missing two kicks, he made a 19-yard field goal with no time left in a 31-28 win over Chicago in early December to leave him one behind Blanda. The next week, he broke the record in grand style. Stenerud kicked four field goals as the Packers defeated Tampa Bay, 12-9, in overtime on Monday night. They would be his last three-pointers as a Packer. The next week, the Packers lost to Chicago on a last-minute field goal and missed the playoffs.

Coach Bart Starr, Stenerud's close friend, was fired hours after the 1983 season ended, and his replacement, Forrest Gregg, made the first of many mistakes when he let Stenerud go. On the first day of the Pack's 1984 training camp, Gregg announced that he had traded Stenerud to Minnesota for an undisclosed future draft pick. That prompted acting Wisconsin governor Ed Garvey, a former NFL Players Association director, to say in jest that he would not abuse the power of the office. "I have, however, canceled the trade of Jan Stenerud to the Vikings," he said. The Vikings, an appropriate team for a Norwegian, were happy to have Stenerud. In September of 1984, he kicked a 54-yard field goal to break a Vikings record and made five kicks in another game. In November, the seemingly ageless veteran of 18 seasons kicked a 53-yard field goal as time expired in a 27-24 win over Tampa Bay. He wound up leading the league in kicking, making 87 percent of his kicks, and went to the Pro Bowl, at age 42, for the fourth time.

In 1985, he finally began to slip when his left ankle, the one he put all his weight on each time he kicked, grew worse. The ankle had bothered him for years, requiring him to wear a brace. He also had a nagging back injury. He made just 15 of 26 kicks that year, well below his career average. He decided to retire when the season ended.

The great Stenerud's career was over. He had made 373 field goals (an NFL record), scored 1,699 points (second behind Blanda), and played in 263 games in 19 seasons. He never missed a game due to sickness or injury. In 1991, he became the first kicking specialist elected to the Pro Football Hall of Fame.

He was in good company. The list of Green Bay Hall of Famers who made field goals—back in the days before kickers were just kickers—includes running back

Curly Lambeau (3 for 12 in field goal attempts in 1921), running back Clark Hinkle (9 for 14 in 1940), receiver Don Hutson (3 for 5 in 1943), and running back Paul Hornung (15 for 22 in 1961).

Stenerud's fame spread around the world; eventually, a street was named after him in Norway.

Stenerud, born on November 26, 1942, still visits NFL stadiums in his post-playing career. Since 1989, he has worked as director of business development for HNTB Corporation of Kansas City; the firm designs new stadiums and helps remodel existing ones. Some of HNTB's projects in recent years have included Arrowhead Stadium in Kansas City, the Meadowlands in New York, Invesco Field at Mile High in Denver, and various college stadiums across the United States. One of three or four such firms in the country, HNTB competed for but did not win the bid to do the Lambeau Field renovation in 2003, Stenerud said.

Stenerud uses his contacts in the sports world and his name to make connections and hopefully make a sale. But just as in his football career, Stenerud is on the field only when needed at HNTB. "I try to go out to visit potential clients only about one or two times a month. I don't like to travel. There are not too many potential clients out there," he said.

PHOTO COURTESY EAU CLAIRE LEADER-TELEGRAM.

Kicker Jan Stenerud, right, and 1960s lineman Fuzzy Thurston reminisce at Lambeau Field in 1989, during a reunion of former Packer players. Stenerud played for the Packers from 1980-83. In 1991, he was inducted into the Pro Football Hall of Fame.

When Stenerud isn't working, he's often wearing a different type of cleat and sending another type of ball through the air and over the grass. A scratch golfer, he competes in about a half-dozen celebrity tournaments each year. He belongs to four golf clubs. Like football, golf was a foreign sport to him until he got to the U.S; Stenerud didn't take it up until about age 30.

With his work, golf, and family life, Stenerud doesn't miss or reflect much on his pro football career. He may watch "Monday Night Football" and highlights but isn't a regular viewer on Sundays. He doesn't miss kicking. "I got the most out of my career that I could. I feel totally fulfilled," he said. However, he still admires the game that he knew nothing of when growing up. Stenerud fell in love with football. "It's the greatest team sport ever invented," he said.

Kicking a football, in some ways, is like ski jumping. Both disciplines require propelling an object through the air as accurately and as far as possible. Ski jumpers, depending on the size of the hill they jump from, can be airborne for 300 feet or more, the length of a football field.

Both actions require power from the legs at the exact moment of impact, whether it's making contact with the ball or timing the liftoff at the end of the ski jump. "If you don't concentrate in ski jumping, the results will be disastrous," Stenerud said.

Ditto for kicking a football. Due to his training as a ski jumper, Stenerud said his ability to concentrate and remain cool under pressure was one of the things that set him apart from his competition as a kicker.

Ski jumping and kicking both produce awe-inspiring sights. The football clears the line of scrimmage and arcs toward the goal posts. The ski jumper lifts off, like the whoosh of a plane, and sails down the middle of the narrow ski hill. Accuracy and distance are essential to both flights.

Stenerud applied the timing, concentration, and grace of ski jumping to the placekick—and football fans have been gazing breathlessly heavenward ever since.

PART FIVE:
BACK IN TIME

PRINCIPAL IN MOTION
Steve Okoniewski (73)

College: Montana
Position: Defensive tackle, 1974–75
Highlight: A part-time starter, he played in 28 games as a Packer.
After football: Principal and assistant football coach at Luxemburg-Casco High
School in Wisconsin.

Dressed in gym shorts and a T-shirt, Principal Steve Okoniewski climbed on an exercise bike in a high school classroom and began spinning at a rapid pace, setting a big silver flywheel in motion with a whirring sound and creating a nice breeze.

I have to admit, I was impressed. Watching him hobble down the hallway moments before, I wasn't sure whether all his joints still were operational. Okoniewski had an obvious limp, and, when we reached a small flight of stairs, he made a considerable effort to lift his left leg eight inches onto each step.

When he took off his sweatpants to exercise in a pair of gym shorts, I saw at least part of his problem—a knee that had a hard, calcified mass on the side about the size of an apple. That wasn't all. One of his shoulders hung low, appearing out of alignment with the rest of his body, which otherwise was still that of a weightlifter and runner. Some of his fingers permanently pointed in various directions.

Despite his physical limitations, Okoniewski pedaled with ease and began pushing and pulling on the bike's movable handlebars, as if they were offensive linemen he were trying to shove aside.

I might have been content simply to watch this former NFL lineman continue to demand performance from his half-mangled body, but I had to keep up. When I told Okoniewski that I was coming to Luxemburg-Casco High School, about 20 miles east of Green Bay, to talk about his old job as a Green Bay Packer and his new job as a principal, he suggested I bring along some exercise clothes. There would be an aerobic workout followed by weightlifting, the principal said. Who was I to disagree? It was his school.

In order to hear his stories, I was going to have to suffer like him, although not quite as badly, thanks to my two good legs and shoulders. So I climbed aboard my own exercise bike, which sat parallel to his, and began to perspire. Sweat soon fell off our faces, onto the bike frames and pooled on the tile floor. As we pedaled forward, Okoniewski took me back.

The halls at Luxemburg-Casco are filled with students who are on the right track. They not only come to school on time every day, they get good grades, study hard for the ACT, take advanced-placement classes, star in athletics or in some other extracurricular program, and have solid career plans.

Other kids, however, don't seem to have it all together. They wind up in one of the four metal chairs in front of Okoniewski's desk, where he tries to figure out what to do with them or what's bugging them.

Okoniewski was once that kind of kid. Football was his salvation. By the time he was out of high school, he had had several encounters with the law. He labeled himself a nonconformist. "I was a wild kid, almost anti-social. I wasn't Honor Society material," he said, although he carried a solid B average in high school.

His academic skills may not have been fully harnessed, but his athletic skills were plain to see. He was a sectional high school javelin champion, one of the best in the state. By the time he was a sophomore at Central Kitsap High School in Silverdale, Washington, across the Puget Sound from Seattle, he knew he had a chance at a college football scholarship.

Securing a football scholarship was important to Okoniewski for another reason besides prestige. His parents had told him they would not be able to support him financially after high school. With the military draft in full swing during the Vietnam War, Okoniewski saw college as his best career choice.

Despite his checkered personal and average academic record, Okoniewski received a football scholarship to the University of Washington in the fall of 1967. "I got so many second chances because I was an athlete," he said.

He needed more second chances in college. After half a year at Washington, he was kicked out because of another run-in with the law. He transferred to Everett Community College, about 30 miles north of Seattle. He played the 1968 football season there, starting both ways and earning junior college all-American honors. Everett was a proving ground for many future NFL players at the time, Okoniewski said, including future St. Louis Cardinals star Terry Metcalf.

With his new chance, Okoniewski said, scholarship offers poured in. "I could have gone anywhere," he said. He chose to return to the University of Washington in the fall of 1969, but his second time around with the Huskies wasn't much better. He suffered a major knee injury and was redshirted. Complicating his life further, he got married and became a father at age 19. His future seemed about as gray as the clouds that frequently hung over Puget Sound.

However, he didn't give up, remembering one thing his dad burned into his psyche: Hard work pays off. Work hard if you want to get somewhere in life. Okoniewski's final chance to salvage his football career and pull himself out of a personal tailspin that went back years came in the spring of 1970 when he decided to leave the University of Washington and transfer to another school. He had been hoping to get out of the Seattle area, where his dad, a tough-as-nails Pole and former military man, worked as a painter in the shipyards.

When Okoniewski was contacted by an assistant coach at the University of Montana and offered a football scholarship, he jumped at it. Montana was the fresh start he needed. He liked the sparsely populated Missoula region, on the western side of the state in the Rocky Mountains, and liked the football program and school. He even thought of homesteading a piece of land up there someday. The college helped Okoniewski and his wife get part-time jobs. The two of them and their daughter had found a home. "They took care of me," Okoniewski said.

He liked the Montana coaches, too, especially the assistant who recruited him, Jack Elway. Jack had a son, a boy about 10 named John, who used to hang out and throw footballs around at the practice field. John seemed to have a pretty good arm for a youngster.

At Montana, Okoniewski enjoyed playing football but didn't necessarily dream of playing in the NFL. He set his sights on something else: becoming a teacher. He changed his major from business to business education as a result of one experience. He worked briefly as a tutor and remembered the feeling that came over him when his pupil made progress and was able to pass a much-needed class. "He was so appreciative," Okoniewski said of the student.

The big, sometimes troubled football player with a knock-'em-down mentality on the field realized he had a talent for and desire to do something else in life. He knew what it was like to be a kid in need of direction. He wanted to be the person who provided that direction to as many kids as he could reach in life—after football, of course.

After a year at Montana, hitting the weight room to add layers of muscle, religiously running up the mountains after practice, and pounding the blocking sled, Okoniewski turned himself into a pro football prospect. He played the game hard, and had good speed and decent size.

He fit the NFL personality mold: He was the kind of guy who didn't flinch at the sight of blood on the field, had a bit of a chip on his shoulder, loved the contact, and could play angry. One *Sporting News* report in May of 1971 said this: "Except for Notre Dame, the campus which had the scouts raving more than any other was, surprisingly, the University of Montana. Montana has two senior offensive linemen who excite the pros— 6-3 $\frac{1}{2}$, 245-pound Steve Okoniewski, a tackle, and Wolfgang Posler, a 6-6, 205-pound guard. It's conceivable Okoniewski could go in the first round [of the NFL draft] next winter."

His prospects of playing in the pros were aided by the fact that he was all-conference and all-American two years for the Grizzlies. During that span, the team went 17-6, won the Big Sky Conference title, and made it into the NCAA playoffs.

He wound up being taken in the second round by Atlanta, reporting for training camp after starting in the College All-Star Game against the Dallas Cowboys. Two Packers draft picks, defensive back Willie Buchanon of San Diego State and kicker Chester Marcol of Hillsdale College in Michigan, also started for the collegians.

Despite his bright prospects, his pro career didn't start well. Switched from offensive tackle to defensive tackle, Okoniewski sprained his arch in Atlanta and could barely move his foot. Falcons Coach Norm Van Brocklin showed little patience, even if he was their second-round draft pick. Okoniewski was cut after 10 games and picked up by Buffalo. He played with the Bills the rest of 1972 and 1973.

Okoniewski, the future teacher, took to heart his first NFL lesson: "I learned one thing in a hurry about the NFL: Don't get hurt," he said.

In the summer of 1974, the 6-foot-3 ¹/₂, 255-pound, bull-strong Okoniewski was on a trout-fishing trip in Montana with some buddies. They were hiking up the side of a mountain when he slipped on some rocks. He fell 30 feet, badly scraping and bruising a leg on the rocky slope. He landed with a thud next to a creek as two people in a canoe floated by.

Okoniewski took one look at his bloody side and knew there was only one thing to do: He walked to the creek, washed the dirt off his wounds, and began to climb. There would be no giving up Montana trout for a little leg wound. If his buddies were shocked to see him disappear head-over-heels down the hill, they were equally amazed to see him reappear at the top, bloody, sweaty, and angry as he clawed his way up.

A few weeks later, still in Montana, Okoniewski was eating a ham-and-cheese omelet at a restaurant at 1 A.M. when a man came up to him with a newspaper in his hand and said, "You've been traded to the Green Bay Packers."

"I had this scab from hip to ankle when I showed up in Green Bay. They must have taken one look at me and wondered what they had traded for," Okoniewski said.

The question wasn't so much what the Packers had traded for but what Okoniewski had been traded to. He didn't know it, but in 1974 the Green Bay Packers were as big a mess as his scabbed-over leg. After going 10-4 to win the 1972 Central Division title, they fell apart in 1973 at 5-7-2 as Coach Dan Devine struggled to find a quarterback. In a desperate attempt to right the ship, Devine made nine trades in 1974, the most in one year in modern Packers history.

To make matters worse, a summer NFL players strike over the issue of free agency left the clubhouse divided between those who would and wouldn't cross the picket lines, those who supported Devine and those who didn't.

The trade that brought Okoniewski may have been a result of that division. Quarterback Scott Hunter would not cross the picket lines, even though Devine offered him $10,000 to do so. After Devine acquired veteran quarterback Jack Concannon, Hunter was traded to the Buffalo Bills the last week of July 1974. The Packers, in return, received Okoniewski and second-year running back Phil Van Valkenburg.

Unaware of the acrimonious situation in Green Bay, Okoniewski crossed the picket lines, too, when he arrived with his nasty-looking leg. He joined a few other Packers in practice, including linebackers Jim Carter and Larry Hefner and kicker Chester Marcol. "I didn't realize it was so political in Green Bay," Okoniewski said.

Devine called Okoniewski and Van Valkenburg "excellent football players." Okoniewski soon proved that when he had two sacks in the Packers' final preseason game against Cincinnati.

The Packers finished 6-8 in 1974, and Devine was finished, too, taking a job at Notre Dame before the Packers could fire him. The next year under Starr was worse; the Packers finished 4-10 in 1975. Packers football hadn't been this bad since the 1950s, before Lombardi arrived.

The losing wasn't for lack of effort on Okoniewski's part. He played defensive tackle, starting some games in 1974 and 1975. By all accounts, he worked as hard or harder than anyone on the team. He was no stranger to pain and all-out effort. Ask any of his 1974–75 teammates and they all say the same thing: Okoniewski could not be outworked.

In the team photos of those years, Okoniewski, number 73, stood out with his wavy black hair, moustache, and thick neck and shoulder muscles, a physical specimen compared with some of the other players in the photograph. In Buffalo the year before, he had been considered one of the strongest men on the team.

Thirty years later on the exercise bike, he still looked like an athlete, the result of years of daily workouts, but he had trimmed off 50 pounds, his hair was turning gray, and it was obvious his body had been through a few battles.

His friends haven't forgotten him. "He's the hardest working guy I've ever seen in my life," said Larry Krause, a running back on the 1974 team who recalled Okoniewski's practice habits and training regimens, which went well beyond what the coaches asked. "Nothing compared to what Okoniewski did. One time we ran the stadium steps, hit the weight room, and ran the stadium steps some more. I said, 'OK, let's go do a hundred 100s [hundred-yard dashes].' I was just kidding, but he said, 'OK.' He would have done it. The guy was like a machine. Every play was 100 mph. He had no concept of difficulty; nothing to him is impossible," said Krause, who is a commercial lending director at American Family Insurance corporate headquarters in Madison, Wisconsin.

All-pro offensive lineman and teammate Gale Gillingham called Okoniewski a kamikaze. "That's the way he played. There weren't a whole lot of guys who lifted weights back then, but you could tell he was one of them," said Gillingham, himself a power lifter then and still today at a gym in his home in Little Falls, Minnesota, where he owns a real estate business.

Mike McCoy, the anchor of the defensive line from 1970 to 1976, summed up the essence of Steve Okoniewski. "He was not tough off the field, but he was on the field. He was a great person," said McCoy, now a Christian speaker and prison ministry leader from Lawrenceville, Georgia.

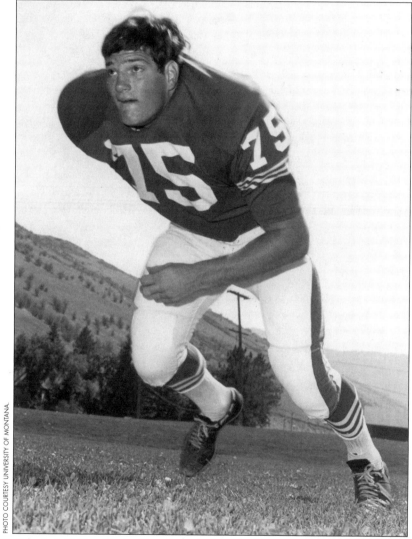

PHOTO COURTESY UNIVERSITY OF MONTANA.

Defensive tackle Steve Okoniewski practices at the University of Montana in the early 1970s. He played for the Packers in 1974 and 1975.

Despite his legendary work ethic, John Stephen Okoniewski lasted just two seasons in Green Bay. He was cut at the end of training camp in 1976, a move by Starr that was criticized by outspoken linebacker Jim Carter on his local television show. Okoniewski was picked up by St. Louis; however, the Cards cut him a few games into the 1977 season. Then he was signed by Cleveland and finished the year with the Browns, coached then by Forrest Gregg.

In 1978, Okoniewski knew he was at a crossroads. He was headed for a career in education, but he decided to play part of the summer with Winnipeg in the Canadian Football League. When the league didn't turn out to be what he expected, he quit on Labor Day weekend, in time to get back to the University of Wisconsin-Oshkosh and enroll in school.

He had seen enough and done enough in football. He had gotten divorced and remarried—to a woman he met while in Green Bay—and was ready for a more stable career and life.

The NFL gave him what he needed—a financial foundation and confidence that he could do whatever he wanted in life with hard work.

Before our after-school workout at Luxemburg-Casco, Okoniewski sat in his office in the center of the sprawling high school and middle school complex, which doubles as a community center. He wore a pressed white dress shirt and tie, and sat behind a modest desk. He talked about his transformation from football player to educator.

When his football career was winding down, Okoniewski began working toward a master's degree in physical education and his teaching certificate at UW-Oshkosh. After he received his degree in 1979, he took a job in Deer Lodge, Montana.

There, he realized that he had made the right career decision. He enjoyed being around young people. At Deer Lodge, he coached the football team to second place in the state in his first year after a 0-8 season the year before. "We had a great group of kids. We meshed," Okoniewski said, summing up an experience that, by the sound of his halting voice, meant much more to him than a trophy.

He had found his calling and an area he loved. An outdoorsman and fisherman, Montana still was his kind of place. He returned nearly every summer for decades to fish and hike. "Deer Lodge was right in the middle of cowboy land. It had the greatest trout stream of my life. It was so easy to fish, it was incredible. I'd make five casts and get five fish, rainbows, cutthroats, browns, every one 12 to 18 inches. I was so damn happy. I was in heaven."

While at Deer Lodge, Okoniewski took more education classes. He moved on to Wibaux, Montana, to become principal, athletic director, and football coach. "They had 2.2 people per square mile. We shot rattlesnakes near the football practice field. This place was like the twilight zone. Everybody had a 30.06 in the back of the truck. We had an eighth-grade dance, and the eighth-grade boys drove to the dance. But come Saturday afternoon, there were thousands of people at the game and not one car moving in town," Okoniewski said.

After leaving Wibaux and spending three years as principal at St. Francis near Milwaukee, Okoniewski took a job at Luxemburg-Casco, a school district formed from two small cities. He and his wife bought a house in Green Bay. Since the late 1980s, he has commuted to Luxemburg, a small city surrounded by farms but with the housing developments of growing Green Bay not far beyond the horizon.

He spends much of his day dealing with unruly students, upset parents, teachers who need help, school board meetings, and various other duties. Some of them aren't so routine. In 2004, he had to announce to the student body that one of the school's recent graduates, Jesse Thiry, of Casco, was killed in the war in Iraq.

After the school day is through, football still is part of Okoniewski's life, and he's thankful for it. As defensive coordinator for the school's team, he can't wait for the school day to end so he can get to the practice field and be with the players and other coaches. He also runs the well-equipped weight room at the school, one that probably is as good or better than the Packers' weight room in the early 1970s.

The high school has taken on the personality of its leader. The football team has been a perennial Packerland Conference contender and state playoff team. One out of every three boys, more than 100 in all, go out for football at L-C, which has about 660 students. The school's winter-season wrestling team, which often gets many of the same kids who play football, has had numerous state champions. The boys and girls basketball teams also have had state-level success.

Getting out of his office, and white shirt and tie, has helped Okoniewski become a more effective principal. When it's football season, he helps coach the defensive linemen, designs the team's defenses, gets to know the kids, and earns their respect.

When he sees students in the hallway, he isn't just another administrator trying to enforce the rules. He knows them, and they know him. "Coaching has made such a difference in my ability to deal with kids. If I wasn't out there, I'm sure my discipline problems with the male population in the building would be a whole lot worse than they are," he said.

Season after season, Pete Kline, head football coach for Luxemburg-Casco, has seen Okoniewski's genuine love for the students and football. "He's an emotional person. When somebody makes a great play or we win a big game, he's overcome with emotion. We see that every year," Kline said. "The kids get to see a different perspective of him. They respond to him and really respect him."

Okoniewski may be the principal, the ex-Packer who students and people in the community admire for his firm hand in school matters, but he's also just one of the guys. He shows up regularly at various school sporting events year-round.

After games, he enjoys stopping at the local restaurants or pubs with parents and booster club members.

He even put on football pads one day to keep a promise. One of the football linemen had been bugging Okoniewski, asking him for a one-on-one duel in football gear. "Mr. O, I want you. Mr. O, we've got to do it," the lineman would say. Okoniewski said he'd do it if the team won the conference. He thought it was a safe bet.

When L-C pulled off some upsets in the Packerland Conference—which has five recent alumni in the NFL—he kept his word. For the first time in more than 25 years, he slipped some shoulder pads over his head. He practiced two weeks for his duel. Then, he battled the L-C player in the wrestling room, bad leg, bad shoulder, and all. "We beat the crap out of each other for 20 minutes. It was pretty much a tie," he said.

Okoniewski firmly believes that sports and other extracurricular activities are a necessary part of an education system because they keep kids focused and teach them invaluable lessons. The school district recently built a $2 million outdoor sports complex.

He talked about one boy at L-C who was into heavy metal music and wore all-black clothing to school. The boy was anti-social and headed in the wrong direction until he found football. "The progress he made from his junior to senior year—it was like a bolt of lightning came down from the football gods. I've never seen anything like it. A lot of guys like that say football was their best experience in high school. He loved to play football. It was his passion," Okoniewski said.

It isn't just the kids who benefit from athletics and from staying in school. Staying close to football and to young people has been a blessing for Okoniewski. Born in 1949 near Seattle, he draws daily inspiration from the zest that young people have for life. It reminds him of the time he hitchhiked down the West Coast to see shifty O.J. Simpson play for Southern Cal.

He wants to hang onto that feeling as long as he can. "People my age are always talking about their aches and pains. It's frustrating. I'd rather be around kids who think they're invincible," he said.

The exercise bikes slowed to a stop, we wiped up the sweat from the floor with paper towels and headed down another hallway to the weight room. About a half-dozen football players were doing their after-school lifting, the machines and weights creaking and clanging. The athletes' faces brightened when Okoniewski arrived to the sound of blaring rock music and the familiar, pungent aroma of sweat-soaked clothing. He asked them to turn down the music, which they did.

It was easy to see the rapport he had with the football players. Okoniewski moved between the machines and the young men like they were old friends, shot the breeze, pumped the iron, and dropped more beads of his sweat in the building where he had spent about a third of his working days.

I gravitated to one of the few machines where I didn't need an operator's manual, lifted a little, and asked one well-muscled player about Okoniewski as a coach. He knew how to motivate them, the player said; he was the kind of guy who knew what to say, and when and how to say it. Once, during halftime of a big game, Okoniewski left the players with a simple image, one that had come no doubt from his years among the ranchers' kids in Montana. "Boys, it's nut-cutting time, and we're going to do the cutting," he told them.

After a full school day and some exercise, Okoniewski had worked up enough of a thirst to go out for a beer. At a local restaurant, which was crammed with people eating their Friday night fried fish, Okoniewski was greeted by old friends and talked about old times.

He didn't have a long NFL career, and he wasn't as big or as talented as many defensive tackles, but he was happy with what he achieved. "If it wasn't for the extra work, I never would have gone to college and played pro football. I wasn't a natural athlete like [Packers teammates] Gale Gillingham or Dave Pureifory."

He lasted six seasons, enough to get an NFL pension, and played with stars like O.J. Simpson in Buffalo and Ted Hendricks in Green Bay. Along the way, he learned that the Green Bay area was a pretty nice place to live, even when the Packers are losing.

Another round was ordered, and he talked about his introduction to the NFL in Atlanta's summer heat: "They were the toughest practices I'd ever been through." Falcons coaches wouldn't let players drink water during practice. As a result, Okoniewski lost 15 pounds a day during training camp.

We started talking Packers again. He recalled teammate Ted "the Stork" Hendricks, the 6-foot-7 all-pro and Pro Football Hall of Fame player who blocked seven kicks in 1974. "His football IQ was off the charts. He would look at the quarterback's eyes and feet. He was the best I ever saw." Hendricks, like Okoniewski, came to Green Bay via a trade in 1974. Devine, in one of his better moves, picked up Hendricks and a second-round draft pick from Baltimore in exchange for linebacker Tom MacLeod and an eighth-round draft pick.

The memories of 1974 and 1975 still were clear. Devine and Starr were not good coaches those years, he said. One of Devine's questionable moves was making linebacker Fred Carr a co-captain of the team. Carr was one of the chief carousers on a team that did plenty of drinking. Drinking was the least of the substance-abuse problems. Players routinely took amphetamines before the games, their pills littering the bathroom stall floors, and some bulked up on steroids.

As he sipped a beer in the crowded bar, Okoniewski said he never was tempted to use steroids in college or in the NFL, where they were readily available to players.

Okoniewski always believed the adage that gain was the direct result of pain. He didn't seem to mind the pain.

It didn't always lead to gain, however. After football, Okoniewski gravitated toward aerobic sports—running, biking, and cross-country skiing—to stay in shape and drop some of his unnecessary football weight. His ugly, almost useless left knee, injured several times in his football career, hasn't benefited from all that exercise. After a knee operation at age 34, his doctor told him he shouldn't run for five years. He didn't heed the advice. Before the knee calcified and developed the mass, he ran seven marathons, including one in a very respectable time of 2 hours, 58 minutes. He finished two half-triathlons that required a 1-mile swim, 50-mile bike ride, and 13.1-mile run.

Okoniewski's days aren't complete without some kind of exercise or adventure, whether it's a trip to the weight room, a visit to the YMCA on his way home, an hours-long bike tour on rural roads, or a late winter afternoon spent by himself on skis.

Physically, he is happiest when he stays active and pushes himself, a carryover from his days in the NFL. He needs knee-replacement surgery but is holding off because he worries that an artificial knee will knock him out of the Birkebeiner ski marathon in Wisconsin. The ski race has become his annual physical test, his chance to prove he still can do the extraordinary.

In his career as an educator, he doesn't have to search for challenges. They come to him at Luxemburg-Casco High School every day—a football team that needs the voice of experience, kids who could use some advice or a few kind words, teachers and parents who depend on him to make the right decisions.

He gave his body to the Packers and the NFL. He has given his heart and most of his life to the noble belief that he can—and will at the end of the day—make a difference in the lives of young people. "The ultimate satisfaction is to occasionally receive feedback that you helped a kid grow and achieve," he said.

THE SPECTER OF STEROIDS

Tom Toner (26)

College: Idaho State
Position: Linebacker, 1973, 1975–77
Highlight: Started nine games during 1975 season.
After football: Sports agent. Died on August 26, 1990, at age 40, in Solana Beach, California.

Rick Scribner (64)

College: Idaho State
Position: Offensive lineman, 1977–78
Highlight: Packers' third-round draft pick in 1977.
After football: Real estate developer. Died on July 6, 1994, at age 36, in Sacramento, California.

One of Phil Luckey's greatest joys as trainer at Idaho State University is getting to know the school's athletes. For more than 30 years, he has helped tape, bandage, and heal them, and he often becomes their friend. When those athletes graduate and move on to bigger and better things, like the NFL, Luckey couldn't be more proud that he played a role in their development.

Sometimes, their college days long since passed, they come back to Pocatello to visit and pay their old trainer a visit. On those occasions, Luckey beams.

In 1989, however, when former Idaho State and ex-NFL football player Tom Toner sat in his office, it wasn't a happy reunion. Toner told Luckey that he had cancer.

Four years later, a similar sad scenario took place. Rick Scribner, another Idaho State football star who went on to the NFL, stopped to see Luckey. He, too, told his old trainer that he had cancer.

Those meetings would be the last time Luckey saw Toner and Scribner. Luckey believes it's more than just a coincidence that the two men, two of the best football players Idaho State has ever produced, both drafted by the Green Bay Packers, died young of cancer. He thinks he knows why they died. "They both sat in my office a year before they died and admitted to taking large amounts of steroids," Luckey said.

Luckey has no way of knowing whether steroids actually caused the cancer that killed two of his favorite Bengals athletes, but he suspects as much. Former NFL star Lyle Alzado blamed steroids as he was dying of brain cancer at age 43 in 1992, although no one really knows what precipitated Alzado's illness. "How are you going to prove that?" Luckey asked of Alzado. "It's all speculation, but how many in that era [from the NFL] have died of cancer? Tom [Toner] simply said he had taken steroids, not that that was the reason he had cancer."

The use of anabolic steroids, drugs that help build muscle tissue, was common in the 1970s and 1980s in the NFL, according to numerous ex-players and coaches from that era. When the health dangers of the hormone-altering drugs became known and ethical questions about their use arose, the NFL began year-round random testing of players for steroids in 1990. The first suspensions of NFL players for steroid use were announced on August 29, 1989. It is believed that far fewer NFL players were using steroids in the 1990s and the first half of the 2000s. For some players, the NFL's actions may have been too late.

In the 1970s and 1980s, steroid use was not illegal in the NFL. The drugs also were used by college football players, who hoped they would gain the edge needed to reach the NFL. "When steroids came out, there was nothing substantiated to say they were bad. None of us knew if there were side effects. It's not fair to say anybody is to blame [for NFL players' deaths]," Luckey said.

Luckey, an Idaho State track and cross-country athlete in the early 1960s, does know one thing: "I don't know if Tom or Rick did [steroids] in college, but they didn't get them from us."

Were the Green Bay Packers to blame? What about the NFL? Is it the players' fault for taking a calculated risk so that they could have longer or better NFL careers? Did steroids even affect their health? All that's really known is that Tom Toner and Rick Scribner died young, leaving wives and friends to tell their stories.

Rick Scribner is a name that only the most diehard Packers fans would remember. He never played in a regular-season game. He was in the NFL for more than two years, however, trying to make the Packers and Oakland Raiders rosters as an offensive lineman.

In 1977, Scribner (not to be confused with 1980s Green Bay punter Bucky Scribner) was the Packers' third-round draft choice. He was the 74th player drafted. Scribner had been a star at Burbank High School in Sacramento, California, then at Consumnes River College in Sacramento, where he met his future wife, and then at Idaho State, where he went on a football scholarship. Scribner played for the Bengals in 1975 and 1976, and was inducted in the school's Sports Hall of Fame in 1991.

In 1977, Scribner was part of a solid Packers draft class. They took defensive ends Mike Butler and Ezra Johnson with their two first-round picks that year, and offensive linemen Greg Koch and Scribner with their next two picks. They also had a second pick in the third round, which was used to take running back Terdell Middleton. All of those draftees—except Scribner—became starters for Coach Bart Starr's Packers.

The Packers, especially offensive line coach Bill Curry who lobbied to draft him, were excited about Scribner's potential to shore up their offensive line. However, the

Packers coaches thought Scribner could add weight and upper-body strength. At 6-foot-4 and 257 pounds, he was light compared with many NFL offensive linemen.

Scribner never had the chance to show Starr's staff and Packers fans what he could do. He spent his rookie season on injured reserve, possibly as a way for the team to hide him because he didn't seem ready to play in the NFL. When he returned in 1978, he suffered a knee injury near the end of training camp just as it appeared he would become one of the starters. Frustrated, he eventually left the team, according to his wife, Wendy.

At some point around the time he was picked up by the Oakland Raiders in 1978, Scribner began using steroids to add weight. "Oakland wanted him to put on weight, about 20 pounds," remembers Wendy Scribner.

Scribner was faced with the choice confronting many an NFL player around that time: Go on a special, high-calorie, high-protein diet and let nature take its course—in other words, eat a ton—or take some pills. Athletes knew there were side effects of steroid use and suspected there may be long-term health effects, but no one knew what those effects would be. To that extent, steroid use may be much like smoking, a social phenomenon whose effects weren't fully known until the cancer death rate began to skyrocket in the 1960s.

Players in Green Bay and around the league have admitted to taking steroids in the 1970s and 1980s. There even were rumors that the Pittsburgh Steelers, who won the 1975 and 1976 Super Bowls, had a competitive edge because of widespread steroid use, according to Jim Haslett, former NFL player and 2005 coach of the New Orleans Saints.

Whether it was in Green Bay or Oakland, Scribner succumbed to the pressure. Wendy Scribner doesn't know the details of her husband's steroid use, other than the fact that he did not use them in college. She did not even know he used them until his career was over.

"At Green Bay, they didn't push him to put weight on. I didn't notice any difference in his personality at Green Bay, but I did at Oakland," said Wendy Scribner, discussing one of the known side effects of the drugs. "He said, 'I had to be in a controlled rage to play ball.' Steroids helped him get some of that edge. He told me it was very difficult to play with that sense of rage. He wasn't that type of person."

After he was cut by Oakland and turned down offers from other NFL teams, he started a career in real estate in the Sacramento area and was doing well financially. The couple had two sons, Mitch and Taylor. About a decade after his brief NFL career ended, however, he came down with flu symptoms that wouldn't go away. Doctors found a tumor.

His wife still remembers early one morning after one of Scribner's first surgeries, to remove the tumor, when a doctor came into his room. The doctor told him that he had bile duct cancer and was surprised because he usually didn't see that illness in 34-year-old men. The disease, which affects as few as 4,000 people a year in the United States, usually strikes between the ages of 50 and 70, according to the American Cancer Society.

The doctor asked Scribner whether he ever had been around toxic chemicals or taken drugs of any kind. When Scribner told him that he had used steroids, the doctor said, "That's what did it," according to Wendy Scribner.

She never will forget her husband's reaction. It hurt her almost as much as the realization that he most likely had a terminal illness. "The look on his face was just awful. His jaw dropped. He said, 'No, no. They told me it wouldn't hurt me,'" she recalled. Rick had feared being afflicted with Alzheimer's disease, which ran in his family. Cancer didn't.

Rick Scribner told the doctor that the steroids he used supposedly were natural and wouldn't harm his body. The doctor replied: "Rick, it's still a drug."

According to Wendy, "He felt betrayed. It's not something you can fix."

For a few years, it seemed as if Rick were winning the battle against bile duct cancer, which usually is terminal. Then, about $3\frac{1}{2}$ years after the tumor was removed, his symptoms returned. He died on July 6, 1994, at his home in Sacramento. He was 38.

"He looked like an AIDS patient, very gaunt, but he was coherent until he died. He took a deep breath, and that was it. He wasn't bitter at all when he died, but he was disappointed he wouldn't see his kids grow up," his wife said.

When he realized he was dying, Rick Scribner helped set up a business for his wife. She eventually left California for Boise, Idaho, where she owns and operates ReSupply Inc. The company creates real estate and building industry products, including a job-site permit pouch that has been marketed nationally. Her grown sons are part of the family-run business, although one of them joined the Marines in 2006.

Although steroid use in pro football was banned in the 1990s, Wendy Scribner knows that some athletes still use them and other similar substances but don't realize that they can be deadly. "When I listen to people talk about steroids on TV, they talk about ethics and the message it sends to kids, but they're missing the point—it will kill you," she said.

Shortly after Rick died, Wendy received a letter in the mail from the NFL. The letter explained that many NFL players were "dying at an alarmingly young age and they wanted to know how Rick's health was," Wendy said. She wrote back and explained, in detail, what had happened to her husband. "I never heard from them again," she said.

Phil Luckey said Tom Toner admitted that day in his office to taking steroids with the Green Bay Packers. In addition, at least one member of the mid-1970s Packers teams told me he was certain that Toner and others used the drugs.

However, Toner never told his wife, Susan. Fifteen years after his death at age 40 on August 26, 1990, she still suspects that he may have used them. "He never said [to me] he took steroids. Am I suspicious? Yes. There was a time when Tom got very big. There was a significant change in his body," said Susan Toner, explaining that his weight rose from about 230 pounds to around 250 when the Packers were considering moving him from linebacker to offensive lineman.

"I do have suspicions. Players popped pills without asking what they were. He brought home packets of pills, and I never knew what was in them," Susan Toner said.

Was Toner's cancer a result of steroid use? Susan Toner doesn't think so. Tom Toner originally was diagnosed with colon cancer, but it had spread throughout his body by the time he died at Solana Beach, California, where 400 people attended a wake. His father also died of colon cancer. "It ran in the family," she said.

Athletic ability also ran in the Toner family. Tom, born on January 25, 1950, in Woburn, Massachusetts, was one of eight boys in an Irish-Catholic family. Many of them went on to star in athletics at the University of Massachusetts. Tom's brother, Ed, played for the Boston Patriots from 1967 to 1969.

Tom Toner starred in athletics at Swampscott High School in Swampscott, Massachusetts. After going to Idaho State, Tom, 6-foot-3 and 225 pounds, was drafted in the sixth round by the Packers under Dan Devine in 1973. He was with the Packers five seasons but played four, missing 1974 with a broken collarbone. He had four career interceptions, one each season, and scored a safety in 1975. He also was a standout on special teams. In 1975, he started nine games after Ted Hendricks was traded but then was supplanted in the lineup by Gary Weaver.

When his NFL career ended, Toner put his experience to work. The use of agents to negotiate contracts for players became increasingly common in the 1970s. After witnessing some disastrous contracts and player investments, Toner saw an opportunity. "He wanted to be an agent with integrity who understood athletes and helped them secure their futures. A lot of them didn't have financial savvy and didn't know what to do with their money," Susan Toner said.

Toner, who had a college business degree, set up shop in 1978 in Boston as Professional Sports Management. He represented players in contract negotiations with teams and partnered with a tax attorney and real estate developer to help players with financial planning and investing. "His business was booming," said Susan Toner; his clients included Otis Wilson of the Chicago Bears, Dan Ross of the Cincinnati Bengals, Joe Morris of the New York Giants, and Karl Swanke of the Packers.

Then, in 1986, 10 days before he and Susan were to move to San Diego, he was diagnosed with terminal colon cancer. His doctor told him that he would live only about nine months. They moved to California anyway, but their world had changed.

Tom Toner never looked like someone who would die young. As a Packer, he lifted regularly in the weight room and had a "chiseled" physique, according to former running back Larry Krause.

Always health conscious, according to Susan, Toner ate healthy foods. Even after his playing days were over, he kept lifting weights and looked like he still could play in the NFL. "He was always in great shape and looked fantastic. He looked like a statue," said Ed Toner Jr., his nephew, who played fullback for the Indianapolis Colts and Pittsburgh Steelers from 1992 to 1995.

Watching a man they admired waste away from cancer was a difficult thing for the Toner family. "He was a guy I really looked up to. He could do no wrong in my eyes," Ed Jr. said. "He was very polished, a happy guy, and he always carried himself well."

After his diagnosis, Tom had one goal. He wanted to battle cancer as long as he could to see his children, Ryan and Polly, grow up. He clearly saved the best physical performance for last. Despite cancer spreading throughout his body, Toner lived four years, enduring colostomy and other surgeries to prolong his life and a sciatic nerve tumor that left one leg paralyzed. He continued to work at home. "He lived in tremendous pain. For two years, he slept standing up, holding onto the canopy on the bed," Susan Toner said.

Shortly before he died, the Toners were at an airport when they ran into Dave "Hawg" Hanner, a Packers defensive assistant coach in the 1970s. By then, Tom was thin and sickly looking and explained his situation to Hanner. "Hawg was very hard on Tom when he played. He was just a tough old guy. He came from the old coaching school where you had to beat it into them. Dave said he wished he could do some of it differently. It was a nice closure," Susan Toner said.

Toner didn't complain or tell his clients that he was sick, but when he neared death Susan Toner called one of the players Tom was closest to, Joe Morris of the Giants. Morris knew that Toner had been sick but not that he had been dying. He flew to California to say goodbye. "Tom was unconscious, but he woke up when Joe arrived and gave Joe a big hug," Susan said. "It was a very touching thing to have happen. It was the last energy we saw from Tom."

Toner died one day later, and his body was flown back to Boston for a wake. A crowd estimated at 2,000 spilled out of a church to pay their respects. "The line went on for blocks, and he had been away from Boston for five years," Ed Toner Jr. said.

Thousands more said farewell, in a sense, in Idaho. Three weeks after he died, he was inducted into the Idaho State Sports Hall of Fame.

Like Wendy Scribner, Susan Toner received a survey from the NFL after Tom passed away. "I completed it, and in it I mentioned that I suspected steroid use and questioned the packets of pills. Like Wendy, I never heard back from them after that."

Ed Toner Jr. won't remember his uncle as the thin man he saw walking with a cane and pulling an oxygen tank a year before his death. He'll remember the robust, story-telling, fun-loving man that he looked up to, the man he called for advice when he was in college. "Even when he was sick, he'd still make time to have a fun day. He was a calming influence on me. He'd always talk about enjoying the moment you're in," Ed Toner Jr. said.

Susan Toner suffered through more triumph and tragedy after Tom died. She became a successful businesswoman. She was involved in charitable fundraising while Tom played in Green Bay, and in 2005 she had risen to executive director of Providence Health Foundation, a Catholic health-care system, in Medford, Oregon.

While raising her children, Ryan and Polly, Susan Toner remarried and divorced. Polly graduated from college, then pursued a master of divinity degree at the University of Chicago. Ryan, in the mold of his father, developed chiseled body features, played college football at Rowan University in Glassboro, New Jersey, and then went into modeling. He appeared in ads for Versace, Polo, Ralph Lauren, and Abercrombie & Fitch.

Thomas "Ryan" Toner died in 2004 at age 26 in Beverly Hills, of respiratory failure, which was brought on by a strict exercise and dieting program, Susan Toner said.

In 2005, Susan Toner and her daughter went back to Green Bay for the first time since Tom's playing days. They drove past the apartments where she and Tom lived as newlyweds in 1973, only months after he was drafted by the Packers. She renewed acquaintances with Packers President Bob Harlan, who in the 1970s was the team's corporate general manager. They saw some of Tom's old teammates, including John Brockington and Jerry Tagge. They went to the Packers Hall of Fame, where they saw Tom in the 1970s team photos.

They were glad they went, Susan Toner said, but two members of their family were missing. "It was a feeling of gratitude to have been part of the Packers, but it was a melancholy, lonely feeling."

A HERO'S LIFE
Harold "Hal" Van Every (36)

College: Minnesota

Position: Running back/defensive back, 1940–41

Highlight: Led the Packers in interceptions in 1941 with three and returned one
of them 91 yards for a touchdown, a team record.

After football: Retired underwriter for Principal Life Insurance in Minneapolis.

On a Saturday in the fall of 2005, Harold "Hal" Van Every rose early with his
wife of more than 60 years, Drexel. They drove off through typically heavy Twin
Cities traffic to the Metrodome in downtown Minneapolis to watch an 11 A.M.
Minnesota Golden Gophers football game.

Battling the busy highways and crowds and hearing the often-intense dome
noise might be too much for some octogenarians, but not the high-spirited Van
Everys. They have season tickets. On this day, however, Hal's spirits were a little down
after the game. You could see it in his tired legs, which were splayed out across a
leather chair that he had sunk into, and hear resignation in his voice. His Gophers had
just been clobbered by Ohio State, ending their hopes for a Big Ten championship.

Van Every, 87, had every right to be upset. Back in his day, the Gophers, coached
by legendary Bernie Bierman, knew the importance of playing tough defense, he said.
I sensed that Van Every had wanted to get out there and help his alma mater. "You've
got to be ready, be sharp, or they'll run right by you," he said of the 2005 Gophers,
whose defense was shredded by the Buckeyes.

It was obvious that one of the oldest living Green Bay Packers not only still fol-
lows but still loves the game of football, especially in Minnesota. Born on February
10, 1918, at Minnetonka Beach, Minnesota, Van Every was a Gophers star for three
years as well as an academic standout. He lettered from 1937 to 1939 and led the
team in rushing as a sophomore and as a senior. He was the team's MVP in 1939,
when he ran for 733 yards.

Van Every was a Gopher when the team was a national power. He helped the
Gophers win Big Ten titles in 1937 and 1938, but he just missed being on a national
title team. The Gophers did win plenty of national championships during the Bierman era, including 1934, 1935, 1936, 1940, and 1941.

UM's great football tradition in the 1930s and 1940s largely is why the Packers
have taken more first-round draft picks (7) and more total draft picks (41) from
Minnesota than any other college in team history. Van Every, who finished his career
fourth on the school's all-time rushing list and in 2005 still ranked 25th, became part
of the Gophers–Packers connection in 1940 when Green Bay made him its number-
one draft pick.

His long devotion to the Gophers and his history with the Packers, however, hardly begin to tell Van Every's story. In their southside Minneapolis home, among their many mementos from a full life together, Van Every and his wife keep a 47-page sketch booklet called "Stalag Luft III." The little publication describes an insidious German prisoner of war camp, and tells more about Van Every's strength, determination, and character than any headline that ever bore his name or any touchdown he scored for the Gophers or the Packers.

Like many of the young men of the early 1940s, Van Every gave the best years of his life—in his case, years that might have been devoted to a burgeoning pro football career—to his country while serving in World War II.

When he returned to the United States in 1946, he met with Earl "Curly" Lambeau, coach of the Pack, at a hotel in Chicago. He told Lambeau about having his plane shot down by the Germans, injuring his back, and becoming a prisoner of war. He never would play pro football again, he told Lambeau. Ironically, Chicago was the same city where Van Every scored a touchdown five years earlier. It would be the last touchdown of his NFL career.

Like many Americans, Van Every's life changed on December 7, 1941, the day the Japanese bombed Pearl Harbor and brought the United States into World War II.

A week earlier, on November 30, 1941, the Packers went to Griffith Stadium in Washington, D.C., and defeated the Redskins, 27-17, to clinch at least a tie for the Western Division championship in their regular-season finale. The Packers were 10-1.

The next week, Lambeau took the team to Chicago to watch the Bears play the Chicago Cardinals. The Bears needed a win in their final regular-season game to tie the Packers and force the first divisional playoff in pro football history. Shortly into the Bears–Cardinals game, the public address announcer told all servicemen in attendance to report to their units, raising a stir among the Packers players and the 43,425 in attendance at Comiskey Park. Then came the announcement that the Japanese had bombed Pearl Harbor. The Bears won, 34-24, but it hardly was the news of the day in Chicago, Green Bay, or elsewhere.

With the United States' military mobilizing, the Packers went to Chicago again the next week, December 14, for the playoff game at Wrigley Field. With the temperature at 16 degrees, the Bears won, 33-17, after scoring 24 points in the second quarter. They held Packers receiving star Don Hutson to just one catch.

Van Every, of course, didn't know it, but it would be the last pro football game of his career. He went out in style, scoring the last Packers touchdown of the game on a 10-yard pass from Cecil Isbell in the third quarter. He knew that he likely would be going to battle. He already had been drafted into the Army in April of

1941 and spent part of the year in military training, arriving late for the Packers' 1941 summer training camp.

He had had a good season. He led the Packers in interceptions in 1941 with three, one more than six teammates, including promising youngster Tony Canadeo. Among his interceptions was one against Pittsburgh on November 23. He returned it 91 yards for a touchdown, a Packers record.

Attesting to his versatility that season, Van Every also completed 11 of 30 passes, rushed 27 times for 127 yards and two touchdowns, caught one pass, returned four punts for a 14.5-yard average, and punted 13 times for a 38.8-yard average.

Although Van Every will say, with some modesty, that he wasn't a star, he was a player on the rise and one of the probable Packers heroes in seasons to come. "You know, I think Harold has a chance to become a greater passer than Cecil Isbell," said Bill Johnson, one of Van Every's Gophers and Packers teammates, after the 1941 season during an interview with a Minneapolis sports reporter. "All 'Van' needs is a little more confidence in an actual game. In practice, he's as good a passer as I ever hope to see. It's going to take a little time, but he'll reach the same point of efficiency under fire. I've never seen anyone who works harder trying to improve his playing than 'Van.' I know he'll eventually rate with the greats," Johnson said.

Hal Van Every, from the University of Minnesota, was the Packers' top draft pick in 1940. He was an all-purpose running back, defensive back, and punter for two years before he left to serve in World War II.

By 1942, Johnson, Van Every, and many other Packers either were serving in the military or soon would be. Van Every spent six months in the infantry, then transferred to the Air Corps, where he trained as a pilot, amassing 500 hours of flying time.

He did play some football, however, starring with the undefeated Second Air Force Bombers, a team of military personnel still stationed in the U.S. The Bombers, who had a few ex-NFL stars, defeated Hardin-Simmons College 13-7 on New Year's Day 1943 to win the Sun Bowl in El Paso, Texas. Van Every scored the decisive touchdown in the second half to hand Hardin-Simmons its first loss of the season.

By late 1943, he was with the Eighth Air Force 447th Bomb Group, 510th Squadron, and piloting a B-17 bomber out of Rattlesden Air Base in England. The B-17, also known as the Flying Fortress, was the United States' biggest plane. Dubbed the "Queen of the Bombers," the B-17G, a newer model of the B-17, carried from eight to 12 bombs weighing up to 6,000 pounds and had thirteen 50-caliber machine guns to provide cover. The B-17G was nearly 75 feet long, and each of its massive wings was more than 103 feet long. Each wing supported two Wright Cyclone engines, which propelled the giant through the skies at speeds of up to 300 mph. It could travel 3,400 miles without refueling. The B-17 was a key part of the punishing $2^{1}/_{2}$ -year daylight bombing campaign of German industrial sites that began in 1942.

Van Every was flying missions over Germany and Poland as soon as he arrived in the European Theatre. Some of his first missions were over Berlin, the well-fortified base of the Third Reich. "They had all the flak in the world. That was a pretty tough target," Van Every said.

He was on his ninth mission—he would have earned a ticket home when he completed 20—when his life changed forever. Flying at 22,000 feet, his plane was hit by German anti-aircraft ground fire. Sitting in his den in Minneapolis more than 60 years later, he recalled the events.

"We were taking flak from down below, and it hit a wing. We lost an engine. I didn't want to hang around too long with the wing on fire, with the gasoline nearby, and the bombs close, too. I ordered everybody out of the airplane. We had to bail out from 22,000 feet. Usually, you like to get down to a respectable altitude to get better breathing [before bailing out]," Van Every said.

"I got up from my seat and got ready to jump, but I didn't have my parachute on. I had to go back and get it. The thing that saved us was the autopilot. A general had taught me really how to set that thing to level out the airplane. With only three engines working, that's what kept the airplane level so we could get out."

Van Every, along with the other nine men in the plane, made it safely to the ground, but he landed on a house near the Germany–Poland border. Figuring he was an easy target for the enemy on the roof, he knew that he had to get down and do it quickly. He jumped but landed on his back and hit a fence post.

Dazed from being shot out of the sky more than four miles high and from two hard landings, Van Every scrambled to his feet to look for a place to hide in some nearby woods. Then a young German soldier with a gun appeared and took him prisoner. It was May 12, 1944, the beginning of an ordeal that would test his will more than any football opponent or red-faced football coach. Van Every became one of about 10,000 Allied prisoners at Stalag Luft III, or Camp Air Three, for captured American and British air personnel. The camp was at Sagan, Germany, about 100 miles southeast of Berlin.

The prisoners were a valuable bargaining commodity for Germany, and the Third Reich took elaborate steps to keep them interred. All the barracks, for example, were above ground to deter tunneling. Monitors were placed in the soil around the camp to detect any tunneling activity.

Still, just before Van Every arrived, 76 men escaped via an ingenious, painstakingly carved tunnel system; most of them were caught, and Hitler had 53 of them executed. (The attempt would one day become the subject of a book and Hollywood movie, *The Great Escape.*) When Van Every arrived in camp, he was met with a sign that read, "Escape is no longer a sport."

The conditions at Stalag Luft III were better than at other POW camps or the concentration camps where millions of Jews and others died, but they still tested a man's will. Prisoners were housed in spartan, cold barracks, where they stuffed newspapers in the cracks to block the winter wind. They received a scant amount of questionable food each day, supplemented by occasional Red Cross packages. The six-compound camp had education classes, sports fields, a dentist, and other facilities to make life bearable, but it also was surrounded by parallel nine-foot-high fences topped with barbed wire. Guards in towers, armed with machine guns, were ready to shoot down anyone who tried to get out.

"The men went hungry, lived in overcrowded quarters, lacked adequate sanitation facilities, had insufficient clothing and bedding, suffered from barbed-wire psychosis, and had inadequate medical care. They lived in constant fear of what the Gestapo and the SS might do to them, were shot at repeatedly inside their compounds, and in some cases were murdered in cold blood," wrote Arthur A. Durand, author of *Stalag Luft III.*

Their lives were to become even more difficult. Russian troops had advanced to within 13 miles of Stalag Luft III, and the Germans feared their prisoners were about to be liberated. On January 27, 1945, the Germans in charge of Stalag Luft III ordered the men out of the barracks and led them on a grueling, mid-winter march to a new camp.

The march began at midnight, two hours after the men had lined up outside; many of them already were freezing. Van Every was used to running through defenders and tackling ball carriers as a two-way player for the Packers. Undoubtedly, his conditioning helped him survive the march, although he did so with an injured back. He could walk, and because of that he received no medical treatment from the Germans, he said.

He walked. The thousands of prisoners walked nearly 62 miles in the next six days in snow that was six inches deep when they started, and the snow kept falling. Temperatures dipped to near zero, and the wind-chill factor was well below zero. Prisoners had frozen hands and feet and fell ill as the march wore on. They slept in a brick factory, roadside inns, and barns.

When they reached Spremberg, they boarded frigid boxcars, which soon became awash in vomit and excrement, 50 men and a guard packed to a car. Only two small windows let in fresh air as the POW train passed through the scarred German countryside, much of which had been bombed by the very prisoners who now were passing through.

At the end of the journey, their reward was a new prison camp at Nuremberg, Germany. For two months, they battled rats and hordes of lice, fleas, and bedbugs, and were fed worm-infested vegetables and soup. The soup, part of their 1,300-calorie-a-day diet, was so bad that the men called it "green death," according to Bob Neary, one of the POWs, who authored the "Stalag Luft III" sketchbook, a copy of which the Van Everys used to help explain Hal's ordeal. The sketchbook described and depicted the conditions in the prison camps and on the marches. The men ate the soup anyway, along with the bitter, black bread with dubious ingredients.

Many of them were sick with dysentery, but with the Russians still advancing the men soon were on the road again. They marched 91 miles in 10 days, in better weather than the first march, to Moosburg, in southeastern Germany. With the guards also suffering from fatigue, some POWs escaped and others freely bartered for food in the small towns they passed through.

Sixteen days later, on April 29, 1945—nearly a year after Van Every had been shot down—he and his fellow prisoners were set free when U.S. General George Patton's Third Army broke through the German lines on its way to Munich and sliced through the barbed wire around the POW camp.

Van Every remembers Patton, who arrived two days later, standing on a polished jeep with a four-star flag as he heard cheers from the Allied prisoners, who now numbered close to 100,000 men from many nations. Standing straight in a pressed uniform and polished helmet, Patton ordered the German flag replaced by the U.S. flag atop the camp flagpole. Then he told the man who took down the German flag to use it as a substitute for toilet paper. "Well, I guess you sons-a-bitches are glad to see me. I'd like to stay with you for a while, but I've got a date with a woman in Munich; it's 40 kilometers away, and I've got to fight every damned inch of the way," he said, and he roared off, according to Durand.

Soon, the Red Cross was there with food and nurses. Although they wouldn't leave camp for another few weeks, the prisoners' lives began to improve: For the first time in a year or more, they tasted freshly baked white bread.

The next day, Adolf Hitler committed suicide in Berlin and the war in Europe was all but over. Van Every probably felt like celebrating but didn't have the strength. Once a well-muscled, 200-pound running back for the Packers, he had become a weakened, 150-pound prisoner of war with a damaged back.

During the war, the Packers and the NFL played on, but the league, like the whole country, wasn't the same.

While Van Every sat injured in Stalag Luft III, the Packers won the 1944 NFL title on December 17 at the Polo Grounds in New York. The Packers defeated the New York Giants, 14-7, behind Ted Fritsch's two rushing touchdowns and Joe Laws' three interceptions.

Oddly, one of the players for the Giants in that game was former Packers star Arnie Herber. He had retired late in the 1941 season (feted at a testimonial dinner that was attended by Packers players [including Van Every], coaches, and fans). Three years later, Herber came out of retirement to help the Giants. With nearly 1,000 NFL players called into service in World War II, many teams suffered severe shortages of players.

Most teams were affected by the war. The Philadelphia Eagles and Pittsburgh Steelers were so short of players that they temporarily merged, becoming the "Steagles." Other teams also merged until players began returning from the war. The Cleveland Rams did not play in 1943 because of a lack of players.

Van Every wasn't alone as a Packer in service to his country during the war. A total of 32 active Packers were called to duty, with up to 27 of them seeing action in 1944. The Packers, however, weren't as adversely affected as some NFL teams. The New York Giants lost 44 players and the Detroit Lions 45.

Some Packers were rejected because of their physical condition, according to Charles "Buckets" Goldenberg, a Packers Hall of Fame guard who played from 1933 to 1945. "One of the reasons more of our players weren't drafted was that we were a bunch of broken-down stumblebums. A bunch of us tried to get in but were rejected. Bill Lee and I went down to volunteer, but when the doctors examined us they said we had knees of 80-year-old men. When we asked them how come we could play pro football and yet be rejected for the service, one doctor said, 'Well, if you're playing in a football game and your knee gives out, they can stop the game and take you out, but in a war you can't call time out during a battle,'" Goldenberg said in a story that originally was printed in *Packer Report*. Lee, however, eventually was accepted and served from 1943 to 1945.

About 14 college players were drafted by the Packers, only to have Uncle Sam's draft notice take priority. Packers Hall of Fame tackle Dick Wildung was the team's number-one draft pick in 1943, but thanks to the war he didn't play until 1946.

Wildung joined the naval officer training program, which allowed him to finish his degree at the University of Minnesota. He saw action in the Philippines, on a PT boat, for one year.

In addition to players whose football careers were interrupted by military service, some players who had retired from the game went on to serve in World War II. Among them was Johnny "Blood" McNally, a running back from 1928 to 1933 and 1935 to 1936 who was inducted into the Pro Football Hall of Fame in 1963. McNally served in the Air Force from 1943 to 1945.

Also in uniform were Canadeo and Clark Hinkle, future Pro Football Hall of Fame inductees. Canadeo served in 1945—originally getting a deferment because he was married and a father—while Hinkle served from 1942 to 1945. Hinkle played with the Packers from 1932 to 1941 but did not return after the war. Lambeau tried to convince Hinkle to return, but he said he had had 10 good years as a Packer and "wanted to go out on top. You know, after a four-year layoff, you can never get your legs back in shape." Gone but one year, Canadeo did return and became the Packers' first 1,000-yard rusher in 1949 in Lambeau's final season as coach. Eleven of the 32 players who served in World War II returned to the team after they were mustered out of service.

Players who weren't called to service did their part for the war effort at home. NFL players used their star power to sell $4 million in war bonds. More than half that total came from one night in Milwaukee, when Packers stars Hutson, Isbell, and Coach Lambeau sold $2,100,000 at a rally. The NFL also held eight exhibition games, with the proceeds going to Army Emergency Relief. The Packers played one of those games, defeating the West Army All-Stars, 36-21.

While many NFL players returned from the war to resume their football careers, others like Van Every were in no shape to play again. Mario "Motts" Tonelli faced a similar situation. The Chicago Cardinals fullback was among 75,000 American and Filipino troops who endured the infamous Bataan Death March. Without food and water, as many as 10,000 of them died during the torturous trek, which lasted seven days and covered more than 60 miles. Captured in Bataan in 1942, Tonelli survived the march and more than 3½ years as a prisoner of war. When he was freed, he weighed 90 pounds. Somehow, he played for the Chicago Cardinals again in 1945.

Nineteen NFL players, an ex-head coach, and a team executive died in the war. Among them was Al Blozis, a massive New York Giants tackle who played in the 1944 championship game against the Packers. Six weeks later, in 1945, Blozis was in France looking for missing members of his platoon when he was shot and killed by machine gun fire in the snow in the Vosges Mountains. Blozis didn't have to go into the Army because he was too big at 6-foot-6 and 250 pounds, but he wouldn't hear of it. During basic training, he set an Army record in the hand-grenade throw.

Another of the 21 NFL men who died was a Packer, Howard "Smiley" Johnson. A guard and linebacker, Johnson played with Van Every on the 1940 and 1941

Packers. Johnson enlisted in the Marine Corps in 1942. In June of 1944, he traveled with the Fourth Marine Division to the Western Pacific, to Saipan. There, he earned a Silver Star when he defended a flank during an attack by the Japanese. He was promoted to lieutenant a month later.

In February of 1945, Johnson was in Iwo Jima when a shell exploded nearby. He was injured by flying fragments from the shell. "Johnson lay on the ground as Navy Corpsmen rushed to his side. Instead of pleading for help, Johnson pointed to the other Marines that had been hit and told the Corpsmen to save them first," wrote Scott Venci of the *Green Bay Press-Gazette*. Johnson then died. He was 28. He left behind a wife and a daughter, who was only a year old.

Johnson had starred for the University of Georgia from 1937 to 1939. By way of remembrance for his sacrifice, the Smiley Johnson Award is given out each year to the outstanding player in the Peach Bowl in Atlanta. In 2005, the Packers Hall of Fame erected a display case in Johnson's honor. The case is at the entrance to the hall, situated between oversized wall photos of Vince Lombardi and George Halas, and the Packers training camp at Rockwood Lodge.

Six decades later, Van Every wasn't aware that one of his former Packers teammates had died in the war. Weeks after I visited his house, I called him and told him about Johnson. Van Every paused and said, "Well, I didn't know that." He paused again, processing the news in his mind, trying to remember Smiley Johnson and dealing for the first time in decades with an old but awful feeling—the reality of war. "That's too bad," Van Every said with sadness in his voice.

Although he was injured, Van Every considers himself one of the lucky war veterans; he returned home alive. A few months after being liberated from the POW camp, he arrived by ship in New York and passed the Statue of Liberty before setting foot on U.S. soil. Van Every went back to Minnesota and was mustered out at Fort Snelling in Minneapolis, ready to begin a new life.

The Germans bent Van Every, but they didn't break him. His bad back required several surgeries and forced him to wear a corset-style brace for support for more than 50 years. In 1997, another surgery finally relieved some of the pain and allowed him to shed the corset and replace it with a special belt for back support.

He built a career in the insurance business as an underwriter for Principal Life. He and Drexel raised a son and a daughter. Through it all, he worked full time into his early 80s, played in state-level amateur golf tournaments, fished, played piano, and became an avid Gophers and Vikings football fan. Van Every cheered for the Packers, too.

During the week of Veterans Day in 2005, he shot an 86, one better than his age, in golf; visited a nearby veterans hospital, and had dinner with his wife and other vets at an American Legion hall in Wayzata, Minnesota.

Van Every and his wife have a shelf full of big, leather-bound scrapbooks that chronicle his college and pro football careers, and his years in the service. A one-inch by one-inch yellowed clipping of a Packers game reads: "Van Every ran 31 yards through right tackle for another six-pointer."

Pictures of Van Every show a strong, square-jawed young man who was all business on the football field. A 1941 picture taken from the stands documents an end-around play, in which Van Every handed off to Hutson for an 11-yard TD run in the fourth quarter to beat the Chicago Cardinals. Another picture from that year captured Van Every leaping to intercept a pass from the arms of the Cardinals' Johnny Clement. Still another photo showed him relaxing in a chair while wearing his football pants but no pads, his "Van Every"-emblazoned warmup jacket next to him. He appeared to be at a hotel, where players used to dress for games.

One of the most heroic football images in the scrapbook is of Van Every in a wide, horizontal shot taken from ground level as he breaks through the Cleveland Rams' line for a seven-yard gain, leaning forward, his head down, and ready to take on another tackler.

Drexel was the keeper of the scrapbooks, and she appears in the early 1940s book with Hal. While Hal was a Packer and a war pilot in training, they were getting engaged and married. "To Wed Golden Gopher Star," one caption read under a picture of Drexel Kay Weck. "Aviation Cadet Harold Van Every Was Athletic Pride of Minnesota," read another. Still another showed Second Lt. Van Every with his bride after they married on July 27, 1942, in Carson, Nevada.

After we paged through some of the scrapbooks and talked about his life, Van Every took me into his basement, gingerly descending the stairs. The paneled, carpeted family room was a box of memories with framed mementos lining the walls and filling the corners. He pointed to the black-and-white 1940 team photo. Van Every was the clean-cut blond in the upper right corner of the photo, wearing number 36. Another image showed him ready to punt the ball, one muscular calf dug into the grass and a strong leg swinging toward the ball, suspended in midair. It was just one moment from his nearly 90 years of living, but it represented something special: Never again would he be that strong and agile, not after the war.

He showed me his first contract, signed by Lambeau. Hanging on the wall, it was a simple, one-page document with just 14 stipulations. Lambeau made Van Every the ninth pick overall in the 1940 draft after he had led the Gophers in running and led the nation in 1939 with nine interceptions. In addition, he lettered as a UM basketball player. Sixty-five years later, Van Every still isn't happy that Lambeau offered him only $4,000 a year. As we talked, he mentioned the $1 million contract signed 50 years later by another Packers number-one draft pick from Minnesota, running back Darrell Thompson. "I'd like to have had his money," Van Every said. "I didn't get enough that year and the next year, either. I didn't really know a lot about salaries. That really burned my butt," Van Every said.

Still, he enjoyed his two seasons in Green Bay. The Packers were one of the elite teams in the NFL at the time, having just won the 1939 championship. They were loaded with talent, including Hutson, who was in his prime as the league's best receiver, halfback Canadeo, fullback Clark Hinkle, and veteran quarterback Arnie Herber, all future Pro Football Hall of Fame inductees.

And, of course, Lambeau. Van Every liked Lambeau, even though he didn't like the paltry contract the coach offered him. "He knew the game and wouldn't put up with any nonsense. He was fun to play for," Van Every said. "He liked all the girls. We always heard about his girlie life. He liked the passing phase of the game. When he got Hutson and Isbell, he could throw that ball all over the place." Van Every did some of that throwing: He threw four touchdown passes among his 12 completions in 1940.

Van Every didn't go back to Green Bay for more than 60 years. Finally, in 2004, he returned for his first Packers game since that Western Division playoff loss against Chicago in 1941. During Packers alumni weekend, a home game every year when ex-players are invited for a weekend of festivities, he toured the remodeled Lambeau Field. He never even had been to the original Lambeau, which was built in 1957; in his days, the Packers played at old City Stadium.

It was a homecoming for Van Every but not a reunion. Of all the ex-Packers there, he didn't know any of them. All his former teammates had passed away. He signed some autographs for fans, however, and met other ex-Packers, most of whom couldn't fathom what it was like playing offense and defense for $4,000 a year with a leather helmet and no face mask—then having to give up your football career to fight in World War II.

And, as is the custom during the annual alumni game, he lined up on the field to be introduced at halftime. Hearing his name once more at a Packers game on a field that was named after his former coach had to make Hal Van Every feel proud again. It resurrected memories of 1940 and 1941, when number 36 in a blue-and-gold uniform scored four career touchdowns and made five career interceptions, before his life, and the world, changed forever.

More than 60 years after Van Every served his country, the war in Iraq hit home for a former Green Bay Packer. In November of 2004, Mike Hunt's son, Isaiah, was killed in a vehicle accident near Baghdad, Iraq. Isaiah Hunt, from Suamico, Wisconsin, was a truck driver and gunner in the 82nd Airborne. He was 20. Mike Hunt was drafted by the Packers in the second round in 1978, behind James Lofton and John Anderson. Hunt, from the University of Minnesota, played linebacker for the Packers from 1978 to 1980.

A VOICE FROM THE PAST
Herman Schneidman (4, 51)

College: Iowa

Position: Running back, 1935–39

Highlight: Played on Packers' 1936 and 1939 NFL championship teams.

After football: Retired; former owner of beer, liquor distributorship in Quincy, Illinois.

In 1935, at age 21, Herman Schneidman was hoping to make the roster for the Green Bay Packers. The chance to play pro football under Coach Curly Lambeau was part of his motivation. He had another motivation, as well, one that was becoming even more pressing. Schneidman needed a job.

He wasn't the only one. That year, in the midst of the Great Depression, 20 percent of Americans were unemployed. Even when they did get work, Americans weren't paid much. Per capita income in the United States in 1935 was $474, or about $9 a week.

In 2005, Schneidman was 93 and living in Sunset Nursing Home in Quincy, Illinois, the small Mississippi River town where he grew up and went to high school. His wife died in 2003. He was in a wheelchair, and his hearing and eyesight were failing, but not his rich memories of the Packers. The team is often the main topic of conversation when Schneidman and his cronies gather for lunch each Tuesday.

Born in Rock Island, Illinois, on November 22, 1913, Schneidman was a football, basketball, and track star at Quincy High School, eventually becoming a member of the school's athletic hall of fame. He went on to the University of Iowa in 1931 to play basketball, but one day in 1932 some of the basketball players said they were planning to go out for the Hawkeyes football team, as well. He thought he'd give it a try.

He didn't know whether he'd make the team until one day he heard a radio sports announcer from WOC in Davenport, Iowa. The announcer, himself a football player who had just graduated in 1932 from Eureka College in Peoria, Illinois, had some inside information to pass along: Herman Schneidman had made the Iowa team. The smooth-talking announcer went by the name "Dutch"—Ronald "Dutch" Reagan.

Schneidman had found a new college sport. He played halfback for the Hawkeyes in 1932, sat out in 1933, and returned in 1934. The Hawkeyes were a combined 3-12-1 in 1932 and 1934, and Schneidman missed most of the latter season with a dislocated shoulder, but he played well enough to catch Lambeau's eye. Lambeau mailed him a free-agent contract for 1935, paying $85 a game. Schneidman signed it. Free-agent contracts were standard operating procedure in the NFL at the time. It was the year before the NFL draft was instituted so all unsigned players, in essence, were free agents.

Schneidman was a Green Bay Packer but still had to make the team; the standards were high. He was walking into a pro football franchise that already was one of the oldest in the league, had won three world titles a few years earlier, and was stocked with talent. Seven members of the 1935 team would go on to make the Pro Football Hall of Fame.

One of those future Hall of Famers was Johnny "Blood" McNally, the unpredictable running back with whom Lambeau had a love–hate relationship. As I talked with Schneidman and brought up McNally's name, it seemed like his memory vault opened wide, taking him back to the late summer of 1935 when he was a strapping young man. It became obvious that McNally was one of Schneidman's best friends and one of his greatest joys as he thought back to his years in Green Bay. A guy like McNally makes an impression for life.

When Schneidman was hoping to get a job as a Packer, he didn't quite know what to think of "Blood" McNally. The Packers played four exhibition games that September, and the only time Schneidman had seen McNally was when the famous Vagabond Halfback ran the ball for two opposing teams. Schneidman once told an interviewer, "I'd have to have a couple of beers before I could talk about 'Blood.'"

I didn't have the beer, but I had some time.

Heading into 1935, Lambeau thought his talented team had a chance to go places. With strong-armed Arnie Herber at quarterback and Don Hutson, a fast rookie receiver from Alabama, Lambeau's hopes were running high. Rumor had it that McNally might even be back with the team. After breaking team rules late in 1933—one of many times he had irritated Lambeau—McNally was sold to Pittsburgh for the 1934 season.

The Packers had won championships in 1929, 1930, and 1931 but nothing since. Lambeau was hungry for another title. So he shook things up. For the first time in their 14-year history, the Packers held training camp outside of Green Bay. Lambeau, 24 players, his son, Donald, assistant coach Red Smith, trainer Bud Jorgensen, and a pile of equipment were loaded on a bus in August 1935, bound for Pinewood Lodge and Lake Thompson, four miles outside of Rhinelander. The team made one stop, at the Muskie Inn in Elcho for lunch, according to a *Milwaukee Journal Sentinel* account, on the 130-mile trip up north.

Schneidman didn't think the team would make it to Rhinelander alive; the bus driver was speeding and recklessly trying to race trains through the crossings. When they did arrive in Rhinelander, banners and hundreds of Packers fans greeted the players and staff.

That week, Lambeau, 37, was all business, although he brought along his new wife, a 26-year-old former Miss California contestant who caught the eye of many of the players. Lambeau let married players bring their wives along too. For one week, players ate breakfast at 8 A.M., practiced twice a day, had evening meetings, and couldn't smoke or drink. Stuck in the woods with no cars, the Packers focused on football. They were bused daily to a practice field at the high school in Rhinelander.

After a week of trying to get in shape, they headed west by bus again to play four preseason games. Schneidman, fearing for his life, didn't ride the team bus. He offered to help the trainer, Jorgensen, load the equipment in exchange for a ride with him. As the team bus rolled on ahead, Schneidman and Jorgensen stopped in one of the small towns and had a cold one.

For the first time since 1921, Lambeau arranged an extensive preseason schedule. From 1922 to 1934, the Packers had typically played only one preseason game a year. In 1935, however, Lambeau scheduled games with semipro teams in Merrill, Chippewa Falls, Stevens Point, and a game at home against La Crosse in a span of eight days. Then they would open the regular season at home on September 15 against the Chicago Cardinals.

It was a successful preseason; the Packers went 4-0 and outscored their opponents, 144-0, as they crossed the state. However, they did have one scare and were part of what would become a historic moment in team history; the appearance of McNally on a semipro town team, and the debut of Hutson in a Packer uniform.

Two days after defeating the Merrill Fromm Foxes, 33-0, before 1,500 fans in Merrill in central Wisconsin, the Packers went to Chippewa Falls, a city of several thousand just north of Eau Claire in the west-central part of the state, to play the Chippewa Marines. It was Labor Day, September 2.

The Marines eagerly awaited them. This collection of local ex-high school players and some former small-college players from Wisconsin and Minnesota had a 37-3-4 record the previous six seasons.

As the Marines practiced for the Packers, McNally showed up in Chippewa Falls. Intent on giving the Packers a good game and knowing he might help bring out more fans, the Marines welcomed McNally aboard. The 6-foot-1, 188-pound halfback wanted to return to Green Bay, despite his run-ins with Lambeau, and figured his best chance was to play against the Packers and show Lambeau he still could run.

McNally wasn't far from home, having grown up in New Richmond, about 75 miles west of Chippewa Falls. He played some college ball at River Falls State in west-central Wisconsin before moving on to play for Notre Dame and St. John's in Collegeville, Minnesota.

Given his history, he seemed like a good fit with the Marines. McNally was prone to drinking, carousing, and stretching team rules on and off the field. McNally became known as the Vagabond Halfback, and the Marines were a vagabond team, men with real jobs who came from nearby towns for a weekly game in the fall. Their lineup included a couple of men who had women's nicknames, "Mary" Luloff and "Kate" Alphonse, a ball carrier nicknamed "Hops," and a quarterback they called "Hoot."

The Marines were serious, however, about beating the Packers. The team brought in a chef during camp to fatten them up for the season. Each Marines player was promised $25 for the Packers game, a windfall compared with their usual paycheck of $10.

The Marines had some talent and size. Their lineup included 235-pound "Wink" Claflin, 250-pound Hank Derleth, and 226-pound Frank Ray. They would need that mass if they hoped to beat the Packers, who themselves had four players who weighed more than 230 pounds, including 260-pound Walt Kiesling, a future Pro Football Hall of Fame player.

By Labor Day, the Marines were ready for the biggest game in team history. A crowd of 6,000 was on hand at the Northern Wisconsin State Fairgrounds football field in Chippewa Falls, more than the Packers would see for two regular season games in 1935.

The Packers didn't disappoint, but neither did the Marines and their new running back. The Marines held the Packers to just a field goal in the first half as the teams mostly traded punts. "Blood" McNally gave Marines fans something to cheer about when he ripped off a 30-yard run in the second quarter, cutting back and reversing field before getting forced out of bounds near midfield. The Packers led just 3-0 at halftime.

Without locker rooms, the players sat on piles of straw next to the field at halftime, and Lambeau let the Packers have it, according to one spectator. "What's the matter with you guys? Here you are, supposed to be professional football players and you're letting this bunch of farmers push you all around," Lambeau said.

One of the Packers replied, "Here's my helmet. You go in there. These guys are some pretty good football players."

Lambeau's speech must have worked, or maybe the Marines had eaten a little too much chef-prepared food that week. In the second half, the Packers pulled away to a 22-0 win. Hank Bruder threw an eight-yard touchdown pass to Al Rose; Clark Hinkle scored on a short touchdown run; and Arnie Herber passed to Milt Gantenbein for another score.

The Marines got some revenge when "Tiny" Bannock, a 220-pound tackle from Stevens Point Teachers College, blocked an extra point by Bob Monnett, who had kicked the first-half field goal.

With victory at hand, Lambeau put his prize rookie on the field for the first time. Don Hutson had played the previous Friday night for the Chicago All-Stars against the Chicago Bears. He then traveled to Chippewa Falls, reaching the team hotel Sunday afternoon. He put on a Packers uniform for the first time and entered the game in the fourth quarter, catching a couple of passes, according to reports. The elusive wide receiver from Alabama signed autographs and was on his way to many NFL records and the Hall of Fame in an 11-year career.

After running their preseason record to 2-0 against the Marines, the Packers won at Stevens Point, 40-0, on September 4. They defeated the La Crosse Old Style Lagers, 49-0, on September 8 to close out the preseason, again with McNally showing up to play for the opponent.

Lambeau had seen enough and re-signed the crafty McNally for 1935 and 1936. "We got back to Green Bay [after the 1935 preseason], and guess who's on the team?" Schneidman said.

Lambeau also had seen enough of Schneidman to know he wanted the tough former Hawkeye on the team. Schneidman recalled the night that he and several teammates waited to hear whether they had made the final roster. "There was a hotel in downtown Green Bay where you could drink beer pretty cheap. One of the old-timers at the hotel told us that Lambeau won't tell you if you're fired or not. He'll put a pink slip in your mailbox at the hotel. We spent half the night running back and forth to check our mailboxes. [The old-timer] was lying to us, of course. Lambeau didn't do that," Schneidman said.

Soon thereafter, sometime before the team's 1935 season opener on September 15 against the Chicago Cardinals, Lambeau personally told Schneidman that he was a Packer, along with a few other rookies, including Hutson. The work was seasonal but at $85 a game, it was close to 10 times more than what the average American was making per week.

Although the Packers didn't live up to Lambeau's expectations in 1935 with an 8-4 record, only good for second in their division, they set the stage for the 1936 season, when they went 11-1-1 and won their fourth NFL championship. That year, Schneidman was a starter and caught a 46-yard touchdown pass, one of his two career scores for the Packers.

Schneidman was a Packer for five seasons, from 1935 to 1939. He was used mostly as a blocker for the other running stars, such as Cal Hubbard, Clark Hinkle, and Joe Laws, but also played defensive back, linebacker, receiver, and on special teams. In five seasons, Schneidman totaled 37 yards rushing and 119 yards receiving.

When McNally left Green Bay in 1937 to become player–coach of the Pittsburgh Pirates, he asked his friend Schneidman to come along, but he decided to stay in Green Bay. "I didn't want to go for $100 a week," said Schneidman, who was making about the same amount with the Packers at the time.

He stayed in Green Bay and played briefly on the 1939 championship team, which finished 10-2. That team capped the season with a 27-0 win over New York in the NFL title game at State Fair Park in Milwaukee. The shutout was the first in NFL championship history, and the 1939 Packers still are considered one of the franchise's greatest teams of all time. Schneidman, however, was injured after one game in 1939 and never returned. He hurt his shoulder when he collided with Hubbard. "I got the hell knocked out of me and told Curly I wanted to quit," Schneidman said.

He retired after the 1939 season but then wound up playing in 1940 for the Cardinals, turning in a career highlight with a 48-yard interception return for a touchdown. Then Schneidman quit the NFL for good and joined the U.S. Navy. He played for the Navy's Great Lakes Naval Station team near Chicago in 1941 and 1942 and did some football coaching while serving in Illinois and North Carolina until 1946. During that time, he and a brother started Schneidman's Distributing Company, a beer and liquor distributorship in Quincy, a business that he remained in until he retired. Quincy, a bustling river town that once had seven breweries and 165 taverns, was a good place to be in the alcohol business.

Schneidman played with McNally for just two seasons, but it was long enough to provide stories that he could tell for a lifetime. True to his legend, McNally was unpredictable, such as the time the Packers all were given expensive wristwatches after winning the 1936 championship. McNally didn't like the watch. "He was coming across the river one day and threw it in," Schneidman said.

Once, McNally made up his own play in the huddle, despite the protest of teammates, who knew that they would get in trouble with the demanding Lambeau. "I'm the damn quarterback, and we're going to run the play," McNally said. "We ran the play, and Hutson caught a touchdown pass," Schneidman said.

Another time, McNally took a team to England to play a half-football, half-rugby game. McNally decided to buy all his Green Bay teammates hats so that they could look as dapper as the Brits. McNally was late for training camp. He called three times and said he needed money, allegedly for the hats, before he could get back home. When he arrived, he had 22 hats, but none of them fit. "The smallest hat was larger than the largest head on the team," Schneidman said with a chuckle.

Like McNally, Schneidman enjoyed a beer or two. They became fast friends on and off the field. "I had good speed," Schneidman said. So did McNally. In 1935, McNally challenged the speedy Hutson to a race in the 100-yard dash. Hutson, the "Alabama Antelope," could run the 100 in 9.5 seconds. He beat McNally, then 33, but just barely.

In 1963, McNally became a charter member of the Pro Football Hall of Fame along with Hutson, Hubbard, and Lambeau. McNally died in 1985 at age 82, and two decades later Schneidman still was telling stories about him—and other late, great Packers. Mention a name and Schneidman could resurrect a half-century-old memory.

What about Arnie Herber, one of the first great long throwers in NFL history? "After every game, he'd buy me a beer and I'd buy him one," Schneidman said. Or

Charles "Buckets" Goldenberg, a star lineman? "He gave everything he had in every play. He was a blocking back, but he went to play guard so that's how I made the starting eleven," Schneidman said.

What stood out about Hutson, who retired in 1945 as one of the greatest players in NFL history? "He was one of the good ones, and I was one of the lousy ones but I made the team. Every play, he ran like it was the play of the game. He was sort of a quiet guy. He changed the game [of football]."

And about Lambeau, the man who made the Packers famous, first as a player–coach and then as the head coach from their first year, 1921, until 1949: "I really liked Curly. He would tell it like it is. If we were down on the scoreboard at halftime, his standard thing was, 'Some of you are playing your hearts out, and some of you are not. If you want to stay on the team, you'd better start playing harder.'"

Schneidman remembered without difficulty that he scored two career touchdowns for the Packers. His 12 points tie him on the team's all-time scoring list with such men as 1960s star Ray Nitschke and Schneidman's old teammate, Cal Hubbard.

At Sunset Nursing Home, Schneidman has a few Packers mementos in his room, including a copy of his final 1939 contract that paid him $135 a game. He still follows the Packers on TV, and friends never get tired of his stories, especially the ones about Johnny "Blood" McNally. "Herman is such an unassuming guy but a high-class guy. It's just a joy to be with him," said Richard Scholz, an old friend who spends time weekly with Schneidman. Scholz already had written Schneidman's obituary.

Someday, the Packers will retire Schneidman's old number, 4. The number first belonged to back Verne Lewellen from 1925 to 1926, then Schneidman from 1935 to 1937 (he wore number 51 from 1938 to 1939). It wasn't used again until quarterback Chuck Fusina wore it in 1986, then kicker Dale Dawson, who wore it for four games in 1988. Then it was given to a young quarterback in 1992, Brett Favre. When the Packers eventually retire the number of one of the greatest quarterbacks of all time, few people outside Quincy, Illinois, will remember that Herm Schneidman also once wore number 4—a generation before Favre even was born.

Time has a way of rounding off the edges and leaving only the core of a thing, be it a mountain, a human body, or a memory. The muscles in Schneidman's once-powerful running back legs no longer are well-defined. Schneidman, however, is strengthened in his final years of life by many memories of the Packers that stay close to his heart. From his wheelchair in a nursing home in Illinois, he happily recalls the days when he and the Packers still were young. He hasn't forgotten his first job.

DOWNFIELD:
THE STORY CONTINUES

In 1996, the year Green Bay brought back the Vince Lombardi Trophy with the Super Bowl XXXI victory, I published my first attempt at catching up on the lives of former Packers. That book, *Downfield: Untold Stories of the Green Bay Packers*, featured short biographies of 45 players and briefly summarized the post-football lives of another 21 men. They ranged from 1930s standouts Lon Evans and George Svendsen to 1980s stars Ezra Johnson and Paul Coffman. I talked with men from the team's forgettable 1950s, including stars Bobby Dillon and Floyd "Breezy" Reid, to men of the championship 1960s, including Ray Nitschke and Bart Starr. I profiled men who had become ministers, firefighters, police officers, doctors, actors, golf pros, farmers, prison guards, sheriffs, security guards, furniture salesmen, car salesmen, businessmen, and attorneys. I talked with the first black Packer, Bob Mann, and the team's first 1,000-yard rusher, Tony Canadeo. Some of the ex-Packers, like Nitschke, never left Green Bay while others, like Jim Carter, the man who replaced Nitschke at middle linebacker, never wanted to come back. Some of them, like Chuck Mercein and Jerry Kramer, were heroes of the Ice Bowl, while others, such as quarterbacks Rich Campbell and Jerry Tagge, left with hardly a good memory.

In the decade since they graciously told their stories, the lives of some Packers in *Downfield* have changed significantly; some have marked milestones of one kind or another, and others have passed away.

John Brockington: A running back from 1971 to 1977, Brockington became the first player in NFL history to rush for 1,000 yards in his first three seasons in the league. In 1971, he was NFL rookie of the year. He was cut by Coach Bart Starr one game into the 1977 season after reaching 5,024 career rushing yards. Brockington, a native of Brooklyn, New York, then moved to the San Diego area and became a financial services broker. He was living comfortably until he ran into the toughest opponent of his life.

In the summer of 2000, at age 52, Brockington's health began to decline. The 6-foot-1, 225-pound fullback had been known for running over defenders, but he suddenly didn't have the energy to take out his garbage. He had pain in his abdomen, swollen ankles, and vomited three times a day. He hadn't seen a doctor in more than 20 years, but he finally agreed to have some tests. He was sent straight to the emergency room. A specialist told Brockington that his kidneys had failed; had he not come to the hospital, he would have been dead within a week.

Brockington had been living with an enlarged prostate, which caused his urine to back up and eventually poison his kidneys. He took medication daily to fight the pain and, in the process, hastened the failure of his kidneys. He had surgery to remove the kidneys and eventually went on dialysis while he waited for a transplant. "I'd never been sick like that before. The pain was unbelievable. I put myself in a bad situation," Brockington said in 2006 from San Diego. "Oh my goodness. I said, 'I can't believe I did this to myself.'"

As he waited for the transplant donor match, a Packers fan from the 1970s stepped forward. Diane Cogan was a graduate student at Marquette University in Milwaukee in 1971 when Brockington was a rookie with the Packers. She watched him play at Milwaukee County Stadium that year and became a big fan of number 42.

In 1993, living in San Diego and teaching college literature, Cogan, then using the name Diane Scott, was introduced to Brockington. They frequented the same deli. They began to date and were together, off and on, for about six years before breaking up around the time Brockington's health declined.

When Scott heard about Brockington's plight, she immediately came to his aid and volunteered one of her kidneys, if it would match. Doctors didn't think a kidney from a 5-foot-3, 128-pound woman would be big enough for a 225-pound man. She insisted on being tested. Amazingly, she was a match and her kidneys were larger than doctors expected. The same day that Brockington received the good news about Scott, he learned that another person awaiting a transplant had 13 relatives tested. None of them matched. "I was truly blessed," Brockington said.

On November 28, 2001, one of Scott's kidneys was transplanted into Brockington. After some minor setbacks in the months after the transplant, his health stabilized and remained good into 2006. He was taking anti-rejection, blood pressure, and cholesterol drugs daily and will be for the rest of his life. "You go one day without your pills, and you're toast. You know what, man? I got religion on this one." He was exercising regularly and working again as a broker at Del Mar Financial in the San Diego area.

Less than two years after the transplant, Scott and Brockington married on August 16, 2003. The two went on to found the John Brockington Foundation in San Diego, the goal of which is to raise awareness about kidney disease and organ donation. Brockington speaks regularly about the importance of being an organ donor. "It's a shame when people take healthy organs to the grave. If you want to be a donor, you have to have that conversation with your family before you're sick or die," he said. One of the foundation's annual events is a fund-raising golf tournament in Manitowoc, Wisconsin, just up the Lake Michigan coast from where Diane Cogan first set eyes on John Brockington.

Carlos Brown: A backup quarterback under Coach Bart Starr in 1975 and 1976, Brown changed his name to Alan Autry and began an acting career in 1988. For years, he was deputy Bubba Skinner in the television drama "In the Heat of the Night." He appeared in numerous other TV shows and in several major motion pictures, including *North Dallas Forty* and *Southern Comfort*. He then turned to politics. In 2006, he was in his second term as mayor of Fresno, California, the state's fifth largest city. Early in 2006, Autry stayed busy as mayor. He met with Governor Arnold Schwarzenegger about economic development, worked on ways to help Fresno keep more of its college graduates from leaving the city, dedicated a new city park in honor of Hmong and Lao veterans, and coordinated a Hurricane Katrina blanket relief project for a sister city in Louisiana. Brown played in 26 games as a Packer and retired after 1976. He completed 29 of 78 career passes for 396 yards and three touchdowns. He had six passes intercepted.

Tony Canadeo: A running back from 1941 to 1944 and 1946 to 1952, Canadeo died on November 29, 2003, at age 84. In 1949, he became the first Packer and only the third player in NFL history to rush for 1,000 yards when he gained 1,052. He crossed the plateau in the final game of the season, which also turned out to be Curly Lambeau's final game as coach of the Packers. Canadeo remained in Green Bay for the rest of his life and was involved with the Packers as a radio announcer in the 1960s and part of the executive committee and board of directors until the 1990s. Canadeo joined the Pro Football Hall of Fame in 1974. His jersey number, 3, is one of only five retired by the Packers.

Mike Douglass: A linebacker from 1978 to 1985, Douglass joined the Packers Hall of Fame in 2003. A fifth-round draft choice from San Diego State, Douglass became one of the Packers' leading tacklers and playmakers in the early 1980s. He was named all-pro by *Sports Illustrated* from 1981 to 1983. After his career, he was active in bodybuilding and opened Midas Touch Physique, a personal training business, in San Diego.

Ken Ellis: A cornerback from 1970 to 1975, Ellis was inducted into the Packers Hall of Fame in 1998. He was part of the 1972 Packers team that won the Central Division title. He was all-pro from 1972 to 1974 and played in the 1973 and 1974 Pro Bowls. He returned three of his 20 interceptions for touchdowns. In early 1976, he was traded to Houston as part of the trade that brought quarterback Lynn Dickey to Green Bay. Ellis played for five teams during the next five seasons and retired prior to the 1980 season. In 1983, he became a minister at Bethany World Prayer Center in Baker, Louisiana, near Baton Rouge. In 2005, he remained an associate pastor at Bethany.

Hank Gremminger: A defensive back from 1956 to 1965, Gremminger died of cardiac arrest on November 2, 2001, near his hometown of Weatherford, Texas. He finished his career as one of Green Bay's all-time interception leaders with 28, including one that set up a touchdown in the Packers' 37-0 win over the New York Giants in the 1961 NFL championship game. He also was part of Packers title teams in 1962 and 1965 before finishing his career with the Los Angeles Rams in 1966. Gremminger owned a ranch outside of Weatherford, near the Dallas-Fort Worth area, and Hank Gremminger Inc., a home construction business. One of his greatest memories of Wisconsin was the people. "They are second to none. They made us feel like one of them," Gremminger said in 1996. He was inducted into the Packers Hall of Fame in 1976.

In 2005, two other players from the 1950s passed away. Billy Grimes, a swift running back and punt returner from 1950 to 1952, died in March in Oklahoma City. He was 77. Howie Ferguson, a fullback from 1953 to 1958, died on December 19, 2005, in New Iberia, Louisiana. He was 75. Cut prior to the 1959 season by new Coach Vince Lombardi, Ferguson rushed for 2,120 yards as a Packer. He joined the Packers Hall of Fame in 1974. Another player from the 1950s, center Clayton Tonnemaker (1950, 1953–54), died in 1996 at age 68. He was the Packers' first-round draft pick in 1950 from the University of Minnesota.

Ezra Johnson: A defensive end with Green Bay from 1977 to 1987, Johnson joined the Packers Hall of Fame in 1997. He finished his 15-year career in 1991 with Indianapolis. Johnson set the Packers' career sack record with 84, including a team record 20 $\frac{1}{2}$ sacks in 1978. After retiring, he moved to the Atlanta area, opened a restaurant, and helped coach at his alma mater, Morris Brown.

Jerry Kramer: The star right guard of the 1960s championship teams eventually followed his teammates into retirement, writing the best-selling books *Instant Replay* and *Distant Replay*, and frequently returning to Green Bay for fantasy football camps, to attend games and reunions, and to raise money for charity, including Vince Lombardi Titletown Legends, a group of mostly ex-Lombardi players who use their star power for special causes. He also became a businessman and motivational speaker. In 2005, he embarked on a new effort to chronicle the Vince Lombardi era, *Inside the Locker Room.* While working on *Instant Replay*, his diary of the 1967 season, Kramer secretly taped conversations and speeches in the team's locker room. With the blessings of his teammates, Kramer released the audiotapes. They include Lombardi's final pregame speech to the Packers, prior to Super Bowl II in 1968.

In a preview of the tape on *www.jerrykramer.com*, there is the sound of a toilet flushing, the current voice of Kramer, and then the coach. "There is very little I can say to you, very little," Lombardi tells his team on January 14, 1968, inside the Orange Bowl in Miami. "You are a good football team, proud football team. You are the world champions . . . ." Another clip is from offensive tackle Bob Skoronski, who chokes back tears to say, "I'm deeply emotional. I really can't say much. A lot of guys who brought the Packers to what they are today might be playing their last game.

I'm asking every guy here to go out and play their [expletive] level best for these guys who've had a lot to do with the Green Bay Packers. Boys, we're wounded but we're not dead," Skoronski said. The Packers defeated the Oakland Raiders, 33-14.

Kramer is selling the CD, including post-game audio, a 14-page picture booklet, and other features. Kramer was one of the subjects of *Downfield* and also wrote the foreword. "Lombardi taught us that the intangibles in life are what's very critical. It's great to have education, etcetera, but if you don't have the need, the want, the burning desire. . . . They were the basic reasons for our success," Kramer said in *Downfield*.

Mark Murphy: A safety from 1980 to 1991, Murphy was inducted into the Packers Hall of Fame in 1998. He led the team in tackles for three seasons, from 1988 through 1990. Murphy, who signed with the Packers as a free agent, returned to his hometown of Canton, Ohio, and became an assistant football coach at Malone College.

Ray Nitschke: A linebacker from 1958 to 1972, Nitschke died of a heart attack on March 8, 1998, while on a trip to Venice, Florida. He was 61. The hard-hitting Nitschke led the Packers defense in the 1960s when the team won five championships. He was named to both the Pro Football Hall of Fame and the Packers Hall of Fame in 1978. His number, 66, was retired by the Packers in 1983. He is considered by some as the greatest middle linebacker in pro football history. He remained in Green Bay after his career, started the *Packer Report* newsweekly, wrote his autobiography, *Mean on Sundays* (with Robert B. Wells), appeared in movies and commercials, and became a goodwill ambassador for the Packers.

"Not a day goes by that people don't bring up number 66 or Lombardi in my life. So I think I'll always be number 66," Nitschke said in *Downfield*. "The game has been so good to me I could never give back what's been given to me. I've really had a wonderful life because of the game of football."

In addition to Nitschke, at least five other 1960s starters died before the year 2000. Lionel Aldridge, a defensive end, died in February of 1998 in Shorewood, Wisconsin, at age 57. Aldridge battled schizophrenia. Lee Roy Caffey, a linebacker, died in 1994 of colon cancer at age 52. Henry Jordan, a defensive tackle, died of a heart attack in 1977 at age 42. Travis Williams, a running back and kick returner, died in 1991 of heart failure in Richmond, California, at age 45 after struggling with alcoholism and homelessness. Ron Kostelnik, a defensive tackle, died in a car accident in 1993 at age 53. Jordan joined the Packers Hall of Fame in 1975, Caffey in 1986, Aldridge in 1988, Kostelnik in 1989, and Williams in 1997. Jordan also was named to the Pro Football Hall of Fame in 1995.

George Svendsen: A center from 1935 to 1941, Svendsen died in 1995 in the Minneapolis area. He was 83. He shared the center duties for a time with his brother,

Earl "Bud" Svendsen, who died in 1996 at age 81. Both men played at the University of Minnesota and both played on the 1939 Packers championship team. George joined the Packers Hall of Fame in 1972 and Earl in 1985. One of George's greatest memories as a Packer was playing the Chicago Bears. "One year we beat the Bears in Chicago [to take the division lead]. There was a parade down Main Street when we got back, and we celebrated all night long," George said in *Downfield*.

David Whitehurst: A quarterback from 1977 to 1983, Whitehurst soon may be watching his son play in the NFL. Charlie Whitehurst, also a quarterback, led Clemson to an 8-4 record as a senior in 2005. In the Champs Sports Bowl, he completed 19 of 27 passes for 196 yards and ran for a touchdown as the Tigers defeated Colorado, 19-10. A three-year starter, Charlie Whitehurst, 6-foot-4 and 225 pounds, was chosen by the San Diego Chargers in the third round of the 2006 NFL draft. He played in the January 2006 Senior Bowl, for the nation's best college players, completing 7 of 9 passes. He set 42 Clemson passing records.

David Whitehurst was the Packers' seventh-round draft pick from Furman University in 1977. David, 6-foot-2 and 205 pounds, started 39 games as a Packer, mostly when Lynn Dickey was injured in 1977 and 1978. In 1985, he started David Whitehurst Homes in the Atlanta area. He and his wife, Beth, also have a daughter, Carrie, who was a forward on the Clemson women's basketball team in 2005–06.

A PART OF THEM LIVES ON

In Green Bay, Packers history can be around any corner. The rich aura of football tradition from neighborhood to neighborhood is a testament to generations of Packers fans throughout Wisconsin who never let the home team leave the NFL's smallest city. In 2006, Green Bay was home to barely more than 100,000 people, the size of a suburb in other NFL metropolitan areas. The Packers made Green Bay famous, but they didn't necessarily make it grow.

Packers players, like politicians in Washington, come and go, but their legacies remain. Fans can find Curly Lambeau's grave in Allouez Catholic Cemetery and just as easily theorize why Curly couldn't win after World War II. They can see St. Willebrord Catholic Church, where Vince Lombardi attended mass every day in an attempt to keep a lid on his ferocious temper. They can have a beer at Title Town Brewing, the old city train depot where 20,000 fans greeted the team in 1929 after the Packers won their first NFL title. One of the beers is named Johnny Blood Red, after the late Johnny "Blood" McNally, a free-spirited man who would be proud that his name still was in a lineup somewhere. Fans still can watch football behind East High School, the site of old City Stadium, where fair-haired southerner Bart Starr played his rookie season in 1956.

The obvious destination for Packers history buffs is Lambeau Field and the Packers Hall of Fame, but if you ask around it's easy to find the house where Lombardi used to live, see the downtown spot at the old newspaper office on Cherry Street where the Packers were founded in 1919, see where Ray Nitschke and Reggie White went to church, where Starr would go out for pizza after a game, or the bar in DePere where the 1989 "Cardiac Pack" used to hang out.

Year after year, team history often as much as the team itself keeps fans coming to Green Bay, in and out of season. In Green Bay, however, fans can do more than see Packers history: They can buy a piece of it. With the resurgence of team pride in the 1990s, owning a share of stock in the Packers or season tickets wasn't enough for many fans.

At Stadium Sports and Antiques, 2041 Holmgren Way, and another shop like it, Packer City Antiques on the other side of Lambeau Field, the book never quite closes on the careers of Packers players and Packers eras. History is recycled with each item that is brought in or goes out the door. Nearly 30 years after Jerry Kramer threw the block that helped the Packers win the Ice Bowl, a replica helmet signed by Kramer was priced at $325 at Stadium Sports. Need a picture of 1930s quarterback Arnie Herber? Consider it done. Collecting 1950s Packers playing cards? You can find them in Green Bay.

The list goes on. Team photos, media guides, newspapers, a signed Brett Favre fishing pole, a box of Frozen Tundra of Lambeau Field ($35), and even used team laundry bags ($20) are on the sales floor at Stadium Sports, where the business motto is "Buying and Selling All Things Green Bay Packer."

Stadium Sports Manager Ken Carriveau hasn't seen everything Packers, but he's come close. There's the bracelet-sized piece of the 1965 championship game goal post for $130 or the ticket stub from that game for $225.95. Both sit, jewel-like, behind glass. Carriveau, a middle-aged man who wears a Packers sweatshirt to work, has gotten so busy on game days that he has resorted to eating some of the stock—old Brett Favre candy bars. He knows the history behind much of what's in his shop, such as the goal post pieces. "The fans carted [the goal posts] out of the stadium. How are you going to stop a mob of tens of thousands of people? The mob came down and even took Vince Lombardi's hat, and he wasn't happy about that," Carriveau said.

Like a curator in a museum, Carriveau values the items he buys and sells because, like his customers, he is more than a collector. He loves the Packers. He loved them even when he moved to California; he loved them more when he came back to Green Bay. Carriveau knows why Brett Favre signed two times on the ball in his showcase. He knows that the Ray Nitschke painting propped up in his store once hung in Nitschke's Green Bay home.

Carriveau says it's rare to find an authentic Lombardi signature, and he's still waiting to set eyes on a football signed by Lambeau or Don Hutson. A ball signed by the 1965 team, including Lombardi, sells for about $5,000, largely because of Lombardi's handwriting. "He signed one of the panels on the ball, and his name was the only name on that panel. It was always that way. Lombardi didn't sign a lot of stuff like that. People think he did, but many of Lombardi's signatures were locker room signatures by other people," Carriveau said, citing one such item that he said likely was signed for Lombardi by fullback Jim Taylor. Lombardi signatures are so rare that an expense check signed by the coach was selling for $325 at Packer City Antiques.

At Stadium Sports, a legend greeted customers at the front door. A full-color, near life-size plaster statue of Bart Starr, getting ready to throw another pass, gazed at the door in the direction of Lambeau Field. The statue was cast around the year 2000; it was one of just 15 made of the player who wore number 15. The asking price: $12,000, although Carriveau would let it go for $10,000. "I hope somebody would find a good home for it," Carriveau said, adding that the Packers Hall of Fame had expressed an interest in it.

In 2005, the Packers Hall of Fame was given something more valuable than the Starr statue. Daniel Flagstad donated a rare Don Hutson jersey. The blue shirt, with gold on the shoulders, was valued at more than $17,000. The owner's parents used to run Rockwood Lodge, where the Packers held training camp from 1946 to 1949. Hutson retired after 1945, but one of his old jerseys still was around in 1946 when Flagstad was told to pick an item out of a trunk as payment for helping the team's equipment manager. He held onto the jersey for nearly 60 years before sending it home to the Packers.

Training camp used to be all about the players. When the Packers began winning again in the 1990s, training camp also became a summer ritual for fans. At Packer City Antiques, owner Mike Worachek's busiest months are July and August, when camp draws thousands of Packers fans. "They're on vacation, and they've got money to spend," Worachek said.

Packers fans aren't the only ones who come through Carriveau's and Worachek's doors. The proprietors have seen recent players Donald Driver, Antonio Freeman, LeRoy Butler, Wayne Simmons, and William Henderson; long-ago players James Lofton, Dave Robinson, John Brockington, Ezra Johnson; and even former Coach Mike Sherman stop in to buy a personal piece of Packers history. Some players enter incognito.

With the success of the team in the 1990s, the value of Packers memorabilia took off. Carriveau saw a Chicago Bears pennant sell for $80 in Chicago and a comparable age and condition Packers pennant sell for $300 in Green Bay. He also saw a shop next door to his come under investigation for possibly selling items with fake Brett Favre autographs. Buying and selling Packers memorabilia can be disheartening if unscrupulous people become involved. Carriveau's greatest joy comes in helping a fan find a treasured, authentic piece of history.

Tom Pigeon has one of the best private collections of Packers memorabilia in the Green Bay area, and there are plenty of Packers pack rats. However, Pigeon considers himself a team historian more than a collector. He doesn't see dollar signs when he looks around his basement. He sees pieces of the Packers story.

Pigeon, 65, has followed that story all his life. His father, Norman, went to the team's first game ever, a 53-0 win over Menominee North End Athletic Club on September 14, 1919. His dad was 11. "I developed a love for the Packers when he started taking me to games in the 1940s," Tom Pigeon said. "I have so many great memories of going to games in the '40s. My dad could go up and down the list and name all the players in the '30s and '40s."

When he grew up, Tom Pigeon went to work in the photo department for Fort Howard Paper Company, which just happened to open its doors in Green Bay in 1919, the same year the Packers made their debut. In retirement, Pigeon is a tour guide at Lambeau Field. He doesn't need a script to talk about team history. "A lot of people on the tours think Packer history started with Lombardi [in 1959]. I like to educate them. People come from all over—70 countries, 49 states, and Minnesota," he said, adding that he usually gets a laugh with that line.

The bulk of Pigeon's home Packers collection is informational. He has hundreds of old game programs, including all but one of the team's championship game programs. He has prints of 2,500 photos from the Lombardi years and stacks upon stacks of the *Green Bay Press-Gazette*, going back decades, all filed chronologically. He has press guides, yearbooks, and tapes of radio game broadcasts since 1971, plus the 1960s championship games. In a tall metal cabinet, out of the sunlight, are Packers highlight videos from the 1940s through the 1960s and videos of all NFL championship games dating to World War II. He also has videos of Packers game telecasts since 1978, but he only keeps videos of the victories. "The losses aren't fun to look at," he said.

There's much more. A 1950 stock certificate, a football signed by General Manager Ron Wolf, the architect of the Super Bowl XXXI championship team, a ball signed by the 1961 championship team, a banner that hung on the new stadium when it opened on September 29, 1957. It read "Welcome to New Green Bay Stadium." That was well before it was named after Lambeau. The Packers defeated the Chicago Bears that day, 21-17. "All that history means a lot to me," Pigeon said.

Pigeon is a respected Packers historian. He has provided research material for ESPN Packers features and other media, helped Bart Starr do research for his biography, and worked with the Packers to make sure their media guides were historically accurate. He even helped write a book about the Packers, *Launching the Glory Years.*

In his modest, ranch-style home on a quiet Green Bay street, Pigeon opened a metal storage cabinet and pulled out a videotape. We watched highlights of a 50-year-old game, the Packers' 1955 season opener against Detroit. Packers stars Al Carmichael, Fred Cone, Bobby Dillon, Billy Howton, Howie Ferguson, and others took the old City Stadium field as 22,217 fans cheered them on. Pigeon pointed out to me—because we couldn't see it on the black-and-white tape—that the Packers still were wearing blue-and-gold uniforms in 1955.

As the highlights played out, set to upbeat music, Pigeon noted that at times when ball carriers apparently were tackled, there was no whistle. They got back up and continued to run. Back then, a player had to be indisputably tackled and held down before the whistle blew. Pigeon pointed out another old rule. "Watch the ball carrier here. When he's being tackled, he'll throw the ball out of bounds to stop the clock," he said. And the ball carrier did just that. Pigeon had watched this video many times. He seemed fascinated by the old game and its quaint rules.

After Pigeon shut off the video, he showed me a replica of the old City Stadium and a picture of that 1955 season opener against Detroit, when Pigeon was 15. Like many a Green Bay youth at the time, he snuck into the stadium without paying, he and friends climbing a 10-foot fence. An oversize photo on his wall shows the game, with teenagers standing in the margin between the field and the stadium.

Pigeon has had Packers season tickets since he was a young man. He saw the Ice Bowl and many other memorable Green Bay victories. However, the virtually meaningless 1955 season opener is his greatest Packers memory. The Lions had won the 1952 and 1953 NFL championships and lost in the 1954 title game. They were an NFL power, led by Bobby Layne and Doak Walker. The Packers had lost to the Lions 12 straight times and hadn't won an NFL title for more than a decade.

On that early fall day, the Packers rallied to defeat the Lions, 20-17, when end Gary Knafelc leaped over three Lions defenders to catch a pass and ran into the end zone with the winning score in the final minute. The touchdown capped a desperation drive by the Packers, led by quarterback Tobin Rote. Pigeon felt like the Packers had won a championship that day. Although the team went just 6-6 that year, Pigeon was hooked for life on the excitement of being a Packers fan.

Late in 2005, several months after we watched the video in Pigeon's basement, one of the players in that game, Howie Ferguson, passed away. He died of heart failure at age 75. Ferguson was a 6-foot-2, 210-pound fullback from Louisiana. He did not play college ball and signed with the Packers as a free agent. He was a good one, leading the Packers in rushing in 1955 with 859 yards, second best in the NFL. He made the Pro Bowl in 1956. In 1974, Ferguson was inducted into the Packers Hall of Fame. He rushed for 2,120 yards in his career with the Pack, which lasted from 1953 to 1958.

Fifty years after he helped provide Tom Pigeon with his greatest Packers memory, Ferguson was gone. He wasn't forgotten, however, not in Green Bay, where love for the Packers has deep roots in the hearts of fans. The Pigeons are examples of that enduring love. Norman and Tom Pigeon have witnessed all of Packers history, more than 85 years of it. They also have collected and preserved tangible parts of the Packers' past and handed down the stories across the generations. Through championship seasons and the most mediocre of years, the Pigeons and legions of other sincere fans like them have unfailingly supported the Packers. Thanks to them, the legend continues.

INDEX